JCMS Annual Review of the European Union in 2007

Edited by

Ulrich Sedelmeier
and
Alasdair R. Young

General Editors: William Paterson and Jim Rollo

WILEY-BLACKWELL

First published 2008 by Blackwell Publishing Ltd

British Library Cataloguing-in-Publication Data applied for
ISBN 978-1-4051-7977-5

Printed and bound in Markono Print Media Pte Ltd

The publisher's policy is to use permanent paper from mills
that operate a sustainable forestry policy, and which has been
manufactured from pulp processed using acid-free and
elementary chlorine-free practices.
Furthermore, the publisher ensures that the text paper and cover board
used have met acceptable environmental accreditation standards.

For further information on Blackwell Publishing, visit our website:
http://www.blackwellpublishing.com

CONTENTS

Editorial: The EU in 2007: Development Without Drama, Progress without Passion

ULRICH SEDELMEIER
London School of Economics and Political Science
ALASDAIR R. YOUNG
University of Glasgow

In our editorial to last year's *Annual Review* (Sedelmeier and Young, 2007), we described 2006 as an '*intermezzo*' year for the European Union (EU). 2004 and 2005 were both quite dramatic – witnessing the accession of ten new members, the signing of the Constitutional Treaty, and its subsequent rejection in France and the Netherlands – and it appeared that 2007 might be equally dramatic in view of the accessions of Bulgaria and Romania and negotiations on replacing the Constitutional Treaty. Indeed, 2006 was relatively quiet, but it turned out not to be the quiet before the storm. While the EU did enlarge further and concluded the Lisbon Treaty in 2007, in many respects these events occurred without great drama.

To be sure there are concerns that Bulgaria and Romania were admitted before they were ready.[1] Political developments in these two newest Member States are discussed for the first time in this volume by Karen Henderson and Nick Sitter, but their accession is noticeable for its absence in the other contributions to the volume. The other macro-level political decisions of 2007 concerned the enlargement of economic and monetary union (EMU) – Slovenia joined in January 2007 and the accession of Cyprus and Malta from 1 January 2008 was agreed (Johnson; Verdun, this volume) – and of Schengen in December 2007 to the new EU members from 2004 except Cyprus (Monar, this volume). And of course there were some tense negotiations in the final stages of the negotiation of the reform treaty, which are covered comprehensively in this volume by Desmond Dinan, complemented admirably by the

---

[1] *The Economist*, 26 April 2008, p. 56.

two presidency reports (Maurer; Ferreira-Pereira, this volume). It is striking, however, how little these events resonated with the wider public.

With respect to the Lisbon Treaty the lack of public resonance was in many respects the result of a choice, particularly by the German Presidency, to favour quiet (even secret) diplomacy over public engagement (Dinan; Maurer, this volume), which, as Andreas Maurer (this volume) points out, may ultimately prove costly. This tendency to avoid publicity and public debate was also reflected in the deliberate presentation of the new treaty as a technical 'reform' treaty and the decision to settle all controversial issues in negotiations on the mandate for the Intergovernmental Conference (IGC), leaving the IGC proper primarily with the task of redrafting the Constitutional Treaty according to the mandate. Moreover, the choice to revert to amendments of the existing treaties, rather than concluding a new treaty, makes it virtually impossible for the uninitiated (and extremely difficult even for the initiated) to read the Lisbon Treaty. This choice facilitated the decisions of a number of Member State governments – notably in France, the Netherlands and the United Kingdom – to avoid ratification by referendums, leaving only Ireland to put the Lisbon Treaty to a popular vote. The avoidance of referendums in turn reinforced the lack of public engagement and awareness of these developments.

In addition to the Lisbon Treaty, a number of developments in 2007 that have direct impacts on EU citizens passed without much public notice. The area of Justice and Home Affairs is now clearly one of the EU's priorities and the Council adopted a record number of texts (Monar, this volume). The EU enhanced police co-operation and provisions for data-exchange and extended the Schengen border-control zone to Malta and the eight central and eastern European Member States that had joined the EU in 2004.

With respect to the single market and competition policy, the European Commission was very active in defence of consumer interests (Howarth, this volume). Often these were very deliberate moves to reconnect with citizens, such as in the Commission's efforts to get mobile phone companies to cut roaming charges before the summer holidays, but even these efforts did not achieve much public acclaim.

Several decisions by the European Court of Justice (ECJ) had significant political implications (Dougan, this volume). In *Viking Line* and *Laval un Partneri* the ECJ clarified the balance struck under Community law between the exercise of economic freedoms and the threat of social dumping within the enlarged EU. The rulings, however, did not attain similar levels of public engagement as, for example, the Services Directive had in the previous year, although they raise very similar issues (Hay 2007). In *Hendrix* and *Morgan* the ECJ extended a Member State's obligation to pay social benefits to its citizens that have moved to another Member State, unless not doing so can be justified by a valid public interest and is consistent with the principle of proportionality. As Michael Dougan points out in this volume, these decisions concern policy areas where EU regulatory power is relatively weak, but established that the Member States' duty to respect the obligations imposed directly under the Treaty exerts an increasingly profound influence on the exercise of their domestic competences. Some of these rulings, notably *Viking Line* and *Laval un Partneri*, were controversial among those paying attention, which raises questions about how far the logic of its legal reasoning can provide the ECJ with legitimacy (Dougan, this volume), but the controversy does not seem to have engaged broader publics.

More generally, as in previous years, the EU got on with the business of governing. This was particularly evident with respect to the high-profile issue of climate change. In March 2007 the European Council set targets of a 20 per cent reduction in green house gas emissions and a 20 per cent share of renewable energy in EU energy consumption by 2020 (20 20 by 2020) (see Maurer, this volume; Damro and MacKenzie, forthcoming). The EU also played a leading role at the Climate Change Conference in Bali in December (see Allen and Smith, this volume).

External relations maintained a high profile on the EU's agenda during 2007. The EU agreed 80 Common Foreign and Security Policy joint actions and common positions and launched four new European Security and Defence Policy operations (in Afghanistan, Chad and the Central African Republic, the Democratic Republic of the Congo, and Kosovo), but the lack of effective strategic thinking continued to be a problem (Allen and Smith, this volume). Two particularly notable EU external relations initiatives in 2007 – the inauguration of an EU policy towards Brazil and the adoption of an Africa–EU Strategic Partnership at the second EU–Africa summit – were both actively promoted by the Portuguese presidency (Allen and Smith; and Ferreira-Pereira, this volume).

Closer to home, 2007 provided further evidence of the limits of political conditionality in EU candidate countries, mainly because of their domestic conditions, but also due to a reduced credibility of the EU's incentives (Lavenex and Schimmelfennig, this volume). Limits to the European Neighbourhood Policy also became more pronounced. Sectoral co-operation in areas of strategic interest to the EU progressed faster than ambitions for broader political change and the gap widened between those countries willing and able to intensify co-operation with the EU and other ENP countries.

As identified in last year's review (Henderson and Sitter, 2007), the sheer number of Member States in the EU now means almost constant flux in the compositions of the Council of Ministers and European Council. In 2007 there were three new prime ministers without changes of government and two presidents were directly elected, while another eight Member States had changes in the governing coalition, including two where there was a complete change in the coalition (Henderson and Sitter, this volume). Beyond the background of instability caused by such changes, some of the domestic political changes – such as the fall of the Law and Justice Party in Poland and the election of President Nicolas Sarkozy in France – had more profound and direct impacts on the EU (see, for instance, Dinan, this volume).

Economic growth in the EU's Member States slowed slightly in 2007, but generally remained strong (Johnson; Verdun, this volume). As in the recent past, the relatively strong economic performances of the euro area Member States meant that they had no trouble meeting the stability and growth pact requirements. Criticism of EMU, therefore, was again muted (Verdun, this volume). The aftershocks of the subprime crisis in the United States, however, have cast a shadow over the economic prospects of all of the EU's Member States (Johnson; Verdun, this volume). The European Central Bank reacted sharply in August by injecting liquidity into the euro area economy, but resisted cutting interest rates because of concerns about inflationary pressures (Verdun, this volume).

As ever the most rewarding and challenging aspect of editing the *Annual Review* is selecting the topics and authors for the keynote article and the review article, not least because we need to make the decisions in early September. In considering suitable subjects for the keynote article, we were influenced by the increasing tensions between Russia and the EU (and the West more generally) during the latter half of 2006 and into 2007. The failure to replace the EU–Russia Partnership Agreement, which expired at the end of 2007, only validated our choice. We were particularly attracted to the topic of EU–Russia relations for two reasons. First, as the EU's neighbouring great power, Russia poses a particularly important challenge to the EU as an international actor. Second, we saw an excellent opportunity to feed into the emerging literature on how other international actors perceive the EU. Margot Light, in the Keynote Article, realizes both of these ambitions admirably. She also underlines that both sides have difficulty dealing effectively with the other: the EU because of tensions between bilateral Member State action and collective responses and Russia because of a lack of understanding of the EU. She argues that although there is strategic rivalry between Russia and the EU, particularly in their shared neighbourhood, each is too important to the other for them not to continue to interact.

Our decision to ask Alberta Sbragia to write the Review Article on comparative regionalism reflects the burgeoning interest in comparative regionalism and our belief it is essential to study the EU in the light of more general theories and of developments elsewhere. A particularly striking point that Alberta Sbragia makes in her excellent review article is that the most note-worthy real-world developments in regional integration are occurring in southeast Asia, where the context of and aims for integration are radically different from those in western Europe. This development poses profound challenges for our understanding of the conditions necessary and sufficient for regional integration. As Alberta Sbragia demonstrates, however, at the moment the emerging comparative regionalism literature poses more questions than it answers.

This volume marks the end of our three-year term as editors. We hope that the readers have found our innovations – such as the review article; the more reflective approach to the articles, which seek to identify key developments in their respective areas rather than providing comprehensive coverage; and, at a smaller level, the key readings – useful. We are pleased to have increased the geographical spread of contributors to reflect more accurately the diversity of the UACES membership and the international standing of the *JCMS*.

We are grateful to UACES and the *JCMS* for entrusting this venture to us and supporting our initiatives. We are grateful to the contributors to the *Annual Review* during our tenure, both the regular contributors to all three issues and the authors of keynote articles, review articles and presidency reports. It is, after all, your contributions that make the *Annual Review* what it is. It is now left to us only to wish our successors Nathaniel Copsey and Tim Haughton well.

References

Damro, C. and MacKenzie, D. (forthcoming) 'Climate Policy and the EU Context'. In Compston, H. and Bailey, I. (eds) *Turning Down the Heat: Climate Policy in Affluent Democracies* (Basingstoke: Palgrave Macmillan).

Hay, C. (2007) 'What Doesn't Kill You Can Only Make You Stronger: The Doha Development Round, the Services Directive and the EU's Conception of Competitiveness'. *JCMS*, Vol. 45, s1, pp. 25–43.

Henderson, K. and Sitter, N. (2007) 'Political Developments in the EU Member States'. *JCMS*, Vol. 45, s1, pp. 183–211.

Sedelmeier, U. and Young, A.R. (2007) 'Editorial: 2006, A Quiet Year?' *JCMS*, Vol. 45, s1, pp. 1–5.

JCMS 2008 Volume 46 Annual Review pp. 7–27

Keynote Article: Russia and the EU: Strategic Partners or Strategic Rivals?*

MARGOT LIGHT
London School of Economics and Political Science

Introduction

Well before 2007, some Russian analysts had diagnosed 'a systemic crisis' in the Russian–European Union (EU) relationship (RUE, 2004). To some western observers, by 2007 the disputes between Russia and the EU indicated that relations had reached 'a critical juncture' (Kempe and Grotzky, 2006, p. 8), or seemed to be 'grinding to a halt' (Haukkala, 2007, p. 117). This article argues that, despite the conflicts that divide the EU and Russia, the relationship has neither succumbed to systemic crisis and nor has it ground to a halt.

Russia–EU relations were troubled in 2007, but to some extent, this reflected a more general deterioration in Russian–Western relations. Differences over the future status of Kosovo, Russian objections to US plans to develop a missile defence system and deploy elements of the system in Poland and the Czech Republic, and the ratification of the Conventional Forces in Europe agreement caused considerable friction and Russia's relations with the EU (the focus of this article) were, at one level, simply a subset of Russia's more general dissatisfaction with the West.

The major failure in Russian–EU relations in 2007 was the lack of agreement on a replacement for the Partnership and Co-operation Agreement (PCA). Although it was due to expire at the end of 2007, no start was made on negotiations on a new agreement. The failure to embark on negotiations was the result of problems in the bilateral relations between Russia and the

* I would like to thank the editors for their help in preparing this article.

EU's newest Member States. On the one hand, these problems demonstrated the extent to which the agenda of EU–Russian relations had become dominated by relations between Russia and EU members that had previously been part of the Soviet bloc. On the other hand, the problems also reflected a host of difficulties in the relationship between Russia and the EU that had accumulated over the years of Vladimir Putin's presidency, and particularly during his second term. As we shall see, one of those difficulties is the tension that often arises between the policy of the EU as a whole and the interests of individual Member States.

This article looks at the difficulties that affect the development of Russian–EU relations. It begins with an account of the problems which arose in Russian–EU relations in 2007 in particular, and the progress which was, nevertheless, made in the relationship. It then turns to an examination of the longer-term complications in the relationship that will need to be tackled if a basis is to be found for a new agreement.

I. The Russian–EU Relationship in 2007

Although some progress was made in the Russian–EU relationship in the course of 2007, a series of specific bilateral disputes between Russia and its former socialist neighbours dominated the relationship. Many of these disagreements had their origins in the years before 2007. For example, a trade dispute between Russia and Poland had erupted in 2005 when Russia claimed that Poland had tried to sell substandard meat on the Russian market by using false sanitary documents. While agreeing that the documents were forged, Poland denied responsibility and claimed that the meat was safe. Unconvinced about the standards of Polish meat, Russia banned Polish meat imports. In return, Warsaw vetoed the start of talks on a new Russia–EU co-operation agreement which had been scheduled to begin in November 2006. Warsaw insisted that its veto would remain in force until Russia lifted the ban. Strenuous efforts on the part of the Commission throughout 2007 failed to break the deadlock and it was only in December, after EU and Russian experts had inspected Polish meat processing plants and, more significantly, an election in Poland had brought to power a new government less overtly antagonistic to Russia, that the ban was lifted.[1]

In February 2007, Lithuanian officials threatened to join Poland in blocking talks on a new EU–Russia agreement. They were reacting to Transneft, Russia's state-controlled pipeline operator, shutting the Druzhba-1 pipeline link to Mazeikiu Nafta, the only refinery in the Baltic states, in July 2006

---

[1] *EurActiv.com*, 21 December 2007.

following a reported leak. Latvia and Estonia also receive supplies from both Mazeikiu Nafta and the Druzhba pipeline. There was speculation in the EU that Russia was using the blockage to prevent the Lithuanians from selling the Mazeikiu complex to the Polish oil group PKN Orlen, rather than to one of the Russian firms that had also bid for it.[2] In October 2006, Lithuania had offered to help Transneft fix the pipeline, but the offer was rejected, with Transneft insisting that the repairs were on schedule. But in February 2007 Transneft warned that if the pipeline could not be repaired, construction of a new one might take up to two years. By May the pipeline had still not resumed deliveries, and the EU Commissioner for Energy, Andris Piebalgs, promised to discuss the issue with Russia. Together with members of the European Parliament, he also made a joint statement urging Russia to stop using energy supplies for political purposes and to resume deliveries to Mazeikiu Nafta. The Russians responded angrily that the EU was artificially politicizing a purely technical incident.[3] On 1 June, Russian Energy and Industry Minister Viktor Khristenko announced that Transneft could not fix the pipeline and would have to rebuild the entire section supplying Lithuania. Russia would continue to send shipments to Mazeikiu Nafta by sea to an offshore terminal at Butinge – which is more expensive – to make up for the cut in supplies.[4]

Russia's relations with Estonia and Latvia, the other two Baltic states, have been fractious ever since the disintegration of the Soviet Union. Russians frequently accuse the two governments of discriminating against the large Russian minorities who live in those countries.[5] There are also great differences in the way in which history, in particular the history of the Second World War, is interpreted by the Balts and the Russians. To Russians, including the Russian minorities who reside in the Baltic states, the Soviet Army liberated the Baltic states from Nazi occupation at the end of the Great Patriotic War and the Baltic states voluntarily joined the Soviet Union. To Balts, the arrival of the Soviet army marked the beginning of Soviet occupation. This has been a constant source of friction between Russians and Balts and the situation became so acute in 2007 that the EU was drawn into the conflict.

In 2006, Estonian nationalists and ethnic Russian activists had clashed at the site of a bronze statue of a Soviet soldier in the centre of Tallinn. To

---

[2] In 2003 Transneft had stopped supplying oil to Ventspils oil terminal in Latvia, apparently in response to Latvian resistance to Russian ownership of Ventspils (*New York Times*, 21 January 2003).

[3] *Kommersant*, 16 April 2007.

[4] *Kommersant*, 1 June 2007.

[5] At the press conference after the Samara Russian–EU summit, for example, Putin called the infringement of the rights of Russian speakers in Latvia and Estonia 'unacceptable and unworthy of Europe' (EU delegation Moscow 2007).

Estonian nationalists, the statue symbolized the Soviet seizure of the country. To Russian community leaders in Estonia, 'remembering the heroism of the Soviet soldier is not a celebration of Soviet power'.[6] In order to prevent future violence, in January 2007 the Estonian government decided to remove the statue to a less controversial spot. Russians in Russia and the Russian minority in Estonia objected, arguing that the decision was symptomatic of a rebirth of fascism in Estonia. Violent protests erupted in Tallinn in April, during which one person died and more than 150 were injured and, to prevent further riots, the Estonian government rapidly moved the monument to a military cemetery, accusing Russia of orchestrating the violence. When Estonia's Prime Minister paid his respects before the monument on Victory Day on 8 May, Russian diplomats refused to participate in the ceremony. Russians themselves celebrate Victory Day a day later, on 9 May, and Russians were particularly enraged that the move had not been delayed until after their Victory Day celebrations. In Moscow the youth movement, Nashi, sealed off and attacked the Estonian embassy, prompting protests from the United States, the North Atlantic Treaty Organization (NATO) and the EU. Sergei Lavrov, the Russian Foreign Minister, accused the EU and NATO of conniving in Estonian attempts to rewrite history.[7] Soon after the riots, Estonia's official websites were disabled by a cyber attack; despite Russian denials, Estonian officials – and most of the Western media – accused Russia of being responsible. A 20-year-old Estonian student was found guilty of participating in the attack in January 2008.

A further long-standing problem that affected EU–Russian relations in 2007 was the issue of trans-Siberian overflights. In November 2006, in the margins of the EU–Russia summit, an agreement had been initialled by EU Transport Commissioner Barrot and the Russian Transport Minister Levitin providing for the abolition of payments for overflights over Siberia for EU airlines not later than the end of 2013 and the gradual reduction of the taxes during the transition period. Under the agreement, Russia was supposed to offer new routes over Siberia that would not be subject to taxes. The charges, which cost EU airlines about €430 million in 2006, are impossible for airlines to avoid since any detour to avoid Siberian airspace is very costly in jet fuel and time lost. The Russians had still not signed the agreement by the beginning of November 2007 and, as a result, a Russian–EU aviation summit scheduled for 16–17 November 2007 was cancelled.[8]

---

[6] *Washington Post*, 9 May 2007.
[7] Lavrov is quoted in *Times OnLine*, «http://www.timesonline.co.uk/tol/news/world/europe/article1763607.ece».
[8] *EU Business*, available at: «http://www.eubusiness.com/Transport/1194532321.61/».

Given these contentious issues, it is perhaps surprising that Russian–EU co-operation evolved and expanded at all in 2007. However, some progress was made. For example, the new Northern Dimension policy which had been adopted at the Helsinki Russian–EU summit in November 2006 came into effect on 1 January 2007. Envisaged as 'a common project and a common responsibility' of the partners – the EU, Russia, Norway and Iceland – with the participation of northern regional councils (the Barents Euro-Arctic Council, the Council of the Baltic Sea States, the Nordic Council of Ministers, and the Arctic Council), it is intended to be a regional expression of the Road Maps towards the Common Spaces.[9] The principle of co-financing from Northern Dimension partners, as well as from international and private financial institutions was accepted. A Parliamentary Conference on the Northern Dimension was held at the end of February and it called for the setting up of a Northern Dimension Parliamentary Forum to meet every two years.

The depiction of the new Northern Dimension policy as a common project, and the expectation that Russia will co-fund projects will, perhaps, ameliorate the Russian perception about EU technical assistance in general, but specifically about the Northern Dimension that, 'EU programmes appear to be designed with solely the EU's interests in mind and that the management of these programmes is insensitive to the concerns of the Russian counterparts' (Prozorov, 2006, p. 47).

On 1 June 2007 two agreements between the EU and Russia on visa facilitation and readmission of illegal immigrants entered into force. The new agreements will simplify visa procedures for certain categories of visitors (diplomats, sportsmen, scientists, students, participants in cultural events), and introduce a uniform fee of €35 for an ordinary and €70 for an express visa.[10] Although there have been complaints about the way in which the agreements are operating (including that so few EU Member States have concluded the readmission treaties with Russia that they insisted should be part of the visa facilitation deal), the agreements symbolize one small step towards Russia's ultimate goal, which is the visa-free movement of Russian nationals across EU borders. The visa-facilitation agreement may, therefore, ameliorate the Russian perception that the extension of the Schengen

[9] *Northern Dimension Policy Framework Document*, available at: «http://ec.europa.eu/external_relations/north_dim/doc/index.htm».
[10] Agreement between the European Community and the Russian Federation on the facilitation of the issuance of visas to the citizens of the European Union and the Russian Federation, *Official Journal of the European Union*, L 129/27, 17.5.2007.

agreement to the enlarged EU is designed to exclude Russia from Europe and denies to Russians their European identity.[11]

There was, therefore, some minimal progress in Russian–EU relations in 2007. Nevertheless, both of the regular Russian–EU summits were affected by the disputes between Russia and its neighbouring EU Member States. The stand-off between Russia and Estonia occurred shortly before the summit scheduled for May, for example, and it almost derailed it. Intense efforts on the part of the German Foreign Minister on behalf of the German EU Council presidency ensured that it took place on 17–18 May at Volzhsky Utyos, in the Samara region of Russia, as scheduled. Unusually no joint declaration was prepared before the summit. Indeed, so low were expectations of the summit that a Russian Foreign Ministry official argued that the mere fact that the meeting was held would be an achievement.[12]

The summit itself engendered further tensions. Before the summit, Russia had appeared to comply with a request from Germany to permit Russian opposition leaders to stage a protest in Samara. Hours before the meeting took place, however, police prevented Garry Kasparov and other opposition activists from flying to Samara, provoking reproaches from both European Commission President Jose Manuel Barroso and German Chancellor Angela Merkel. Putin responded by questioning whether the EU was really concerned about the human rights records of its allies – citing the lack of EU protest about the abuse of terror suspects at the US prison at Guantanamo Bay. Despite this exchange of barbs, both Putin and the EU leaders claimed that progress had been made at the summit on economic co-operation measures, such as simplifying border controls and exploring ways to facilitate investments in trade, and they pledged to continue 'constructive dialogue' and to extend EU–Russia cross-border trade, visa issues and scientific and technical co-operation (EU Delegation Moscow, 2007).

There were similarly low expectations of the summit that took place in Mafra, Portugal in October 2007. Neither the dispute over Polish meat exports nor the trans-Siberian overflight problem had been resolved. Again, both Putin and EU leaders put a positive spin on the meeting, at which a Memorandum of Understanding was signed between the European Monitoring Centre of Drugs and Drugs Addiction and Russia as well as an Agreement on Trade in certain Steel Products which increases the quantities of steel that

---

[11] For an interesting discussion of how the Schengen system has led to the development of an exclusionary and conflictual discourse in Russia on Russian–EU relations, see Prozorov (2006, chapter 2).
[12] *Moscow Times*, 16 May 2007.

Russia can export to the EU to take into account the accession of Bulgaria and Romania.[13] An agreement was also reached to set up an early warning system in the event of disruptions of Russian oil and gas supplies to Europe. EU leaders were, however, rather alarmed by Putin's claim during the summit that there was a similarity between the proposed US missile defence facilities in central and eastern Europe and the Cuban missile crisis of the 1960s.[14] According to Putin, 'For us the situation is technologically very similar. We have withdrawn the remains of our bases from Vietnam, from Cuba, and have liquidated everything there, while at our borders, such threats against our country are being created'.[15]

Putin's proposal to set up a new human rights institute in a European capital city, to parallel the institutes, which EU supports in Russia, also confused European leaders. The Portuguese Prime Minister, Jose Socrates, suggested that the centre would be set up jointly, but Sergei Yastrzhembsky, Putin's senior aide on EU relations, responded that there was little need for co-operation and suggested that the institute would study European human rights issues such as neo-Nazism, ethnic tensions, minority rights and immigration.[16]

In the absence of a new agreement, the PCA was simply extended for a year. Apart from the framework set out in the PCA, the development of the Russian–EU relationship also relies on the more ambitious 'roadmaps' for the projected Four Common Spaces, which had been adopted in 2005. The roadmaps 'set out shared objectives for EU–Russia relations as well as the actions necessary to make these objectives a reality and determine the agenda for co-operation between the EU and Russia for the medium-term'.[17] Some Russian analysts believe that the roadmaps could become the basis of a new agreement. But there are a number of longer-term problems in Russian–EU relations which have led to confusion as to the kind of relationship a new PCA should embody and both sides will have to sort out their priorities if they are to reach an agreement.

---

[13] Press release of the 20th EU–Russia Summit, Mafra, 26 October 2007, available at: «http://www.eu2007.pt/UE/vEN/Noticias_Documentos_20071026RUSSIACOM.htm».
[14] Although missile defence indirectly affects Russian–EU relations, the EU is not involved in the deployments.
[15] *International Herald Tribune*, 25 October 2007.
[16] *Moscow Times*, 29 October 2007.
[17] Conclusions – Four Common Spaces, EU–Russia Summit, Moscow, 10 May 2005, available at: «http://europa.eu.int/comm/external_relations/russia/summit_05_05/index.htm#fsj». For the road maps, see Final Road Maps, «http://ec.europa.eu/external_relations/russia/summit_05_05/#ces».

II. Longer-Term Problems in Russian–EU Relations[18]

The disputes between Russia and the EU in 2007 reflected two of the problems that have beset the relationship throughout the Putin presidency and particularly during his second term: Russia's reaction to the enlargement of the EU and the effect on the EU of Russia's energy policy. I shall begin this section by examining these two problems, before turning to other, equally important difficulties affecting the relationship, such as EU reactions to domestic developments in Russia and the growing resentment in Russia of the EU's normative agenda. I shall end with a brief examination of two longer standing structural problems that undermine EU–Russian relations.

Russia's Reaction to the EU Accession of Post-Socialist States

Throughout the 1990s Russians had a very benign attitude towards EU enlargement. However, in 2003 and 2004 two sets of problems arose as a result of the imminent accession of the post-socialist states of central and eastern Europe to the EU. The first concerned the states that would become the EU's new neighbours after the accession, while the second centred on Russia's relations with the states joining the EU.

As enlargement loomed closer, the European Commission began to consider how it would affect the countries on the external borders of the enlarged EU, that is, Belarus, Moldova, Russia and Ukraine (the western Newly Independent States, NIS, in the Commission's terminology). The attainment of security, stability and sustainable development *within* the EU was deemed to require political reform, social cohesion and economic dynamism in the EU's new neighbourhood. The Commission (2003, p. 3) proposed 'a differentiated, progressive and benchmarked approach' to its new eastern neighbours. Russian officials were horrified that the EU appeared to put Russia into this neighbourhood, in the same category as Belarus and Moldova. Deputy Foreign Minister Vladimir Chizhov (2004, p. 85) made it clear that 'Russia does not regard itself either as an object or subject of this policy.' Russia was duly left out of the European Neighbourhood Policy and instead it was decided to develop the EU–Russian strategic partnership through the creation of Four Common Spaces (Commission, 2004a). In effect, this represented recognition that the European neighbourhood was a shared neighbourhood, as much Russia's as the EU's. It is in this shared neighbourhood that some of the most serious difficulties in EU–Russia relations have arisen.

[18] This section draws on the discussion of the long-term problems in Russian–EU relations in Allison *et al.* (2006), the research for which was funded by the UK Economic and Social Research Council under grant RES-00-23-0146. See also Light (forthcoming).

Ever since Putin became president of Russia, geopolitical realism has predominated in Russian foreign policy thinking. The highest value is accorded to the preservation of sovereignty, territorial integrity and independence, while the most important principle of international law is considered to be the principle of non-intervention. Geopolitical realism also leads to a tendency to see international relations in zero-sum terms. This means that any increase in EU influence is perceived to cause a diminution of Russian influence. Because Russians are so sensitive about foreign influence in an area which they believe is Russia's 'natural' sphere of interest, in relation to the shared neighbourhood, it is often more accurate to talk of strategic rivalry or competition rather than strategic partnership.

The second problem that became acute as enlargement grew closer concerned Russia's relations with the acceding states themselves. The EU expected Russia to extend automatically the PCA to all ten new members prior to the enlargement on 1 May 2004. At the end of January 2004, however, Chizhov announced that 'the issue of extending the PCA is not merely a technical procedure that can be implemented automatically'. He presented a document listing Russian concerns, most of which related to trade and tariff issues, but also included access to Kaliningrad and the status of ethnic Russians in Latvia and Estonia. The EU responded curtly; unless the PCA was applied to the EU-25 'without pre-condition or distinction by 1 May 2004', Russian–EU relations would be seriously affected.[19] The Russians were offended – this response did not accord with the respect with which Russia, as a great power, should be treated. Chizhov declared that Russia expected to participate in European affairs as an equal partner, while Dmitry Rogozin,[20] chairman of the Duma International Relations committee, announced that 'Russia is not about to act on orders from Brussels'. Representatives of the accession states attended the Council meeting that issued the EU's response and this exacerbated Russian fears that the former socialist states would turn the EU against Russia.

Both sides seemed to recognize that compromise was essential. On 27 April Russia signed a protocol extending the PCA to the new members. A joint statement was attached which listed the 'outstanding issues' that both

---

[19] Russian concerns are set out in a report, 'The Effect of the EU Enlargement on Russia's Economy', Moscow, 2004, available at: «http://www.europe2020.org/en/section_voisin/doc/EU_eng.pdf»; Chizhov's statement can be found in Press release 161-30-01-2004, Ministry of Foreign Affairs of the Russian Federation, and the EU response is in 2563rd External Relations Council meeting – Brussels 23.02.2004, Press 49 Nr: 6294/04, available at: «http://ue.eu.int/ueDocs/cms_Data/docs/pressData/en/gena/79150.pdf».
[20] See, for example, *Izvestiya*, 26 February 2004; *Moscow Times* 25 February 2004.

sides undertook to address.[21] These included the transit of goods between Kaliningrad and Russia and the specification of a transitional period during which the terms of some bilateral agreements would continue to operate. Nevertheless, Russians remained convinced that the new Member States would turn the EU against Russia and when the EU sided with Poland, Estonia and Lithuania in their disputes with Russia in 2007, this seemed to confirm their conviction.

Russia's Energy Policy

A new problem arose in Russia–EU relations in 2006: energy security. As a result both of EU enlargement and of increasing consumption, the proportion of Russian energy in the EU's total energy imports increased from 24 per cent in 2001 to 27.5 per cent in 2005. The EU is, therefore, heavily dependent on Russian energy. Russia, however, is also heavily dependent on the European market; 60 per cent of Russia's oil exports and 50 per cent of Russia's natural gas exports go to the EU.[22] Although there are huge potential markets in the Far East, Russia's oil and gas pipeline networks run from east to west and it will take years to construct pipelines from Russia to China or the Pacific coast.

The arrest and trial of Mikhail Khodorkovsky, head of Yukos, then Russia's largest oil company, and the take-over of Yuganskneftegaz, the most valuable Yukos asset, by the state-owned Rosneft in December 2004 caused the first alarm in the EU about Russia's energy policy. When Gazprom, the 51 per cent state-owned gas monopoly, bought Sibneft, Russia's fifth-largest oil firm in October 2005, the EU became worried that the Russian government was seeking state control of Russia's energy resources to use energy as a political lever.

These fears appeared justified when Gazprom raised the highly subsidized price Ukraine paid for gas, effectively quadrupling Ukraine's costs. Although there were good market reasons for increasing the price Ukraine paid for gas – Russia had been subsidizing Ukrainian gas since the disintegration of the Soviet Union and world energy prices had risen hugely – both the timing – the Ukrainian parliamentary election campaign had just begun – and Putin's personal involvement in the dispute made it appear that political motives were as important as economic factors. When negotiations broke down, Gazprom

---

[21] Protocol to the Partnership and Co-operation Agreement, Brussels, 27 April 2004, available at: «http://www.europa.eu.int/comm/external_relations/russia/Russia_docs/protocol_0404.htm» and Joint Statement on EU Enlargement and EU–Russia Relations, 27 April 2004, available at: «http://www.europa.eu.int/comm/external_relations/russia/russia_docs/js_elarg_270404.htm».

[22] *EU–Russia Trade Relations*, p. 8, available at: «http://trade.ec.europa.eu/doclib/docs/2006/may/tradoc_113440.pdf». See also, «http://ec.europa.eu/external_relations/russia/intro/index.htm». According to the official Russian website for its G8 chairmanship, 90 per cent of Russia's energy exports go to Europe. See «http://en.g8russia.ru/agenda/nrgsafety/russianrole/».

cut off Ukraine's gas supply and, since 80 per cent of European gas supplies from Russia is transported through the pipelines through Ukraine, the EU's supply was briefly disrupted, according to Gazprom, because Ukraine was siphoning off gas.[23] Alarmed, the EU launched a debate on the necessity of diversifying the EU's energy supplies and called on Russia and Ukraine to resolve the dispute. The European media accused Russia of launching a gas war, remaining silent about Ukraine's role in the dispute. The Russian government was highly offended and insisted that Russia is a reliable supplier.[24]

A year later, at the beginning of 2007, there was an energy dispute between Belarus and Russia, involving both gas and oil, and, since Belarus was a loyal Russian ally, this made the Russian argument that increases in the price of energy were based on market principles rather than political factors seem more credible. The gas dispute was resolved quite quickly, averting a threat to supplies to western Europe via the Yamal network. The oil dispute was more difficult to resolve and it resulted in a brief interruption to the flow of oil to the Czech Republic, Germany, Hungary, Poland, Slovakia and Ukraine. Once again, the disruption was caused by Belarus siphoning off oil, and again the western media blamed Russia. By 11 January the dispute had been resolved and the oil flow through Belarus had reached full volume. By then, however, there were renewed calls for the EU to diversify its energy sources.

Three production-sharing agreements made in the mid-1990s with Royal Dutch Shell, ExxonMobil, and Total SA have also run into trouble. According to the agreements, in lieu of taxes, Russia takes part of the oil and gas produced once the investors' costs are covered. But Shell announced in 2006 that the costs of its Sakhalin-II project had doubled. The Russian Ministry of Natural Resources responded by threatening to suspend its licence in Sakhalin because of alleged environmental violations. In December 2006 Shell agreed to sell a majority share in Sakhalin-II to Gazprom. There were also allegations that Exxon Mobile and Total were infringing the technical provisions in their contracts and threats that their licences might be revoked. Further, in June 2007 TNK-BP was forced to sell a 62.9 per cent stake in its Kovykta gas field to Gazprom (*Novosti*, 22 June 2007). In all these cases, the real problem appears to be that Russia wants to regain state control over its oil and gas industries. This has exacerbated the EU's apprehension that the Russians will use energy as an instrument of foreign policy (Bradshaw, 2006, p. 19).

The EU concerns persist despite a number of multilateral initiatives intended to deal with Russian–EU energy security. In 2000, for example, a

---

[23] *Itar-Tass Weekly News*, 2 January 2006.
[24] See Prime Minister Fradkov's message to the European Council in *Itar-Tass Weekly News*, 3 January 2006.

Russian–EU Energy Dialogue was established to consider security of supply, including 'rationalization of production and transport infrastructures, European investment possibilities, and relations between producer and consumer countries'.[25] In October 2005 a Russia–EU Energy Forum, a platform for the business community to discuss energy co-operation, was set up to supplement intergovernmental energy co-operation. There is also the international Energy Charter Treaty (ECT), established on the initiative of the European Commission in 1994 as a legally-binding multilateral instrument to deal with issues pertaining to investment, trade, transit, competition and environmental concerns and inter-governmental co-operation in the energy sector.[26] Although Russia signed the ECT, it has not ratified it, despite the Commission's strenuous efforts over the years to persuade it to do so.

Although the Russian–EU energy relationship remains contentious, the Energy Dialogue made a little progress in 2007. A new thematic group on Strategies, Forecasts and Scenarios was set up and it held its first meeting in September 2007 and, as we have seen, Russia and the EU agreed at the Mafra summit to set up an early warning system in the event of disruptions of Russian oil and gas supplies to Europe.[27]

Russia's attempts to change the terms of the production-sharing agreements with western oil companies and its reluctance to ratify the ECT are indications of how Russian foreign policy, including its policy towards the EU, has changed. Russia signed the production-sharing agreements and the ECT at a time when its economy was extremely weak. As the economy recovered (in large part because of huge rises in the world price of energy), however, Russian officials began to display a new assertiveness in the pursuit of domestic and foreign policy goals. International agreements, such as the ECT, would no longer be permitted to impinge on Russia's national interests. Putin insists that the ECT cannot be ratified until it is amended to take account of those interests. He objects, in particular, to the ECT's requirement that Russia should open up access to its pipelines, which are currently under the monopoly control of Gazprom and Transneft. His objection coincided with Russian demands that European states should open up their downstream operations to enable Gazprom to buy into their distribution and retail natural gas infrastructure, which prompted the Commission to propose a 'reciprocity clause' for energy relations with third countries, a move that is widely seen to be targeting Gazprom.[28] Since Gazprom is believed to be synonymous with

---

[25] European Union–Russia Energy Dialogue, available at: «http://ec.europa.eu/energy/russia/overview».
[26] *The Energy Charter Treaty and Related Documents* at: «http://www.encharter.org/index.php?id=7».
[27] EU–Russian Energy Dialogue, Eighth Progress Report, 2007, available at: «http://ec.europa.eu/energy/russia/joint_progress/index_en.htm».
[28] *EurActiv.com*, 20 September 2007.

the Kremlin, its possible acquisition of downstream assets within the EU conjures up visions of Kremlin control over European domestic gas markets.

On one level, therefore, Russian–EU energy relations appear to have reached an impasse. Paradoxically, however, those relations continue to expand. Just before the Russia–Ukraine gas dispute began, for example, Russia and Germany had agreed to build a pipeline under the Baltic Sea. This 1,200 km-long North European Gas Pipeline will make it possible for Russia to supply Germany and the rest of the EU with gas without relying on transit via Poland and Ukraine. And, despite the EU's policy debate about the need to diversify EU energy supplies, the pipeline will increase the EU's dependence on Russian gas (Hughes, 2006). This highlights the difficulty that the EU has in co-ordinating its energy policy towards Russia. Many European leaders prefer to deal with Russia on a bilateral basis rather than via the EU, pursuing their own energy interests, even when those interests conflict with the interests of the EU as a whole or with the interests of other Member States. In negotiating the North European gas pipeline, for example, Germany showed scant regard for the concerns of Poland (as well as Ukraine and Belarus) that the pipeline gives Russia the potential to cut them off from gas supplies or for the environmental concerns of Finland and Sweden. Similarly, Hungarian and Bulgarian readiness to buy into Gazprom's proposed South European gas pipeline to take Caspian gas to Europe undermines the potential of the Nabucco pipeline, favoured by the EU.

Putin's Domestic Policy

The domestic policies that have been adopted by Putin since he became President in 2000, and which have turned Russia into, at best, a 'regulated democracy', have also caused a great deal of disquiet in the EU. It is not difficult to see why Putin felt that it was necessary to introduce changes in the domestic political system. Throughout the 1990s there were constant conflicts between the Duma, the lower house of parliament, and the president, his administration and his government. There was also strife between the president and his government; between March 1998 (when Viktor Chernomyrdin was dismissed) and August 1999 (when Putin became prime minister, at the same time becoming Yeltsin's designated successor) there were five different prime ministers in Russia. Putin believed that it was essential to bring an end to the conflict between the legislature and the executive and to ensure stability of government.

Putin also believed that Russia was on the brink of disintegrating. Russia is a multinational federation, and, although there is a federal treaty binding the units to the centre, many of the units had signed separate treaties with the central government in the 1990s, arrogating political and economic power to the regional government. This resulted in a very asymmetric federation and an impoverished central government. Despite the great constitutional power accorded to the president in the 1993 constitution, the central government became extremely weak between 1993 and 2000. Putin believed that unless power was returned to the central government, Russia would disintegrate as the Soviet Union had done a decade before.

Putin therefore set about constructing a strong state (or, in his terminology, re-establishing the 'power vertical'). His first step was to establish a strong 'party of power' – now called United Russia – to support presidential policies. United Russia holds 315 of the 450 seats in the current Duma and it can count on the co-operation of two of the other three parties represented in parliament. The President has no difficulty now in persuading the Duma to adopt the legislation he proposes. His second step was to change the composition of the Federal Council, the upper house of parliament. It had previously consisted of the elected governors/presidents and the heads of the legislatures of the federal units. It now consists of two representatives of each federal unit, one chosen by the governors/presidents, the other by the legislatures. Third, in an attempt to ensure that central laws were implemented across the country, Putin established seven federal districts encompassing the 89 federal units, each presided over by a governor-general representing the president. Putin also clamped down on the media – particularly the electronic media critical of the government.

These changes caused some concern in the EU, but in the wake of the Beslan tragedy in September 2004,[29] President Putin introduced two more changes that were far more serious in their impact on Russian democracy. First, governors/presidents of the federal units who had previously been elected by popular vote would now be nominated by the president and confirmed by the regional legislature. Second, Putin changed the electoral law so that in the 2007 parliamentary election, the Duma was elected entirely on the basis of proportional representation (previously half the deputies were elected from single-mandate constituencies). Although Russian officials explain this as a means of strengthening political parties, the effect has been to increase the distance between Russian voters and their parliamentary representatives, making it more difficult for them to hold their representatives accountable. At the same time, the threshold for parties to be represented in the Duma was raised from 4 to 7 per cent and smaller parties were no longer

---

[29] Armed terrorists took more than 1,200 school children and adults hostage on 1 September 2004 in the town of Beslan in North Ossetia. On the third day, gunfire broke out between the hostage-takers and Russian security forces. According to official data, 344 civilians were killed, 186 of them children, and hundreds more wounded.

permitted to form electoral alliances to enable them to win seats in the Duma. This has effectively prevented smaller political parties from gaining any seats. These political measures have reduced the political choices Russian citizens can make, made it more difficult for a plurality of opinions to be heard, and removed the possibility of the political opposition influencing Russian policy.

Putin's reforms have also had implications for EU–Russian relations. At a practical level, Putin's centralizing measures have had a negative impact on particular aspects of EU policy, for example, the regional interdependence and cross-border co-operation explicitly fostered by the Northern Dimension. Internal differences notwithstanding, EU actors have also frequently expressed disapproval of Russia's retreat from democracy and criticized the conduct of Russian elections. For example, the Commission (2004b, p. 6) recommended that 'a partnership must be [also] founded on shared values [. . .]. This implies discussing frankly Russian practices that run counter to universal and European values, such as democracy, human rights in Chechnya, media freedom and some environmental issues.' The EU and individual governments also complained about the treatment of ODIHR election observers in the December 2007 and March 2008 elections. These criticisms have provoked a steadily increasing resentment in Russia of the EU's normative agenda.[30]

Another issue that has affected Russian–EU relations is the war in Chechnya. The Russian government has always maintained that the situation in Chechnya is an entirely domestic matter, whereas EU officials and the governments of a number of Member States believe that the way in which the Chechen wars have been prosecuted infringes both the letter and the spirit of the principles which Russia endorsed by signing up to the PCA and to other international agreements. When Russia launched the second war in 1999, the EU responded by temporarily suspending TACIS funding for all programmes except for specific priority areas including human rights, the rule of law, support for the development of a civil society and nuclear safety. President Putin has always asserted that Russia is fighting international terrorism in Chechnya and, after the terrorist attacks on the US on 11 September 2001, the international community, including the EU, appeared to give some credence to his assertion. Although the EU consequently moderated its public criticism of Russian conduct, Chechnya did not cease to be a contentious issue in Russian–EU relations. When the Danish authorities declined to ban a meeting of the World Chechen Congress in Copenhagen in 2002, for example, the venue for the Russian–EU summit had to be moved. The Russian government

---

[30] That the EU criticized neither President Yeltsin's very many undemocratic actions nor the administrative manipulation of elections in the1990s makes Russians believe that its criticisms of Putin are particularly objectionable.

was angry when the Danish and British courts refused to extradite Akhmed Zakaev, Chechen President Aslan Maskhadov's envoy to Russia, and when the British courts granted him political asylum in November 2003.[31] According to the Russian government, in refusing to label Chechens as international terrorists the EU is guilty of double standards. After the Beslan siege in September 2004, when Dutch Foreign Minister Bernard Bot (the Netherlands held the EU Council presidency at the time) expressed EU sympathy but also asked 'how this tragedy could have happened',[32] Russian resentment of the EU's response to Chechen terrorism became far sharper. The diplomatic row in 2004 was smoothed over and the Russian government agreed to an EU proposal to establish regular consultations on human rights, the first of which took place on 1 March 2005.[33] Nevertheless, Russians continue to resent EU criticisms of Russia's democratic deficit and of its policy in Chechnya, while the EU, in turn, appears to question Russia's commitment to core universal and European values and the pursuit of democratic reforms (see e.g. Commission, 2004b).

Russian Rejection of the EU's Normative Agenda

The promotion of democratic values and the rule of law are very prominent aspects of the EU's policy towards Russia. Russia's growing hostility to the imposition of Western values and norms and to the intrusive nature of EU policy has, therefore, become an impediment to deepening relations. Particularly during Putin's second term, Russian officials have rejected the incorporation of 'common European values' into the Russia–EU relationship, since they believe that these values are determined exclusively in the EU and are simply proclaimed by EU officials for Russia to adopt.

The official Russian position by 2004 was that Russia would participate in European affairs 'not as an object of "civilizing influences" on the part of other states or groups thereof, but precisely as an equal among equals'.[34] Putin and other Russian officials often argue that values such as democracy should reflect Russian traditions. The term 'sovereign democracy', proposed and promoted by Putin's deputy chief of staff, Vladislav Surkov, appears to embody this conviction that Russians should define their own democracy and protect themselves from values exported from outside.[35] Sovereign democracy is very different from the democracy proposed by and practiced in the

---

[31] *Itar-Tass Weekly News*, 3 December 2002; 28 November 2003.
[32] *RFE/RL Newsline*, 6 September 2004.
[33] See Russian Ministry of Foreign Affairs, Press Release, Russia, European Union Human Rights Consultations in Luxembourg, 397-02-03-2005, 2 March 2005.
[34] Deputy Foreign Minister Vladimir Chizhov, *Izvestiya*, 25 February 2004, p. 2.
[35] *Moscow News*, 12 July 2005.

EU, since it 'embodies nostalgia for the old European nation state and nostalgia for a European order organized around the balance of power and non-interference in the domestic affairs of other states' (Krastev, 2008, p. 75).

Russian hostility to the EU's normative agenda has been reflected in the dismissal of European anxiety about Putin's political reforms as well as in resentment of the EU's reaction to Russian policy in Chechnya. But the most obvious manifestation of hostility is Russia's response to the perceived role of the democracy promotion programmes of the EU (and the US) in instigating the 'colour revolutions' in Georgia, Kyrgyzstan and Ukraine.

Since Putin is a very popular leader and the opposition in Russia is small and divided, it is extremely unlikely that a significant challenge to either Putin or President Dmitry Medvedev will arise in the foreseeable future. Neverthe-less, the Russian government has reacted harshly to attempts by the opposi-tion to stage public protests against government policy, lest these demonstrations turn into the mass protests that sparked the 'colour revolu-tions'. Moreover, ever since the 'Orange Revolution' in Ukraine in 2004, it has also been determined to prevent any foreign intervention in Russian politics. The law on non-governmental organizations (NGOs) is one mani-festation of this determination. Since NGOs, particularly foreign funded ones, were credited with organizing opposition forces against the regimes in Georgia, Kyrgyzstan and Ukraine, a law was adopted in Russia in January 2006 that severely limits the ability of foreign NGOs to function on Russian territory. The law denies local registration to foreign NGOs if their 'goals and objectives [. . .] create a threat to the sovereignty, political independence, territorial integrity, national unity, unique character, cultural heritage and national interests of the Russian Federation'. Only individuals who are 'legally domiciled in the Russian Federation' may create, participate, or be a member of a Russian NGO. NGOs have to undergo a lengthy, arduous and expensive process of registration with a regulating agency that has the task of evaluating whether the organization's activities are in line with its stated goals and which oversees its funding and expenditures through an annual review of its activities and financial statements.[36]

The EU has criticized the NGO law. In its resolution on the Mafra summit, for example, the European Parliament (2007) stressed that the law has had a negative impact on the work of many NGOs, and it supported initiatives to simplify procedures for registering NGOs. Russians have ignored the criticism and it is clear that, although they may pay lip service to normative commit-ments they have already undertaken in agreements with Western partners, they

---

[36] A translation of the law can be found at: «http://www.russiaprofile.org/resources/ngos/ngolaw/index.wbp». For an interesting discussion of all the means Russian officials have used to prevent a colour revolution in Russia, see Ambrosio (2007).

believe that Russian–EU relations should be based on shared interests and not on the accommodation by Russia to a set of EU values and norms.[37]

Structural Problems

Two structural problems will need to be resolved if a mutually acceptable basis is to be found for a new Russian–EU agreement. The first is the inadequate administrative infrastructure and the lack of proper co-ordinating mechanisms within Russia to deal with the EU. Russians do not understand how the Brussels bureaucracy works and they complain bitterly about its 'rather woolly decision-making procedure' (see e.g. Lukin, 2005, p. 58). They resent the EU's inflexibility and its reluctance to compromise. But they are even more critical of the inadequacies of their own bureaucracy, arguing, for example, that there are too few experienced negotiators in the Ministry of Trade to deal with the economic consequences of enlargement.[38] According to Russian EU specialists, '[Russian] policy towards the EU suffers [. . .] from a weakness of bureaucratic support'.[39] One Russian specialist on the EU argues that there is a 'catastrophic shortage of qualified experts, in addition to the marked disunity among government agencies' in Russia as a result of which it is very difficult to form an efficient task force to negotiate a new agreement (Bordachev, 2006, p. 115). Russian EU specialists propose that the role of co-ordinating Russian policy should be assigned to an existing institution, or else a special agency should be established to 'co-ordinate efforts to work out and advance a single Russian position on all aspects of relations with the European Union'.[40]

The result of this lack of capacity is that the Russian government tends to respond to policy proposals emanating from Brussels, rarely putting its own initiatives forward. This, in turn, gives rise to complaints that the EU treats Russia as the 'junior partner'. Moreover, Putin's 'power vertical' has meant that substantive progress on contentious issues has increasingly depended on agreements at very high levels and, since summits have been liable to being hijacked by issues of high politics, co-operation on issues of low politics has faltered.

The second structural problem – the preference for bilateralism – afflicts both Russia and the EU. On the Russian side, the preference for engaging

---

[37] For a fuller discussion of Russia's attitudes to the EU's normative agenda, see the final chapter in Allison *et al.* (2006).

[38] *Razshireniya ES: ugroza ili shans dlya Rossii?* RUE, Moscow, 2002, pp. 17–18.

[39] *Otnosheniya Rossii i Yevropeiskogo Soyuza: sovremennaya situatsiya i perspektivy,* Situatsionnyi analiz pod rukovodstvom S.A. Karaganova. Moscow, 2005, p. 18.

[40] *Otnosheniya Rossii i Yevropeiskogo Soyuza: sovremennaya situatsiya i perspektivy,* Situatsionnyi analiz pod rukovodstvom S.A. Karaganova. Moscow, 2005, pp. 21–2.

with individual EU Member States rather than the EU as a whole predates President Putin – it was a prominent feature of President Yeltsin's diplomacy – but Putin particularly cultivated personal relationships with individual European leaders (for example, former German Chancellor Gerhard Schröder, former French President Jacques Chirac and Italian Prime Minister Silvio Berlusconi) and has used those relationships to exploit differences of opinion between EU Member States.

Putin's approach is possible because European leaders are also prone to cultivate personal relationships with Russian leaders and to raise issues on a bilateral basis, even when the EU as a whole could or should address the issues and even when their actions undermine EU policy (Shuette, 2004, pp. 1–2). Some European leaders believe that Russia is too important a partner to let the EU lead (Smith, 2005, p. 286). The EU's 1999 Common Strategy was intended to ensure co-ordination between EU and Member State policy towards Russia (European Council, 1999), but recognition that it had not achieved this goal led to a review of EU policy in 2004 (Commission, 2004b). As we have seen particularly in relation to energy, some European leaders continue to deal with Russia bilaterally in order to pursue their own interests.

Conclusion

The term 'strategic partnership' is frequently used by both EU and Russian officials to refer to the relationship between the two parties (for recent examples, see Commission, 2007; Putin, 2007b). However, it has become increasingly difficult in recent years to understand exactly what they mean by the term. Initially, it was intended to depict co-operative interaction over an increasingly extensive agenda, stopping short of Russian accession to the EU. But, as we have seen, there have been so many tensions in their relations in recent years that, arguably, 'strategic rivalry' is the more appropriate term to use to depict some aspects of the relationship.

Nevertheless, EU officials frequently reiterate that Russia is the EU's biggest and most important neighbour.[41] Putin (2007b) similarly often points out that Russia's biggest partner is the EU and that Russia's 'ongoing dialogue with the EU creates favourable conditions for mutually beneficial economic ties and for developing scientific, cultural, educational and other exchanges. Our joint work on implementing the concept of the common spaces is an important part of the development of Europe as a whole'.

In other words, Russia and the EU agree that their inter-relationship is crucial to both. The Russian–EU relationship may be experiencing difficulties

---

[41] See, for example, Javier Solana's interview with *Kommersant*, 23 October 2007.

and they may continue to vie for influence in their common neighbourhood but, whether the PCA is indefinitely extended or whether a mutually acceptable basis is found for a new agreement, Russia and the EU are doomed or destined to continue to interact.

References

Allison, R., Light, M. and White, S. (2006) *Putin's Russia and the Enlarged Europe* (London/Oxford: Blackwell/Royal Institute of International Relations).

Ambrosio, T. (2007) 'Insulating Russia from a Colour Revolution: How the Kremlin Resists Regional Democratic Trends'. *Democratization*, Vol. 14, No. 2, pp. 232–52.

Bordachev, T. (2006) 'Toward a Strategic Alliance'. *Russia in Global Affairs*, Vol. 4, No. 2.

Bradshaw, M. (2006) 'Battle for Sakhalin'. *World Today* (November).

Chizhov, V. (2004) *International Affairs* (Moscow), No. 6.

Commission of the European Communities (2003) 'Wider Europe – Neighbourhood: A New Framework for Relations with our Eastern and Southern Neighbours'. COM(2003)104, 11 March.

Commission of the European Communities (2004a) 'European Neighbourhood Policy Strategy Paper'. COM(2004)373, 12 May.

Commission of the European Communities (2004b) 'Relations with Russia'. COM(2004)106. Available at «http://europa.eu.int/comm/external_relations/russia/Russia_docs/com04_106_en.pdf».

Commission of the European Communities (2007) *The European Union and Russia: Close Neighbours, Global Players, Strategic Partners*. Directorate-General for External Affairs, Brussels.

Council of the European Union (1999) 'Common Strategy of the European Union on Russia', 4 June; Official Journal, L157/1, 24 June.

EU Delegation Moscow (2007) Joint Press Conference of Vladimir Putin, Jose Manuel Barroso and Angela Merkel following the Russia–European Union Summit Meeting on 16 May. Available at «http://www.delrus.ec.europa.eu/en/images/pText_pict/559/Transcript.doc».

European Parliament (2007) 'Resolution on the EU–Russia Summit', 14 November. Available at «http://www.europarl.europa.eu/sides/getDoc.do?Type=TA&Reference=P6-TA-2007-0528&language=EN».

Haukkala, H. (2007) 'The Tomorrow is Now: the Case for Rejuvenating the Ailing EU–Russia Relationship'. *Russia in Global Affairs*, Vol. 5, No. 4, pp. 116–23.

Hughes, J. (2006) 'EU Relations with Russia: Partnership or Asymmetric Interdependency?' In Casarini, N. and Musu, C. (eds) *The EU's Foreign Policy in an Evolving International System: The Road To Convergence* (Basingstoke: Palgrave).

Kempe, I. and Grotzky, D. (2006) 'Crossroads of Co-operation: The Future of EU–Russian Relations and the Impact of the Baltic States'. *Lithuanian Foreign Policy Review*, Vol. 18, pp. 8–38.

Krastev, I. (2008) 'Russia as the "Other Europe" '. *Russia in Global Affairs*, Vol. 5, No. 4.

Light, M. (forthcoming) 'Russia and Europe and the Process of EU Enlargement'. In Wilson, E. and Torjesen, S. (eds) *The Multilateral Dimension in Russia's Foreign Policy* (London: Routledge).

Lukin, V. (2005) 'In 2004, Russian Foreign Policy Moved Ahead Cementing its Achievements and Never Losing Initiative'. *International Affairs* (Moscow), No. 1.

Prozorov, S. (2006) *Understanding Conflict between Russia and the EU: The Limits of Integration* (London: Palgrave Macmillan).

Putin, V. (2007a) Press conference after the Mafra EU–Russian summit, *Itar Tass Daily*, 26 October. Available at «http://dlib.eastview.com/sources/article. jsp?id=12815549».

Putin, V. (2007b) Annual Address to the Federal Assembly, 26 April. Available at «http://president.kremlin.ru/eng/speeches/2007/04/26/1209_type70029type 82912_125670.shtml».

RUE (2004) *Russia and the Enlarged European Union: The Arduous Path Towards Rapprochement*. Russia in a United Europe Committee.

Shuette, R. (2004) 'EU–Russia Relations: Interests and Values – A European Perspective'. *Carnegie Papers*, No. 54.

Smith, K.E. (2005) 'Enlargement and European Order'. In Hill, C. and Smith, M. (eds) *International Relations and the European Union* (Oxford: Oxford University Press), pp. 270–91.

Review Article: Comparative Regionalism: What Might It Be?

ALBERTA SBRAGIA
University of Pittsburgh

Introduction

The term 'comparative regionalism' has entered into common usage as the study of regionalism has become both increasingly fashionable and multi-dimensional. This review article first discusses the movement toward extra-European regionalism, which has been accompanied by the rejection of the European 'model' of supranational regional integration as well as the scholarship linked to that model. This combination has led to an ill-defined field of 'comparative' regionalism as well as confused use of the terms 'region', 'regionalization' and 'regionalism'. The article goes on to analyse how economists and political scientists differ in their respective approaches to the study of regions. Given its momentum and importance, the new Asian regionalism is then discussed. The article concludes with a brief analysis of three recent books which illuminate different ways of analytically approaching the comparative study of regionalism.

I. Regionalism: Beyond Europe

Regionalism beyond the European Union (EU) has become both a reality and an object of study as the international system has recalibrated itself after the end of the cold war, globalization has proceeded and multilateral negotiations designed to liberalize trade under globally-applicable rules have been very difficult to conclude. Earlier attempts at regionalism were modelled on the

European Economic Community and the first scholarly attempts at studying regionalism beyond Europe were inspired by the work of Ernst Haas (1961), the leading theoretician of early European integration. However, the more recent experience of regionalism has not imitated the EU, nor has the scholarly work related to 'the new wave of regionalism' imitated its EU-related counterpart (Mansfield and Milner, 1999; Mansfield and Milner, 1997; Higgott, 2007).

That scholarship in fact has been carried out by both political scientists and trade economists. The former have included mainstream scholars of international political economy (IPE) as well as those who view the study of regionalism as a way to escape from the 'methodological orthodoxy which shaped much of the substantive output of mainstream IPE' (Gamble and Payne, 2003, p. 46). International Relations scholars, for their part, have also approached the study of regionalism from a variety of perspectives (Hurrell, 2005). Partially due to the variety of sources from which the literature on regionalism draws, a common vocabulary has not developed. Nor has that literature developed established boundaries.

The term 'new regionalism', for example, can refer to a wide variety of subjects and theoretical approaches. The actual emergence of post-cold war regionalism or the 'neoliberal counter-revolution in development thinking' can both fall under this rubric (Doidge, 2007, p. 2). Alternatively, it can include analyses that view regionalism as being closely tied to globalization or approaches that want to declare their independence from 'American dominated definitions' of IPE – in which case it is often referred to as the New Regionalism Theory (NRT) or the New Regionalism Approach (NRA) (Warleigh-Lack, 2006; Soderbaum and Shaw, 2003; Hettne and Soderbaum, 2000). 'New regionalism' is therefore a broad tent rather than a single analytic approach, and the approach is claimed by some, but certainly not by all, scholars of contemporary regionalism (Payne and Gamble, 1996; Murphy and Tooze, 1991; Cox, 1986; Soderbaum, 2003).

Most scholars do, however, reject a definition of regionalism modelled on the legalism, institutions, and acceptance of supranationality à la European integration. The study of European integration clearly falls into the 'old regionalism' category. Fredrik Soderbaum (2003, p. 4) pithily expresses the rejection of European regionalism as a model by concluding that 'the new regionalism is both global and pluralistic, compared to the old regionalism, which was Eurocentric and narrow.'

In fact, the study of post-cold war regionalism does not rely on either neo-functionalism or intergovernmentalism, historically the dominant theoretical paradigms in the study of European integration. Much of the current political science literature on regionalism is informed by the general theoretical debates within that discipline or by debates within the relevant area studies community, rather than by the literature on the contemporary EU. As the EU's institutional capacity has strengthened over the decades, EU scholarship has shifted its focus away from integration to governance broadly defined (see, for example, Hix, 1994; Kohler-Koch and Rittberger, 2006; Jørgensen et al., 2006; Pollack, 2005). As a consequence, the gap between the work on European regionalism (defined as the EU) and that on regionalism in other parts of the world has widened. The two are now separate professional communities within political science.[1]

Scholars of regionalism who are engaged in broader disciplinary debates have been joined by scholars interested in a particular geographic region of the world and working within an area studies framework. The latter rely on what Peter Katzenstein (2005, xi) has termed 'area-based knowledge'. Such scholars are interested in patterns of co-operation that have been developing in a particular region of the world. They have a deep knowledge of the politics, economics and cultures within the geographical region with specialized knowledge of some of the states in that particular region.

Their work is typically theoretically informed, but their core interest has to do with the region under study rather than with contributing to theoretical debates in either international relations or IPE. Theory is essential to their work, but the latter has the primary objective of placing area-based knowledge within a social science perspective rather than contributing to theoretical debates as such. Amitav Acharya (2005) has referred to this group of scholars as 'discipline-oriented regionalists'. Much work on the relatively institutionalized forms of regional integration – the North American Free Trade Agreement (NAFTA), the Common Market of the South (Mercosur/Mercosul), the Asian-Pacific Economic Co-operation forum (APEC) and the Association of South-East Asian Nations (ASEAN) would fall in this category (Telo, 2007; Laursen, 2003).

The study of regionalism is also attractive to 'non-western' scholars who are interested in developing a body of theory which is not dominated by the Western experience and who view it as possibly contributing to the development of 'a non-Western international relations theory'. From this perspective,

> [. . .] much of Western international relations theory is drawn from Western history [. . .] [it] has also been excessively concerned with rather narrow, rational choice, views of motive in power politics, strategy and economics. It is only beginning to come to terms with the wider range of possibilities such as identity, honour, tradition, etc. (Acharya and Buzan, 2007, p. 293)[2]

---

[1] For an overview of the conflicts – of the 'disciplinary politics' – within EU studies, see Rosamond (2007).
[2] For a discussion of non-western International Relations theory, see Aggarwal et al. (2007).

The debates and perspectives of economists, for their part, inevitably shape at least some of the work of political scientists, as well as framing the discussion of economic regionalism. Definitions and analyses by international institutions, such as the World Trade Organization (WTO), shape the parameters of trade economists' scholarly work so that the economics literature tends to frame regionalism within the broader context of the multilateral system governing trade. In general, that perspective views multilateral arrangements as preferable to regional groupings, for the former are inclusionary while the latter are by definition exclusionary. Since regionalism can be defined as 'the form of plurilateralism defined by geographic proximity' (Hettne, 2005, p. 272), trade economists are bound to be sceptical of its overall benefit for the health of the world's trading system.

Studies of regionalism that draw on economics as a discipline are basically different from those that draw on other paradigms. The prominent trade economist Jagdish Bhagwati (1993, p. 22) has defined regionalism as 'preferential trade agreements among a subset of nations'. For those working within the paradigm of economics and multilateral institutions such as the GATT/WTO, regionalism has been triggered by preferential trading arrangements that were often seen as potentially undermining the multilateral system designed to limit preferential trade. Bjorn Hettne (2003, pp. 24–5; see also Hettne *et al.*, 1999, 2001), whose work has developed the relationship between regionalism and globalization through the NRA, argues that such an economic lens views 'regionalism as a trade promotion policy [. . .] [whereas] for the NRA regionalism was a comprehensive multidimensional programme, including economics, security, environmental and many other issues'. On the other hand, Mansfield and Milner (1999, p. 606), in an influential article reviewing the political foundations of the 'new wave' of regionalism, conclude that membership of preferential trade arrangements 'stimulate[s] liberal economic and political reforms [. . .] and may contribute to both commercial openness and political co-operation'.[3]

II. The Ambiguities of 'Comparative Regionalism'

The study of 'comparative regionalism', not surprisingly, is ill-defined.[4] Scholars often use the term loosely to refer to the study of practically any

---

[3] Trade agreements negotiated by the US or the EU may also lead to other political changes such as in the area of human rights (Hafner-Burton, forthcoming).

[4] In the study of comparative politics, the term 'cross-regional' usually refers to comparisons of individual states in different geographic regions – i.e. Europe, South America, Africa. For an example of this type of usage, see Huber (2003). The term 'region' in this context refers to simply geographic region and does not refer to the kinds of works which are thought of as belonging to 'comparative regionalism' however defined.

form of regionalist project involving various forms of political or economic co-operation outside of the EU whether or not they are interested in comparison. To make matters even more confusing, the literature on comparative regionalism overlaps with the literature on comparative regional integration understood in terms of regional institution-building. At times, the two terms are used almost synonymously, while at others the term regional integration implies an institutionalization and a degree of (intergovernmental) political direction that is not a necessary requirement for regionalism *tout court*. While scholars focused on the EU typically do not view themselves as participating in either the study of comparative regionalism or comparative regional integration, scholars focused on regionalism in other parts of the world often do so even if they are not comparing regions. The term 'comparative' regionalism thus often refers to the study of a single regionalist project outside of Europe.

That said, both work that is explicitly comparative and that which is focused on a single (non-European) region often incorporate the EU as a focal point if only to argue that the EU is unique.[5] The EU, given its institutional structure and the high degree of regional economic integration it has attained, is often (if only implicitly) seen as the 'gold standard' of regional integration. Indeed, Breslin and Higgott (2000, p. 341) have argued that the assumption that the EU is the exemplar of integration is 'one of the major obstacles to the development of analytical and theoretical comparative studies of regional integration' (see also Hurrell, 2005, p. 39). For their part, EU scholars, in sharp contrast, are generally unfamiliar with the work on comparative regionalism or with regionalism in any of its variants, including explicit integration projects, in other parts of the world.

If the field of comparative regionalism exists, its boundaries are certainly permeable – just as is its subject. Its character is interpreted in many ways depending on the perspective of the author, the area of the world with which the author is most familiar, and the theoretical orientation applied. Given that diversity, no commonly accepted definition of 'region' or 'regionalism' or 'regional integration' exists. Even the role of geography, for example, is becoming more variable as trade agreements and co-operative arrangements more generally are now characterized as 'inter-regional,' 'cross-regional' or 'transcontinental' (see, for example, Maull and Okfen, 2003).

The vastness and 'loose-limbed' nature of the literature arises from the importance of both economics and politics in the study of regionalism. Some would argue that a region is essentially an economic unit, while others would maintain that a region is 'politically made' (Katzenstein, 2005, p. 9), while

---

[5] Telo (2007) explicitly compares regional projects to the EU.

still others are interested in the role of regions in international security (Buzan and Waever, 2003; Adler and Barnett, 1998). The term 'comparative regionalism' is therefore imprecise, fluid, and open to numerous interpretations. The ambiguities inherent in the term are multiplied by the fact that the relevant scholarly community is unusually global, for the phenomenon of regionalism, however defined, has captured the interest of scholars from a wide range of countries (in this article, I refer only to works written in English, but there is a relevant literature written in, for example, Portuguese and Spanish).

Since the terms 'region', 'regionalization', 'regionalism' and 'regional integration' are attached to so many different definitions, usages and analytical approaches, the literature that can be viewed as reasonably belonging to the field of 'comparative regionalism' is very large, diverse, and expanding. This article can do no more than mention a small portion of the relevant literature while alerting the reader that the study of comparative regionalism understood broadly is largely detached from the study of the internal dynamics of the EU. Students of comparative regionalism are grappling with an international arena and with dynamics of globalization which have been often ignored by scholars focused on the EU.[6] Such scholars have been able to construct their own scholarly community partially because the EU, constituted by wealthy industrialized states, plays a very different role in the international arena than do the countries that constitute regional groupings in the developing world (Sbragia, 2002).

III. EU Exceptionalism

While regionalism outside of Europe confronts the complexities of globalization, the EU for its part has been a shaper of globalization rather than simply its object. Helen Wallace (2000, p. 381) has argued that 'Europeanization is sufficiently deeply embedded to act as a filter for globalization'.[7] It is telling that the EU was not subject to the financial crises of 1997–99 that had major impacts on regional projects in both southeast Asia and Latin America. The vulnerability of non-European regionalism to the forces of globalization and, by contrast, the ability of European regionalism to 'filter' those same forces, testifies to the structural difference that sets European regionalism apart from regionalism in the developing world. That structural difference certainly arises from the institutionalized character of the EU, but it also reflects the wealth and social stability of its Member States.

---

[6] For a discussion of how Europeanization and globalization may intersect, see Snyder (1999) and Longo (2003).
[7] It is also viewed as powerful within WTO trade negotiations (Elgstrom, 2007).

Finally, the EU is so deeply institutionalized that its internal political and inter-institutional dynamics are unique within the world of regional integration. Whereas other regional projects are concerned with the process of integration, however defined, the EU is now struggling to come to terms with the degree of integration it has already achieved. The difference between the process of integration and the governance of that integration is such that scholars focused on the process outside of Europe do not find the literature on European governance to be especially pertinent.

IV. Economic Regionalism and Security Communities

Economic regionalism is extensively discussed in the comparative regionalism literature. The term has been used to indicate two types of relationships. One is focused on production and supply networks centred on relationships among firms in different nation-states, typically found in East Asia, while the other refers to a project of regional integration with some kind of formalized institutional component. The first is society-centred while the second is more state-centred.

The term 'regionalization' is now often (but not consistently) used to refer to relationships among firms across national borders, while economic 'regionalism' usually refers to intergovernmental co-operation, often in the form of a preferential trade agreement, among a group of geographically contiguous states. Such a preferential trade agreement may exist alongside regularized consultation among national leaders oriented toward achieving co-operation outside of the economic arena. Economic regionalism, therefore, may exist alongside non-economic forms of co-operation, but the literature tends to be divided, with scholars focusing on either one or the other.[8]

Some would argue that all regional trading agreements should qualify for study under the rubric of regionalism whether or not they involve geographically contiguous signatories. Other scholars would focus on economic linkages and networks within a contiguous geographic area, without regard to the existence of such agreements. Still others would stress the existence of specific organizational and institutional characteristics of a more or less well-defined geographically-based regional grouping. While the terms regionalization and regionalism tended to be used synonymously in early literature, a (relatively) common usage of the term regionalization has

---

[8] A recent analysis comparing trade agreements and co-operation agreements in arenas other than trade concludes that 'states co-operate disproportionately more in the domain of trade than in other domains' (Estevadeordal and Suominen, 2008, p. 129). In the case of the US, however, 'political and geostrategic motivations' influence the selection of countries with which it is willing to negotiate unilateral preferential trade agreements (Lederman and Ozden, 2007, p. 236).

recently emerged. In Hurrell's (1995, p. 39) words, 'the most important driving forces for economic regionalization come from markets, from private trade and investment flows, and from the policies and decision of companies'.

Regionalism, for its part, may well include regionalization, but it tends to be a more complex and multi-dimensional arrangement. 'Regions', understood as political actors, and regionalism are often used synonymously. Hurrell (1995, pp. 37–45) argues that scholars tend to analyse regions in terms of identity, regularized patterns of consultation, policies designed to achieve some level of economic integration through preferential trade agreements and the attainment of cohesion such that the group can play an international role and/or play a role in the formulation of policy within the region.

The work on the 'new regionalism' does not draw on Ernst Haas's works on neo-functionalism, although Haas had explicitly explored the utility of neo-functionalism in understanding regional integration in non-European contexts (Haas, 1961, 1967; Haas and Schmitter, 1964, 1965). Walter Mattli (2005) argues that a key reason for the contemporary absence of neo-functionalist analysis is the failure of the original theoretical work to deal with disintegration as well as integration. Although work on the EU is carried out under 'the shadow cast by neo-functionalism', that shadow is absent in the study of comparative regional integration (Rosamond, 2005, p. 238).[9]

V. Regionalism and Security

The influence of early work on regional integration is much greater in the area of security. Although security communities have received less attention than regional projects concerned with trade, the literature on security communities explicitly draws on Karl Deutsch's work, especially on his *Political Community and the North Atlantic Area: International Organization in the Light of Historical Experience* (1957). Works in Deutsch's tradition have contributed to the development of constructivism in international relations (Adler and Barnett, 1998; Buzan and Waever, 2003), with southeast Asia (Acharya, 2001), and the Mediterranean region (Adler *et al.*, 2006) receiving sophisticated attention within that theoretical tradition. Deutsch's influence on security communities is very evident, though as Adler and Barnett point out (1998, p. 9) 'Deutsch's study was often cited but rarely emulated'.[10]

---

[9] An exception is Acharya (2006) who compares the impact of the Asian financial crisis on east Asia with the impact of the crisis of 1973 on the European Community.
[10] For an analysis of ASEAN which, drawing on Jervis (1982), argues that it is a security regime rather than a security community see Collins (2007).

The society-centred view put forth by Deutsch stood in contrast to the framework put forth by Haas in the arena of economic integration which emphasized international bureaucracies and functional policy elites. Neither framework, however, tied economics to security in the way that Peter Katzenstein's (2005) *A World of Regions* has done. Similarly, neither addressed the issue of regional international institutions in both arenas in the way that Acharya and Johnston (2007) have done.

VI. Regionalism: Economists and Political Scientists

Regional (as well as bilateral) approaches to trade liberalization have been triggered by several dynamics. These include the difficulties encountered by multilateral negotiations, the unilateral liberalization of domestic economies in developing countries (Milner and Kubota, 2005), and the deepening of regional integration in the EU and the US (through NAFTA), two key export markets for the developing world.

Economists, for their part, view preferential trading arrangements as nearly synonymous with regionalism (Panagariya, 1999) and debate whether such arrangements are in fact GATT/WTO compliant. In general, they fear that regional agreements will exclude more efficient competitors in third countries (Bhagwati and Panagariya, 1996). Some evidence has been found for this point of view in the case of NAFTA (Morgenstern *et al.*, 2007). Such agreements differ in the range of preferences that they grant the participating members as well as the depth of those preferences.

The linkage between regionalism and multilateralism, therefore, is a focus of both scholarly and policy debate (Baldwin, 2006; for a legal perspective see Devuyst and Serdarevic, 2007). In general, economists have treated the growth of regionalism as damaging to the overall expansion of global trade. Jagdish Bhagwati (1993) coined the now universally-used image of a 'spaghetti bowl' to symbolize the complex set of trade agreements that, because of their distinct rules of origin and various forms of protection, economists believe threaten a multilateral system of trade-friendly rules and enforcement procedures.

The literature specifically concerned with regionalism and trade policy is shaped by the WTO regime, and the definition of a 'region' is being re-thought as the geographic shape of trade agreements undergoes change. Regional trade agreements, as defined by the WTO, are increasingly involving 'cross-regional or cross-continental partners' and can be bilateral as well as plurilateral (WTO Secretariat, 2003, p. 2).

Focusing on preferential trade agreements leads to a different view of 'region' than does a focus on the more institutionalized regional arrangements such as the EU or NAFTA (Sbragia, 2007). According to the WTO, nearly 400 regional trade agreements (RTAs) are likely to be in force by 2010.[11] Although, as Pomfret (2007) argues, that figure overstates the importance of RTAs to the world economy, it does reflect the widespread acceptance of bilateral and pluri-lateral trade agreements. States are joining a variety of RTAs, each with its own rules, which can lead to difficulties in implementation and high costs of compliance for traders.

As the number of preferential trade arrangements has skyrocketed, the term 'regionalism' has become used in widely differing ways. As indicated, an RTA does not necessarily involve states within one geographic region. Neither does it necessarily imply the kind of institutionalization found in traditional regional projects such as Mercosur or NAFTA.

Regionalism therefore incites passionate debate among those who worry about the ability of the multilateral system to regulate international trade. The study of comparative regionalism is very much tied to policy debates about the pros and cons of negotiating preferential trade agreements which provide preferred access to markets to some and not to others. Given that the most-favoured nation (MFN) basis of international trade has been a core element of the GATT/WTO system, the rise of regional trade agreements which offer privileged access to some countries has raised a number of alarms that are reflected in at least one portion of the relevant literature.

VII. Political Scientists and Regionalism

Political scientists, for their part, tend to define regions differently from economists and view the advent of regionalism with a good deal more equanimity. They tend to view a region as a group of contiguous countries that have adopted 'arrangements designed to bring together neighbouring countries [. . .]. In this sense, the term *region* carries a meaning that is not only geographic but also geopsychological' (Pempel, 2005, p. 3). Thus, while some regions are made up of countries that have signed a trade agreement, others have a different basis. Given the 'geopsychological' nature of such regional groups, political scientists tend not to restrict themselves to viewing such groups as simply members of a preferential trade agreement.

While economists have a 'thin' view of regions, most political scientists view them as incorporating a relatively dense set of interconnections. Nonetheless, political scientists have not arrived at a common definition of regions,

---

[11] Available at WTO Regional Trade Agreement gateway «http://www.wto.org/english/tratop_e/region_e/region_e.htm». For a discussion of the literature on the political reasons for pursuing RTAs, see Damro (2006).

regionalism, or regionalization. The role of identity formation, for example, is not settled. Camroux (2007, p. 552), for one, argues that 'regionalism' is '[. . .] defined as being essentially ideational, implying degrees of identity and the construction thereof'. Other perspectives on regionalism, by contrast, privilege institutionalized economic relationships or arrangements for regularized consultation.

VIII. Asian Regionalism

The 'rise of Asia' is triggering a rebalancing of geopolitical and geo-economic power. The concomitant emergence of regionalism in Asia raises new questions about how 'regions' are created, defined, and expanded, questions which will help redefine the field of comparative regionalism in political science. Regionalism in Asia ranges from ASEAN, the oldest and most institutionalized form of regional co-operation, to the third East Asia Summit (EAS) in 2007, which represents a very loose form of regional dialogue. The surprising – given Asia's diversity and history of conflict — move from economic regionalization to regional co-operation was triggered by the perceived inadequacy of the international response to the devastating Asian financial crisis of 1997–8 (Breslin *et al.*, 2002; de Brouwer and Wang, 2004; Higgott, 2007). The paralysis of Mercosur in Latin America's Southern Cone (Vasconcelos, 2007) and of integration in the Americas as a whole (Guedes de Oliveira, 2007) along with the counter-intuitiveness of both regionalism in Asia and ASEAN's ability to adopt and maintain a key role in the construction of such regionalism[12] have enhanced the importance of Asian regionalism in the literature on comparative regionalism.

The non-communist states of southeast Asia took the first step toward successful regional co-operation in Asia in 1967 by launching ASEAN so as to ensure peaceful relations between Indonesia, Malaysia and the Philippines (Antolik, 1990, p. 8). The organization gradually became known for the 'ASEAN Way', which focused on socialization, non-interference, the construction of norms and the slow building of consensus. Amitav Acharya (1993, 2001, 2004, 2006, 2007; Acharya and Buzan, 2007; Acharya and Johnston, 2007) has written extensively on the evolution of ASEAN, very significantly contributing to both the comparative regionalism and International Relations literatures.

Asian regionalism beyond ASEAN has, until the creation of the East Asian Summit in 2005, incorporated an Asia-Pacific dimension through APEC,

---

[12] Acharya (2004, pp. 258–9) identified the establishment of the ASEAN Regional Forum (ARF) in 1994 as a milestone in that 'for the first time in history, Southeast Asia and the Asia Pacific acquired a permanent regional security organization'; see also Michael Leifer (1996).

established in 1989. It initially brought together the United States, Australia, Canada, ASEAN, Japan, China, and South Korea into an 'open' regional grouping committed to unilateral economic liberalization integrated into the world economy (Ravenhill, 2001). Gorbachev's Vladivostok speech of July 1986, increased intra-Asia-Pacific trade, the rising economies of East Asia, the increased role of foreign direct investment, difficulties with the Uruguay Round, fears that the US was moving away from its long-stated commitment to multilateralism, guarantees that ASEAN would play a key role and the sophisticated leadership of Australia (in concert with Japan)[13] all contributed to the creation of APEC (Ravenhill, 2001, pp. 62–89; see also Aggarwal and Morrison, 1998; Komori, 2007). The geopolitical and geo-economic environment, including the difficulties being faced by the Uruguay Round, were clearly key factors in the formation of APEC and in deciding its membership. However, APEC's failure to help the Asian states hard hit by the Asian financial crisis of 1997 dramatically reduced its effectiveness and importance (Ravenhill, 2008).

ASEAN, for its part, began to focus on economic integration. The ASEAN Free Trade Area (AFTA), announced in 1991, has achieved mixed results but has been reaffirmed and expanded in scope by the now 10-member organization. Nesadurai argues that 'elite governance politics' – understood as the balance between a focus on economic growth on the one hand and 'maximizing the wealth of particular groups' (the domestic business class in particular) on the other – is key to explaining the negotiation and most particularly the implementation of AFTA (Nesadurai, 2003, pp. 19 and 53).

Partially in response to APEC, the Asia–Europe Meeting (ASEM), first meeting in 1996, established a 'region-to region dialogue' which not only has helped to institutionalize 'the concept of interregionalism' (Gilson, 2005, p. 308),[14] but also helped the process of region-building in East Asia. Hostilities between China, Japan and South Korea have been so deeply-rooted that their leaders had not met during the entire post-Second World War period.

ASEM, for its part, depended on (East) Asian states forming themselves into a 'region' if only for the sole purpose of holding a dialogue with the EU. ASEAN took the lead (Komori 2007). The first meeting between ASEAN and the leaders of China, Japan, and South Korea took place in 1995 during an APEC meeting when an 'informal lunch [. . .] [was held] to prepare for the first ASEM meeting in Bangkok in 1996'(Terada, 2003, p. 262). Thus, 'Asia' had to be created in order to serve as an interlocutor for the EU. Given the geopolitics

---

[13] For an analysis of why both Japan and Australia have found it difficult to 'belong' to East Asia, see Beeson and Yoshimatsu (2007).
[14] The EU began focusing on Asia much later than on other parts of the world. (Holland, 2002, pp. 59–84) By contrast, the EU–Mercosur interregional relationship is far more institutionalized (Santander, 2005).

of Asia, however, the East Asian Summit process, initiated in 2005, has added Australia, New Zealand, and India to that earlier definition of 'Asia'.

IX. Comparative Regionalism: How to Compare

It is with the backdrop of Asian regionalism and Japan's role in the construction of that regionalism that Peter Katzenstein's (2005) *A World of Regions: Asia and Europe in the American Imperium* must be approached. Katzenstein's contribution to the understanding of Asian regionalism has been so important that the *Journal of East Asian Studies* recently published a roundtable devoted to his work (Aggarwal *et al.*, 2007). Through his earlier groundbreaking work on Germany, Katzenstein draws on a very rare area competence on Japan, Germany and the EU, and is regarded by many as the most important study in comparative European–Asian regionalism. In this article I can only alert the reader to its centrality rather than provide an in-depth review. Wide-ranging, utilizing 'area-based knowledge', drawing on realism, liberalism, and while sociological approaches to international relations linking American power with the 'regional orders' that have emerged in both Europe and East Asia,[15] the book will serve as a referent for future work for many years to come. In a similar vein, the excellent articles brought together in the roundtable offer a variety of thought-provoking assessments (which should be assigned to students) of the strengths and weaknesses of the analysis. Katzenstein's (2005, p. 42) core argument that 'world politics is now shaped by the interaction between porous regions and America's imperium' views regions as open to both globalization and internationalization rather than constituting 'blocs'. Due to their inclusion in the American imperium, 'Asia and Europe are not part of a rich trilateral club or a cohesive tripolar bloc' (Katzenstein, 2005, p. 37).

Katzenstein, however, acknowledges the limits of regional autonomy. The United States play a key role in the 'world of regions' and so do Germany and Japan, the 'core states'. The latter two, having been defeated and occupied in the Second World War were 'client states that eventually rose to become core regional powers' (p. 3). They are the ones who support American aims and power within their own regional orders as well as being tied in many ways to the United States. In this analysis, Asia and Europe as regions are not political actors *à la* literature on inter-regionalism.

Although he draws from the major theoretical traditions in international relations, Katzenstein's own approach is, in his own words, 'eclectic' (p. 39).

---

[15] 'Asia' refers to east and southeast Asia (p. 36). Other authors on Asian regionalism include southeast Asia in their definition of east Asia. The literature on Asian regionalism is not uniform in this area.

Nonetheless, he is clear about those analyses with which he disagrees (pp. 39–42). Drawing on both materialist theories and critical theories of geography, Katzenstein argues that 'regions are the creation of political power and purpose' (p. 21) and that 'the United States plays the central role in a world of regions' (p. 43). Although American power is the commonality across the two regions, he argues that Europe and Asia are very different along many dimensions. He is thus not searching for regularities across the two areas.

Whether the dynamics identified by Katzenstein will prove to have laid the foundations for the Asian 'regional order' in the 21st century is, however, unclear. They may prove to have shaped what will seem to be a bygone era. Japan holds such a prominent place in the analysis that the role of China in East Asia is understated, if only perhaps in retrospect. In a similar vein, it is very likely that the lack of attention paid to India will seem strange to future readers. However, scholars are still catching up with the extraordinarily rapid rise in importance of India, symbolized by its invitation to join the East Asian Summit (EAS) in 2005. Naidu (2005, p. 715) rightly argues that the inclusion of India in the EAS represents 'a remarkable turnaround in fortunes' as it was not initially invited to join either APEC or the ASEAN Regional Forum. The unexpected rise of China, and even more startlingly of India, raises the question of the limits of the American imperium with its reliance on core states whose role in regional politics is being at the very least trimmed.

A World of Regions is theoretically eclectic, based on area knowledge, and does not use the language of 'variables'. By contrast, Walter Mattli's (1999) *The Logic of Regional Integration: Europe and Beyond* is a self-conscious social science study of regional integration. Mattli (1999, p. 3) believes 'that there is a general logic to regional integration' and he thus asks 'the reader to think scientifically about integration and to be wary of so-called explanations that fail basic tests of scientific inference'. Whereas Katzenstein's analysis illuminates the key differences between Asia and Europe in both material and ideational arenas, Mattli (1999, p. 17) deliberately 'play[s] down the many significant differences among regions [. . .] [in order] to capture general tendencies and to explain those fundamental traits that are common to most cases'. Finally, 'economic factors' are the key explanatory variables with ideational concerns omitted from the analysis. Mattli's analysis offers a sharp contrast to the assumptions, research styles, and method of gathering data used by Katzenstein.

Mattli's work is important in that he is trying to explain variation in the success and failure of economic integration agreements. His objective is thus far narrower than is Katzenstein's but points to a key problem in the 'real world' – agreements aimed at increasing intra-regional trade are ceremoniously signed but fail. Mattli's work is especially relevant for the Latin

American experience as well as for ASEAN's. Given his focus on economic integration, it may not be surprising that he finds that in order to obtain successful integration, 'the potential for economic gains from market exchange within a region must be significant' (p. 42). The lack of economic complementarity among regional members contributes to the failure of the attempt (p. 42).

Nonetheless, attempts at economic integration in the developing world seem to downplay the role that extra-regional export markets play for many developing countries. Increasing intra-regional trade remains a focus for integration efforts even though it might be more advantageous to focus on increasing co-operation in areas other than trade. The EU 'model' which has focused on economic integration among wealthy countries with highly developed market structures may have provided a misguided roadmap for many developing economies. Put simply, it made economic sense for the countries of western Europe to try to increase intra-regional trade in the 1950s. By contrast, Latin America or southeast Asia are so dependent on extra-regional export markets that the opportunities for intra-regional trade are more limited than they are for wealthy countries trading with each other. It is important to remember that four of the G7 are EU members and two are NAFTA members – precisely the two regional projects focused on economic integration that have succeeded in substantially increasing intra-regional trade.

In the case of ASEAN, for example, the attempt to create an ASEAN Free Trade Area (AFTA) has been less successful than has ASEAN's attempt to co-operate in non-economic policy arenas, external relations in particular. It may be, however, that gains in trade should not be the indicator of a successful integration agreement. A trade agreement negotiated among states with non-complementary economies may actually be a way to attract foreign direct investment (FDI) rather than to increase trade. Nesadurai (2003, pp. 20 and 184), for example, argues that in the case of the ASEAN Free Trade Area, attracting foreign capital for 'capital and production rather than [a focus] on trade and exchange' were key. Nonetheless, Mattli's emphasis on outcomes in terms of intra-regional trade as part of a consistent explanation across cases for the failure of many economic integration agreements provides a strong contribution to the regional integration literature.

Mattli (1999, p. 42) argues that 'the demand for regional rules, regulations, and policies by market players is a critical driving force of integration'. Such regional rules and regulations are the focus of Francesco Duina's (2006) *The Social Construction of Free Trade: The European Union, Nafta, and Mercosur*. Duina, a sociologist, seeks to explain why Mercosur, NAFTA, and the EU differ. He is, like Katzenstein and unlike Mattli, interested in difference rather than similarities. Law and legal systems lie at the core of his analysis, and he analyses the degree of standardization that regional officials have pursued. Such standardization is tied to the region's legal tradition. Regions that rely on civil law are more likely to 'codify the world a priori' (Duina, 2006, p. 6; see also p. 52). By contrast, systems underpinned by common law exhibit a 'gradual approach to regulation' (pp. 6 and 52). NAFTA, relying on common law, asks market actors to rely on international standards and mutual recognition, for example (p. 72), while the EU and Mercosur, both based on civil law, standardize a great deal. If Duina had included the Asia-Pacific in his study, however, NAFTA would have appeared as a highly legalized system (Abbott, 2000) compared to the Asia-Pacific region (Kahler, 2000, p. 550). Nonetheless, Duina's analysis highlights the substantive consequences of legal traditions and provides an important alternative approach to Mattli's economic analysis.

In conclusion, the field of comparative regionalism reflects a process that is so complex and geographically expansive that it can fruitfully accommodate a wide variety of theoretical and methodological approaches. Most interestingly, non-Western scholars will undoubtedly help shape its future evolution.

References

Abbott, F.M. (2000) 'NAFTA and the Legalization of World Politics: A Case Study'. *International Organization*, Vol. 54, No. 3, pp. 519–47.

Acharya, A. (1993) *A New Regional Order in South-East Asia: ASEAN in the Post-Cold War Era* (London: Brassey's/International Institute for Strategic Studies).

Acharya, A. (2001) *Constructing a Security Community in Southeast Asia: ASEAN and the Problem of Regional Order* (New York: Routledge).

Acharya, A. (2004) 'How Ideas Spread: Whose Norms Matter? Norm Localization and Institutional Change in Asian Regionalism'. *International Organization*, Vol. 58, pp. 239–75.

Acharya, A. (2005) 'International Relations and Area Studies: Towards a New Synthesis? (With Special Reference to Asia)'. Revised Version, Paper presented to the 'Workshop on the Future of Interdisciplinary Area Studies in the UK'. St. Anthony's College, Oxford, 6–7 December.

Acharya, A. (2006) 'Europe and Asia: Reflections on a Tale of Two Regionalisms'. In Fort, B. and Webber, D. (eds) *Regional Integration in East Asia and Europe: Convergence or Divergence?* (London: Routledge).

Acharya, A. (2007) 'The Emerging Regional Architecture of World Politics'. *World Politics*, Vol. 59, pp. 629–52.

Acharya, A. and Buzan, B. (2007) 'Why is there no Non-Western International Relations Theory? An Introduction'. *International Relations of the Asia-Pacific*, Vol. 7, September, pp. 287–312.

Acharya, A. and Johnston, A.I. (eds) (2007) *Crafting Co-operation: Regional International Institutions in Comparative Perspective* (Cambridge: Cambridge University Press).

Adler, E. and Barnett, M. (eds) (1998) *Security Communities* (Cambridge: Cambridge University Press).

Adler, E., Crawford, B., Bicchi, F. and Del Sarto, R. (eds) (2006) *The Convergence of Civilizations: Constructing a Mediterranean Region* (Toronto: University of Toronto Press).

Aggarwal, V.K. and Morrison, C.E. (eds) (1998) *Asia-Pacific Crossroads: Regime Creation and the Future of APEC* (New York: St. Martin's).

Aggarwal, V.K., Koo, M.G., Acharya, A., Higgott, R., Ravenhill, J. and Katzenstein, P.J. (2007) 'Roundtable: Peter J. Katzenstein's Contributions to the Study of East Asian Regionalism'. *Journal of East Asian Studies*, Vol. 7, No. 3, pp. 359–412.

Antolik, M. (1990) *ASEAN and the Diplomacy of Accommodation* (Armonk, NY: M.E. Sharpe).

Baldwin, R.E. (2006) 'Multilateralizing Regionalism: Spaghetti Bowls as Building Blocs on the Path to Global Free Trade'. *The World Economy*, Vol. 29, No. 11, pp. 1451–518.

Beeson, M. and Yoshimatsu, H. (2007). 'Asia's Odd Men Out: Australia, Japan, and the Politics of Regionalism'. *International Relations of the Asia-Pacific*, Vol. 7, pp. 227–50.

Bhagwati, J. (1993) 'Regionalism and Multilateralism: An Overview'. In De Melo, J. and Panagariya, A. (eds) *New Dimensions in Regional Integration* (Cambridge: Cambridge University Press).

Bhagwati, J. and Panagariya, A. (1996) 'The Theory of Preferential Trade Agreements: Historical Evolution and Current Trends'. *American Economic Review*, Vol. 86, No. 2, pp. 82–7.

Breslin, S. and Higgott, R. (2000) 'Studying Regions: Learning from the Old, Constructing the New'. *New Political Economy*, Vol. 5, No. 3, pp. 333–52.

Breslin, S., Higgott, R. and Rosamond, B. (2002) 'Regions in Comparative Perspective'. In Breslin, S., Hughes, C.W., Phillips, N. and Rosamond, B. (eds) *New Regionalisms in the Global Political Economy* (New York: Routledge).

Buzan, B. and Waever, O. (2003) *Regions and Powers: The Structure of International Security* (Cambridge: Cambridge University Press).

Camroux, D. (2007) 'Asia . . . whose Asia? A "Return to the Future" of a Sino-Indic Asian Community'. *The Pacific Review*, Vol. 30, No. 4, pp. 551–75.

Collins, A. (2007) 'Forming a Security Community: Lessons from ASEAN'. *International Relations of the Asia-Pacific*, Vol. 7, pp. 203–25.

Cox, R. (1986) 'Social Forces, States, and World Orders: Beyond International Relations Theory'. In Keohane, R.O. (ed.) *Neorealism and Its Critics* (New York: Columbia University Press), pp. 205–54.

Damro, C. (2006) 'The Political Economy of Regional Trade Agreements'. In Bartels, L. and Ortino, F. (eds) *Regional Trade Agreements and the WTO Legal System* (Oxford: Oxford University Press).

de Brouwer, G. and Wang, Y. (eds) (2004) *Financial Governance in East Asia: Policy Dialogue, Surveillance and Co-operation* (New York: Routledge Curzon).

Deutsch, K. (1957) *Political Community and the North Atlantic Area: International Organization in the Light of Historical Experience* (Princeton: Princeton University Press).

Devuyst, Y. and Serdarevic, A. (2007) 'The World Trade Organization and Regional Trade Agreements: Bridging the Constitutional Credibility Gap'. *Duke Journal of Comparative & International Law*, Vol. 18, No. 1, pp. 1–75.

Doidge, M. (2007) 'From Developmental Regionalism to Developmental Interregionalism? The European Union Approach'. NCRE Working Paper No. 07/01.

Duina, F. (2006) *The Social Construction of Free Trade: The European Union, NAFTA and Mercosur* (Princeton, NJ: Princeton University Press).

Elgstrom, O. (2007) 'Outsiders' Perceptions of the European Union in International Trade Negotiations'. *JCMS*, Vol. 45, No. 4, pp. 949–67.

Estevadeordal, A. and Suominen, K. (2008) 'Sequencing Regional Trade Integration and Co-operation Agreements'. *The World Economy*. Vol. 31, No. 1, pp. 112–40.

Gamble, A. and Payne, A. (2003) 'The World Order Approach'. In Soderbaum, F. and Shaw, T.M. (eds) *Theories of New Regionalism: A Palgrave Reader* (New York: Palgrave Macmillan).

Gilson, J. (2005) 'New Interregionalism? The EU and East Asia'. *Journal of European Integration*, Vol. 27, No. 3, 307–26.

Guedes De Oliveira, M.A. (2007) 'The Southern Cone Model'. In Roy, J. and Dominguez, R. (eds) *After Vienna; Dimensions of the Relationship between the European Union and the Latin America-Caribbean Region* (Jean Monnet Chair, University of Miami and Miami-Florida European Union Center of Excellence).

Haas, E.B. (1961) 'International Integration: the European and the Universal Process'. *International Organization*, Vol. 15, No. 3, pp. 366–92.

Haas, E.B. (1967) 'The Uniting of Europe and the Uniting of Latin America'. *JCMS*, Vol. 5, No. 4, pp. 315–43.

Haas, E.B. and Schmitter, P. (1964) 'Economics and Differential Patterns of Political Integration: Projections About Unity in Latin America'. *International Organization*, Vol. 18, No. 4, pp. 705–37.

Haas, E.B. and Schmitter, P. (1965) *The Politics of Economics in Latin American Regionalism: the Latin American Free Trade Association after Four Years of Operation* (Denver: University of Denver Press).

Hafner-Burton, E.M. (forthcoming) *Coercing Human Rights:Why Preferential Trade Agreements Regulate Repression* (Ithaca: Cornell University Press).

Hettne, B. (2003) 'The New Regionalism Revisited'. In Soderbaum, F. and Shaw, T.M. (eds) *Theories of New Regionalism: A Palgrave Reader* (New York: Palgrave Macmillan).

Hettne, B. (2005) 'Regionalism and World Order'. In Farrell, M., Hettne, B. and van Langenhove, L. (eds) *Global Politics of Regionalism: Theory and Practice* (London: Pluto Press).

Hettne, B. and Soderbaum, F. (2000) 'Theorizing the Rise of Regionness'. *New Political Economy*, Vol. 5, No. 3, pp. 457–73.

Hettne, B., Inotai, A. and Sunkel, O. (eds) (1999) *Globalism and the New Regionalism* (Basingstoke: Macmillan).

Hettne, B., Inotai, A. and Sunkel, O. (eds) (2001) *Comparing Regionalisms: Implications for Global Development* (London: Palgrave).

Higgott, R. (2007) 'Alternative Models of Regional cooperation? The Limits of Regional Institutionalization in East Asia'. In Telo, M. (ed.) *European Union and New Regionalism: Regional Actors and Global Governance in a Post-Hegemonic Era* (Aldershot: Ashgate).

Higgott, R. (2007) 'The Theory and Practice of Regionalism in East Asia: Peter Katzenstein's Value Added'. *Journal of East Asian Studies*, Vol. 7, pp. 378–87.

Hix, S. (1994) 'The Study of the European Community: the Challenge to Comparative Politics'. *West European Politics*, Vol. 17, No. 1, pp. 1–30.

Holland, M. (2002) *The European Union and the Third World* (Basingstoke: Palgrave).

Huber, E. (2003) 'The Role of Cross-Regional Comparison'. *APSA-CP Newsletter*, Vol. 14, No. 2, pp. 1–6.

Hurrell, A. (1995) 'Regionalism in Theoretical Perspective'. In Fawcett, L. and Hurrell, A. (eds) *Regionalism in World Politics: Regional Organization and International Order* (Oxford: Oxford University Press).

Hurrell, A. (2005) 'The Regional Dimension in International Relations Theory'. In Farrell, M., Hettne, B. and Van Langenhove, L. (eds) *Global Politics of Regionalism: Theory and Practice* (London: Pluto Press).

Jervis, R. (1982) 'Security Regimes'. *International Organization*, Vol. 36, No. 2, pp. 357–78.

Jørgensen, K.E., Pollack, M.A. and Rosamond, B. (eds) (2006) *Handbook of European Union Politics* (London: Sage).

Kahler, M. (2000) 'Legalization as Strategy: The Asia-Pacific Case'. *International Organization*, Vol. 54, No. 3, pp. 549–71.

Katzenstein, P.J. (1996) 'Regionalism in Comparative Perspective'. *Co-operation and Conflict*, Vol. 31, No. 2, pp. 123–59.

Katzenstein, P.J. (2005) *A World of Regions: Asia and Europe in the American Imperium* (Ithaca: Cornell University Press).

Kohler-Koch, B. and Rittberger, B. (2006) 'The "Governance Turn" in EU Studies'. *JCMS*, Vol. 44, s1, pp. 27–49.

Komori, Y. (2007) 'The Construction of Regional Institutions in the Asia-Pacific and East Asia: Origins, Motives, and Evolution'. PhD dissertation, University of Pittsburgh.

Laursen, F. (2003) *Comparative Regional Integration: Theoretical Perspectives*. (Aldershot: Ashgate).

Lederman, D. and Ozden, C. (2007) 'Geopolitical Interests and Preferential Access to US Markets'. *Economics & Politics*, Vol. 19, No. 2, pp. 235–58.

Leifer, M. (1996) *The ASEAN Regional Forum: Extending ASEAN's Model of Regional Security* (London: International Institute for Strategic Studies).

Longo, M. (2003) 'European Integration: Between Micro-Regionalism and Globalism'. *JCMS*, Vol. 41, No. 3, pp. 475–94.

Mansfield, E.D. and Milner, H.V. (1997) *The Political Economy of Regionalism.* (New York: Columbia University Press).

Mansfield, E.D. and Milner, H.V. (1999) 'The New Wave of Regionalism'. *International Organization*, Vol. 53, No. 3, pp. 589–627.

Mattli, W. (1999) *The Logic of Regional Integration: Europe and Beyond* (Cambridge: Cambridge University Press).

Mattli, W. (2005) 'Ernst Haas's Evolving Thinking on Comparative Regional Integration: of Virtues and Infelicities'. *Journal of European Public Policy*, Vol. 12, No. 2, pp. 327–48.

Maull, H.W. and Okfen, N. (2003) 'Inter-Regionalism in International Relations: Comparing APEC and ASEM'. *Asia Europe Journal*, Vol. 1, pp. 237–49.

Milner, H.V. and Kubota, K. (2005) 'Why the Move to Free Trade? Democracy and Trade Policy in the Developing Countries'. *International Organization*, Vol. 59, No. 1, pp. 107–43.

Morgenstern, S., Tamayo, A.B., Faucher, P. and Nielson, D. (2007) 'Scope and Trade Agreements'. *Canadian Journal of Political Science/Revue canadienne de science politique*, Vol. 40, No. 1, pp. 157–81.

Murphy, C.N. and Tooze, R. (eds) (1991) *The New International Political Economy* (Boulder: Lynne Rienner).

Naidu, G.V.C. (2005) 'India and the East Asian Summit'. *Strategic Analysis*, Vol. 29, No. 4, pp. 711–16.

Nesadurai, H.S. (2003) *Globalization, Domestic Politics and Regionalism: The ASEAN Free Trade Area* (London: Routledge).

Panagariya, A. (1999) *Regionalism in Trade Policy: Essays on Preferential Trading* (London: World Scientific).

Payne, A. and Gamble, A. (1996) 'Introduction: The Political Economy of Regionalism and World Order'. In Gamble, A. and Payne, A. (eds) *Regionalism and World Order* (New York: St. Martin's Press).

Pempel, T.J. (2005) 'Emerging Webs of Regional Connectedness'. In Pempel, T.J. (ed.) *Remapping East Asia: The Construction of a Region* (Ithaca: Cornell University Press).

Pollack, M.A. (2005) 'Theorizing the European Union: International Organization, Domestic Polity, or Experiment in New Governance?' *Annual Review of Political Science*, Vol. 8, pp. 357–98.

Pomfret, R. (2007) 'Is Regionalism an Increasing Feature of the World Economy?' *The World Economy*, Vol. 30, No. 3, pp. 893–1032.

Ravenhill, J. (2001) *APEC and the Construction of Pacific Rim Regionalism.* (Cambridge: Cambridge University Press).

Ravenhill, J. (2008) 'Asia's New Economic Institutions'. In Aggarwal, V.K. and Koo, M.G. (eds) *Asia's New Institutional Architecture: Evolving structures for Managing Trade, Financial, and Security Relation* (Berlin: Springer).

Rosamond, B. (2005) 'The Uniting of Europe and the Foundation of EU Studies: Revisiting the Neofunctionalism of Ernst B. Haas'. *Journal of European Public Policy*, Vol. 12, No. 2, pp. 237–54.

Rosamond, B. (2007) 'European Integration and the Social Science of EU Studies: the Disciplinary Politics of a Subfield'. *International Affairs*, Vol. 83, No. 1, pp. 231–52.

Santander, S. (2005) 'The European Partnership with Mercosur: a Relationship Based on Strategic and Neo-Liberal Principles'. *Journal of European Integration*, Vol. 27, No. 3, pp. 285–306.

Sbragia, A.M. (2002) 'Building Markets and Comparative Regionalism: Governance beyond the Nation-state'. In Jachtenfuchs, M. and Knodt, M. (eds) *Regieren in internationalen Institutionen* (Leske + Budrich, Opladen).

Sbragia, A.M. (2007) 'European Union and NAFTA'. In Telo, M. (ed.) *European Union and New Regionalism: Regional Actors and Global Governance in a Post-Hegemonic Era* (Aldershot: Ashgate).

Soderbaum, F. (2003) 'Introduction: Theories of New Regionalism'. In Soderbaum, F. and Shaw, T.M. (eds) *Theories of New Regionalism: A Palgrave Reader* (New York: Palgrave Macmillan).

Soderbaum, F. and Shaw, T.M. (eds) (2003) *Theories of New Regionalism: A Palgrave Reader* (New York: Palgrave Macmillan).

Snyder, F. (1999) 'Globalization and Europeanization as Friends and Rivals: European Union Law in Global Economic Networks'. EUI Working Papers, Law No. 99/8 (Florence: European University Institute).

Telo, M. (ed.) (2007) *European Union and New Regionalism: Regional Actors and Global Governance in a Post-Hegemonic Era*, 2nd edn (Aldershot: Ashgate).

Terada, T. (2003) 'Constructing an "East Asian" Concept and Growing Regional Identity: From EAEC to ASEAN+3'. *The Pacific Review*, Vol. 16, No. 2, pp. 251–77.

Vasconcelos, A. (2007) 'European Union and MERCOSUR'. In Telo, M. (ed.) *European Union and New Regionalism: Regional Actors and Global Governance in a Post-Hegemonic Era* (Aldershot: Ashgate).

Wallace, H. (2000) 'Europeanization and Globalization: Complementary or Contradictory Trends?' *New Political Economy*, Vol. 5, No. 3, pp. 369–82.

Warleigh-Lack, A. (2006) 'Towards a Conceptual Framework for Regionalization: Bridging "New Regionalism" and "Integration Theory" '. *Review of International Political Economy*, Vol. 13, No. 5, pp. 750–71.

WTO Secretariat. (2003) 'The Changing Landscape of RTAs'. Paper presented to the seminar on Regional Trade Agreements and the WTO, WTO Secretariat, Geneva, 14 November. Available at «http://www.wto.org/english/tratop_e/region_e/sem_nov03_e/sem_nov03_e.htm».

The German Council Presidency: Managing Conflicting Expectations

ANDREAS MAURER
Stiftung Wissenschaft und Politik, Berlin

Germany acceded to the Presidency of the European Union (EU) in January 2007 at a difficult time and with much expected of it. It faced the challenging task of finding a replacement for the European Constitutional Treaty, which had been scuppered by the Dutch and French referendums, in the face of considerable reservations about the further integration envisaged in the Constitutional Treaty. At the same time several Member States had high expectations for the Presidency to meet this challenge. First, as a large state, Germany had – at least in principle – the material and staff resources necessary to fulfil the various management tasks of a Presidency. Second, the domestic conditions in Germany were more conducive to taking on a leadership role than those in other states such as France, the Netherlands and the United Kingdom, where the scope for action was considerably restricted through changes in leadership (see Henderson and Sitter, this volume). Thus, the German Presidency was regarded as the last opportunity in the medium term to resume the negotiations on the Constitutional Treaty and pave the way for institutional reforms.

Moreover, failure to advance institutional reform would also have had a negative effect on the Presidency's chances of making progress in other policy areas. The German government therefore decided to emphasize key issues such as climate policy and the fight against terrorism and organized crime instead of launching another 'broad debate' on the key objectives of the EU. Berlin prioritized four main themes: the socio-economic modernization of Europe; strengthening the European area of justice; launching international peace initiatives, particularly in the EU's neighbourhood; and agreeing on how to proceed with regard to the Constitutional Treaty (German Federal Government, 2007).

Instead of simply tallying the Presidency's goals against its achievements, I intend to evaluate the German Presidency's performance within the scope and limits set for EU Presidencies in the academic literature. Following the approach proposed by Schout and Vanhoonacker (2006), I concentrate on the question what kinds of demands particular situations placed on the German Presidency in terms of management, brokering and so on, and whether the Presidency efficiently and effectively matched its various functions to these demands. Accordingly, the article will focus on the particular resources the Presidency had at its disposal, how it used them, the particular *modus operandi* that it adopted, which national contextual factors defined its scope for action and which 'external' factors affected its capacity to meet these demands. The analysis of the tasks performed by the Presidency is thus judged against a more nuanced background taking account of divergent contextual factors and the different scope for action which these contexts offered.

I. Evaluating the Performance of the German EU Presidency

The following analysis starts from the premise that each Presidency has to fulfil a number of different functions in the EU political system (Heyes-Renshaw and Wallace 2006, pp. 133–61; Kietz, 2007b): to organize the political process at the European level; to act as broker on all levels of negotiation, as well as to place short-term negotiations in the long-term perspective of European integration; to represent the EU both internationally and internally; and to serve as a contact point for all EU institutions at the Council. In terms of organizing the work of the Council, the German Presidency planned, co-ordinated and implemented up to 4,000 Council meetings on all levels. Efficient management is a key condition for activating and fulfilling the other functions of the Council, in particular its broker function. The extensive administrative and human resources of the largest Member State greatly facilitated this task for Germany. The challenges in preparing the meetings were greatest when the negotiations had reached an advanced stage and the focus was on policy issues that were very sensitive for some Member States (Kietz and Maurer, 2007). The management and brokerage functions were closely linked. The requirement for efficient management was increased when compromise packages were being finalized under pressing deadlines. Management demands further increased when the negotiations in the Council involved the European Parliament (EP) under the co-decision procedure (especially on migration policy and police co-operation) and third countries in foreign policy.

II. Conditions for Successful Management and Brokering

Setting out early and clearly the priorities of the Presidency in both the overall work programme and the programmes of the individual ministries helped to focus the management and broker functions. On the national level the preparations for the German Presidency began after the change in government in autumn 2005. The relevant German actors then co-ordinated intensively with their Finnish predecessors, resulting in strong continuity.

A further condition for the management and brokerage success was the early communication of largely realistic timetables, e.g. dates, deadlines for initiatives and/or reactions to tabled policy drafts and draft agendas. The smaller Member States in particular expected sufficient time to elaborate their negotiating positions in the area of justice and home affairs, climate and energy policy. The comprehensive resources which were made available by German governmental departments, meanwhile, permitted the Presidency to set a fast pace and an ambitious workload in the various Council working groups. However, in some cases this led to a situation where smaller Member States were close to the limits of their ability to act. Parkes' (2007) case study on migration policy illustrates that the pace of the German Presidency overwhelmed delegations that needed more time to formulate their own positions or indeed to consult with their respective national parliaments and other institutions.

A third factor contributing to success was a confident leadership style in the Council working groups that did not allow discussions to get out of hand and exerted pressure on the national delegations to make concessions in situations where sensitive issues required unanimous decisions. One such area was police co-operation, where the assertiveness of the German Presidency led to discontent amongst some Member States (Finland, Italy, Spain) (Kietz, 2007a), but even these delegations admitted that this style prevented extensive debates and encouraged good performance. Many Member States seemed to recognize that decision-making in sensitive policy areas is almost impossible when it requires 27 national delegations to make a unanimous decision.[1] The resolute leadership of Council working groups was therefore welcomed rather than criticized and given legitimacy through the recognition by other states of the Presidency's expertise and powers of persuasion.

---

[1] Background briefing with the Permanent Representatives of Belgium, Ireland, Slovenia, and Austria, Brussels, Permanent Representation of Austria to the EU, 8 November 2007.

III. Balancing Mediation and Representation

Brokering a consensus (whether within the Council, between the Council and other EU institutions, or between the EU and third countries) requires the broad perception that the Presidency is fair and neutral. The balance between mediating and representing national interests was particularly delicate for Germany because of its political and administrative weight.

When the time frame for dealing with new dossiers was very tight, Council negotiations took place on the basis of unclear positions or positions that had been deliberately muddied by individual states (see the analysis on the negotiations on the 'Berlin Declaration' and partly also the revision of the Constitutional Treaty by Maurer, 2007; and Schwarzer, 2007). In these cases the Presidency, and in particular Chancellor Angela Merkel and her closest advisers, had to exhibit especially intensive management and a sure instinct in their brokering efforts between those who sought to bury the Treaty, those who wanted to rescue it and the self-declared 'bridge-builders' that opted for some kind of Treaty of Nice-plus-X or Constitutional Treaty-minus-X solutions. The final success of reaching an agreement on the mandate for an Intergovernmental Conference was mainly due to the organization of discretionary negotiations on the basis of informational asymmetries between the Presidency's 'focal points' on the one hand and their counterparts of the other Member States and EU institutions on the other.

On those issues where Germany had a distinct national preference, the Presidency's neutrality was maintained by skirting the issues via the EU institutions or coalitions of like-minded Member States. The German government thus used its influence to have the European Council instruct the Commission under the Finnish EU Presidency to put forward a report on migration from the former Soviet Union that was in line with its own ideas. Berlin also ensured that its ideas on the development of the European Neighbourhood Policy (ENP) were included in Commission papers that were authorized by the Finnish EU Presidency and as such could not be directly linked to Germany. In the negotiations over the Constitutional treaty, Germany's favoured position was indirectly represented by the activities of like-minded Member States in the so-called 'friends of the constitution' group, in which Germany did not officially partake in order to remain neutral (Maurer, 2007). These examples show that a presiding government that wants to reconcile its own national interests with the role of a neutral broker must start work long before its official tenure.

Council presidencies are also increasingly required to act as inter-institutional mediators between the Council and the EP, not least because of the co-decision powers of Parliament which it acquired in 2005. This situation was particularly acute in justice and home affairs, where the negotiations with the EP presented a challenge to Germany's mediating abilities (Kietz, 2007a; Parkes, 2007). The German Presidency had visible difficulties in negotiating with Parliament over sensitive proposals, including the Visa Information System and the Immigrant Returns Directive (Parkes, 2007). However, it finally recognized the necessity of intensive and compromise-oriented efforts to mediate with regard to the EP.

The Council Presidency received some assistance in its negotiation efforts from third parties, including the Commission, the EU Special Representatives and the High Representative for the Common Foreign and Security Policy. In general, however, the German Presidency made only limited use of these institutions. During the negotiations on the Berlin Declaration and the reform of the Constitutional Treaty, for instance, the Commission acted as party to the negotiations rather than as an additional broker supporting the Presidency (Schwarzer, 2007; Maurer, 2007). During the negotiations with Russia, the German government was less dependent on the Commission because of its close bilateral relations with Russian (Lindner, 2007). Similarly, the German government did not rely on the support of the Commission in the Middle East conflict due to its direct links to Russia and the United States (Asseburg, 2007).

IV. Limits on the Presidency's Ability to Act in Foreign Policy

In foreign policy, the Presidency's ability to act was restricted by various external factors. When there are as many actors, such as in the Middle East conflict (the United States, Russia, Israel, the Arab states, the United Nations, etc.) the Presidency's management and mediation abilities faced huge challenges. The complexity of the issue required Berlin to mediate intensively and in parallel at a number of negotiation tables (Asseburg, 2007).

On other issues, the search for a common European position was influenced by bilateral disputes involving individual EU countries. Thus, during the German Presidency Baltic–Russian and Polish–Russian tensions influenced the negotiations between the EU and Moscow over a new partnership and co-operation agreement (see Light, this issue). The complexity of the Russia dossier in turn hindered the intensification of EU relations with its neighbours in Eastern Europe and the southern Caucasus as originally sought by the German Presidency (Lang, 2007; Lindner, 2007; Schmitz, 2007). Thus Presidency priorities could not be insulated from related issues that impeded progress.

V. Prioritization, Consultation and Firm Commitment as Success Factors

In addition to remaining neutral and being a credible broker, a further factor contributing to the success of the German Presidency was the early and strategic concentration of negotiation resources on a limited set of priorities. Reviving the negotiations on the Constitutional Treaty was the main priority of the German Presidency to which it subordinated goals in other policy areas. In order to secure the reform of the Constitutional Treaty, Berlin accepted far-reaching compromises in policy areas unrelated to the Treaty to the advantage of countries such as Poland and France, whose approval of the Constitutional Treaty was particularly problematic. These included compromises in trade policy, in particular on the Doha negotiations, a rhetorical turn against more concessions of the EU in the field of agriculture and services, more outspoken criticism of Russia's energy and energy supply policy, and the clear focus of the ENP towards some kind of a renewed '*Ostpolitik*'). This weighting of priorities was possible only because the ministries leading on these issues had consulted closely from a very early stage and the Chancellor's Office co-ordinated their positions during the actual negotiations on replacing the Constitutional Treaty.

VI. A Mixed Review of the Strategic Guidance Function

The Presidency has a responsibility to offer strategic guidance by placing conflict-laden, stalled or blocked negotiations into the long-term perspective of EU integration in order to make the Member States more willing to compromise and to defer their short-term interests. To this end, with regard to migration policy the German Presidency emphasized social, foreign and economic aspects of the European asylum and migration policy, which had been called for by the 2004 Hague Programme. The heavily polarized and therefore stalled debate on legal economic migration was to be reinvigorated ahead of impending legislative drafts of the Commission. It also had to drive forward the measures to extend the exchange of personal data between national law enforcement bodies and simultaneous strengthening of data protection which had been called for in the Hague Programme but which had in practice been inadequately implemented. In negotiations on energy and climate policy the Presidency facilitated finding compromises by referring to a number of declared long-term objectives on European energy and climate policy contained in Commission drafts (Parkes, 2007).

An assessment of the Presidency's strategic guidance role yields a mixed result. In energy and climate policy the Presidency's substantive goals coincided with the measures contained in Commission drafts (reduction of greenhouse gases and support of renewable energy), which facilitated the task of strategic guidance for the Presidency (Dröge and Geden, 2007). There were also several important issues where the Presidency's balancing of its mediating and representing roles was criticized as Germany's national interests were seen as standing in the way of successful and timely discussions. In migration policy the Presidency gave the impression that it intentionally delayed addressing various aspects of legal economic migration and that it left key conceptual debates on the issue unresolved because it was unwilling to concede its own position (Parkes, 2007).

VII. Risky Games: The Success of the Presidency and the Potential Cost to the Union

The German Presidency's performance was facilitated by the extensive personal and administrative resources of the German federal government and the state governments. Because of its resources, the German Presidency did not have to rely on the Commission and Council Secretariat, but could employ more independent and laborious methods, such as frequent bilateral consultations outside formal negotiation venues (see Dinan, this issue). Its administrative capacity also enabled it to make progress on a number of policy fronts as well as on the negotiations over the Constitutional Treaty.

Analysis of the negotiation on the Berlin Declaration and the Constitutional Treaty (Schwarzer, 2007; Maurer, 2007), however, raises the question of whether the *modus operandi* chosen by the German Presidency – discretionary negotiations on the basis of informational asymmetries – should become the rule and be a model for other presidencies. Under the German Presidency such negotiating tactics proved effective, thanks to the high degree of confidentiality of the negotiations, the use of 'Sherpas' or 'focal points' proved suitable for achieving consensus in a very short timeframe in a highly sensitive negotiation among 27 Member States. At the same time, this success negates the original goal of the Constitutional process of bringing the debate over integration out from behind closed doors and into a larger inclusive framework, such as the European Convention. The lack of public engagement becomes problematic when integration steps are agreed that, in the long term, must rely on a broad societal consensus. The broader the consensus, the less Member State governments are tempted to ignore the compromises at a later date. Instead of including broader civil society and parliaments in the decision-making process or using the input from the EU-wide debates on the future of Europe in an effort to create a deep-rooted consensus within society, Berlin prioritized brokering compromises between democratically legitimated governments. This strategic decision is inherently risky, as in referendums on the Reform Treaty citizens could reject the agreement. Irrespective of whether referendums put a brake on the integration process, there is the danger that growing discontent will be articulated in other elections (through votes for eurosceptic or populist parties at EP elections) with the result that the core European institutions are irreparably damaged. At the end of the German Presidency it is valid to ask whether a new and lasting European political consensus was created between the governments and their citizens: the political conjuncture lent itself to such efforts, even if the German government did not take the opportunity.

References

Asseburg, M. (2007) 'Die Ratspräsidentschaft und der Nahostfriedensprozess: Begrenzter Handlungsspielraum, Vorrang der Diplomatie'. In Kietz, D. and Perthes, V. (eds) *Handlungsspielräume einer EU-Ratspräsidentschaft. Eine Funktionsanalyse des deutschen Vorsitzes im ersten Halbjahr 2007*, SWP-Studie, No. 2007/S 24, pp. 87–92.

Dröge, S. and Geden, O. (2007) 'Weitreichende Grundsatzentscheidungen für eine integrierte Energie- und Klimapolitik'. In Kietz, D. and Perthes, V. (eds) *Handlungsspielräume einer EU-Ratspräsidentschaft. Eine Funktionsanalyse des deutschen Vorsitzes im ersten Halbjahr 2007*, SWP-Studie, No. 2007/S 24, pp. 48–52.

German Federal Government (2007) 'Europe – Succeeding Together'. Presidency Programme, 1 January–30 June 2007, Berlin.

Heyes-Renshaw, F. and Wallace, H. (2006) *The Council of Ministers* (Houndsmills: Palgrave).

Kietz, D. (2007a) 'Heimspiel in der Polizeikooperation. Spannungen zwischen Impulsgebung und Vermittlung'. In Kietz, D. and Perthes, V. (eds) *Handlungsspielräume einer EU-Ratspräsidentschaft. Eine Funktionsanalyse des deutschen Vorsitzes im ersten Halbjahr 2007*, SWP-Studie, No. 2007/S 24, pp. 60–7.

Kietz, D. (2007b) 'Methoden zur Analyse von EU-Ratspräsidentschaften', SWP Diskussionspapier, No. 2007/05, Berlin.

Kietz, D. and Maurer, A. (2007) 'Handlungsanreize und Handlungsbeschränkungen der EU-Ratspräsidentschaft. Eine Bilanz des deutschen Vorsitzes im Lichte des Reformvertrags'. In Kietz, D. and Perthes, V. (eds) *Handlungsspielräume einer EU-Ratspräsidentschaft. Eine Funktionsanalyse des deutschen Vorsitzes im ersten Halbjahr 2007*, SWP-Studie, No. 2007/S 24, pp. 101–17.

Lang, K.-O. (2007) 'Das deutsche Präsidentschaftsprofil in der ENP: Dosierte Stimulation und vielschichtiges Brokern'. In Kietz, D. and Perthes, V. (eds) *Handlungsspielräume einer EU-Ratspräsidentschaft. Eine Funktionsanalyse des deutschen Vorsitzes im ersten Halbjahr 2007*, SWP-Studie, No. 2007/S 24, pp. 68–74.

Lindner, R. (2007) 'Das Russland-Dossier der deutschen EU-Präsidentschaft: Zwischen Realinteressen und Nachbarschaftskonflikten'. In Kietz, D. and Perthes, V. (eds) *Handlungsspielräume einer EU-Ratspräsidentschaft. Eine Funktionsanalyse des deutschen Vorsitzes im ersten Halbjahr 2007*, SWP-Studie, No. 2007/S 24, pp. 80–6.

Maurer, A. (2007) 'Le sauvetage du traité constitutionnel. Retour sur un dossier prioritaire de la présidence allemande'. Note du Cerfa, No. 46, Institut Français des Relations Internationales, Paris, September.

Parkes, R. (2007) 'Asyl- und Zuwanderungspolitik: Die effiziente Realisierung eines bescheidenen Vorhabens'. In Kietz, D. and Perthes, V. (eds) *Handlungsspielräume einer EU-Ratspräsidentschaft. Eine Funktionsanalyse des deutschen Vorsitzes im ersten Halbjahr 2007*, SWP-Studie, No. 2007/S 24, pp. 53–9.

Schmitz, A. (2007) 'Effizienz als Leitmotiv: Die "Strategie für eine neue Partnerschaft mit Zentralasien" '. In Kietz, D. and Perthes, V. (eds) *Handlungsspielräume einer EU-Ratspräsidentschaft. Eine Funktionsanalyse des deutschen Vorsitzes im ersten Halbjahr 2007*, SWP-Studie, No. 2007/S 24, pp. 75–9.

Schout, A. and Vanhoonacker, S. (2006) 'Evaluating Presidencies of the Council of the EU: Revisiting Nice'. *JCMS*, Vol. 44, No. 6, pp. 1051–77.

Schwarzer, D. (2007) 'Die Berliner Erklärung – Testlauf für die Verhandlungen zum Verfassungsvertrag'. In Kietz, D. and Perthes, V. (eds) *Handlungsspielräume einer EU-Ratspräsidentschaft. Eine Funktionsanalyse des deutschen Vorsitzes im ersten Halbjahr 2007*, SWP-Studie, No. 2007/S 24, pp. 20–6.

Portugal and the 2007 EU Presidency: A Case of Constructive Bridge-Building

LAURA C. FERREIRA-PEREIRA
University of Minho, Braga

I. Learning-by-Doing: From 1992 to 2007

On 1 July 2007, Portugal took over the rotating Presidency of the Council of the European Union (EU) for the third time. The previous time Portugal held the EU Presidency in 2000, it was expected to launch the Intergovernmental Conference (IGC) to revise the Amsterdam Treaty and to implement the European Security and Defence Policy (ESDP). Seven years later, José Sócrates's government sought to play a leading role in advancing the EU's agenda at a propitious juncture both domestically and at the EU level.

Domestically Sócrates could count on an absolute parliamentary majority and reasonable time until the next general elections (scheduled for 2009). This allowed him to devote time and energy to the EU's Presidency without fearing internal criticism for concentrating on European matters. Within the EU, the Prime Minister benefited from the unprecedented advantage of having a Portuguese President of the European Commission, José Manuel Durão Barroso, who from the outset openly voiced his commitment to proving that Portugal had an important role to play within the EU (Barroso, 2007, p. 23).

Furthermore, Portugal's third EU Presidency could confidently draw on the experience accumulated through a 'learning-by-doing' process of two decades of engagement in the integration process, and particularly from the second Portuguese Presidency, during which the country has managed to assert itself as a full-hearted advocate of the European project. At the time of

its first EU Presidency, in 1992, national authorities still nurtured reservations
regarding the European political integration process which had been, since
Portugal's accession to the European Community in 1986, subject to widespread scepticism which contrasted with prevailing positive views regarding
the economic integration dynamics. Only later, during the period of implementation of the Maastricht Treaty, did Portugal come to embrace a more
inclusive view of the Community-building process that included the reinforcement of the political and security dimension.

The increased acquiescence to collective efforts to endow the EU with an
international political *persona* under the Common Foreign and Security
Policy (CFSP) contributed positively to the 'conscientious resolve' exhibited
by the Portuguese foreign policy makers during the first semester of 2000
(Edwards and Wiessala, 2001). This helped to pave the way for the third
Portuguese presidency to be marked by the government's strong desire to
reaffirm its firm commitment to the EU (Sócrates, 2007a, p. 11).

II. Towards a 'Stronger Europe in a Better World': Presidency Priorities and Ambitions

When Portugal took over the EU's Presidency during the second half of 2007
it did so under the newly-created trio presidency, or 'troika' system. This
meant that Portuguese authorities were *a priori* committed to advancing the
implementation of a programme that had been agreed with Germany (its
predecessor) and Slovenia (its successor). At the same time, the Portuguese
government prepared an individual agenda that mirrored the idiosyncratic
features stemming from the country's foreign policy identity.

Under the motto 'A Stronger Europe for a Better World', the Portuguese
Presidency programme revolved around three major lines of action: the treaty
reform process, the strengthening of Europe's role in the world and an agenda
for modernizing European economies and societies. Although the latter featured formally as a priority, the vast majority of the presidency's energy went
into the treaty reform and the EU's external relations. These two main issues
were viewed as intimately intertwined. The Portuguese authorities recurrently
associated enhancing the EU's role in the world with reforming its institutions to be able to tackle global challenges and opportunities. A new European
treaty was, therefore, a strategically important device to enable the EU to play
an international political role on an equal footing with both traditional and
new global players. Thus, during the historic informal European Council in
Lisbon on 18–19 October 2007 José Sócrates pressed his European peers to
agree the Reform Treaty by arguing that the EU would be in a stronger

position going into the impending summits with Russia, China and India (see Allen and Smith, this volume) if the institutional question was resolved.[1]

Portugal's concern with enhancing EU's external capacity and role can be traced back to its history as a global power and particularly to the 15th and 16th centuries, during which Portugal led the European expansion and subsequently, as national diplomats like to evoke continually, 'introduced Europe to the world'. In 2007, this historical global outlook led José Sócrates and his team to make the second EU–Africa Summit the external priority of the Presidency (see below). From the outset, therefore, the success of the Portuguese tenure became inextricably connected to two flagship events: the approval of the new EU treaty and the materialization of the second African Summit.[2]

III. The IGC and the Lisbon Treaty: The Future of the EU Back on Track

From the beginning of the preparatory work for the EU Presidency, the Portuguese government knew that it would have to address institutional reform and the deadlock over the Constitutional Treaty. As Angela Merkel increased political pressure towards bringing the 'shadow of intra-European divisiveness' to an end, it became clear that the 'period of reflection' was to give place to a phase of action. At the European Council in Brussels on 22 June, the 27 Member States sanctioned what was judged as a 'clear and precise mandate' for a new treaty (see Maurer, this volume). This called for opening an IGC and negotiating a revised text based on what had been agreed in Brussels with the view to attaining a final agreement on a new treaty by the end of 2007.

Unsurprisingly, therefore, when the Portuguese Prime Minister presented his country's presidency's priorities before Parliament on 27 June, the negotiation and agreement on a new treaty figured as *the* objective (Sócrates, 2007a, p. 11). Most of the labours of the national diplomatic apparatus were directed at reaching agreement on a reform treaty under the aegis of a new ICG, which was inaugurated on 23 July. The Portuguese government particularly sought to secure agreement on the new legal text during its presidency. It, therefore, drove forward the political and technical exercise of giving substance to the mandate agreed under the German Presidency.

The Portuguese inherited a generous legacy from the Germans: a mandate that pointed to a new treaty that no longer aspired to be constitutional in nature or to replace the existing treaties, but resumed the tradition of

---

[1] *Visão*, 25 October 2007, p. 26.
[2] *El Mundo*, 27 October 2007, p. 9.

introducing amendments to agreed legal texts (see Maurer, this volume; Dinan, this volume). The mandate also maintained the previously established European institutional architecture and the sharing/division of powers between institutions, but abolished the EU's pillar structure (see Dinan, this volume). Finally, it preserved the intergovernmental character of both the Common Foreign and Security Policy (CFSP) and the European Security and Defence Policy (ESDP). While there was a broad consensus on these aspects of the mandate, Portuguese authorities repeatedly noted that, 'a mandate was not a Treaty' (Sócrates, 2007a, p. 12). Rather, the mandate pointed to a path ahead that had to be walked and this still entailed 'demanding, intensive and complex work' (Sócrates, 2007a, p. 12).

That Lisbon was given 'clear and precise' mandate to supervise the institutional reform process should not obscure the fact that between July and the eve of the October summit considerable hurdles had to be overcome. Initially the issue was the final date of Polish general elections, during the run-up to which the Polish president and prime minister were reluctant to make concessions. Later there was the Italian reluctance to lose a member in the new European Parliament and the Polish demands to reinforce the Ioannina Compromise (see Dinan, this volume). Throughout the IGC the intricate negotiations with London over *opt outs* related to the Justice and Internal Affairs dossier caused apprehension within the Portuguese diplomatic establishment (Antunes, 2008, p. 6). Management of these difficulties required diplomatic competence, clever tactics, leadership skills and continued determination. It also required finding technical formulae and legal engineering to produce a mutually acceptable text.

When the Reform Treaty was formally signed on 13 December 2007 in Lisbon, the Portuguese authorities had plenty of reasons to celebrate along with their European partners who flew to Lisbon for the signing ceremony since Portugal insisted that the treaty be signed there and enter the annals of European integration as the 'Lisbon Treaty'. Their endeavours to reach a comprehensive political compromise by building bridges between specific (and sometimes conflicting) needs and concerns of different Member States had thoroughly succeeded. The new treaty represented the 'confirmation of European unity and solidarity' (Barroso, 2007, p. 23). The successful conclusion of the Treaty also 'place[d] Portugal in the front line of the Community-building process'.[3] Therefore, one of Sócrates's prime ambitions was achieved: putting down the name of Lisbon – and of Portugal for that matter – in European integration history.[4]

---

[3] *Visão*, 25 October 2007, pp. 24–5.
[4] *El Mundo*, 27 October 2007, p. 8.

IV. Look South! Reintroducing Africa onto the Union's Agenda

Since the mid-1970s, although directing their ambitions towards member-ship in the then European Community, successive generations of Portuguese political leaders have sustained relations with (Portuguese-speaking) Africa – particularly Angola, Cape Verde, Guinea Bissau, Mozambique and São Tomé e Príncipe – as a top national foreign policy issue. This has not been without resonance for the country's European strategy. Since the early 1990s, Portugal has been vocal in arguing for the European partners not to 'abandon their friends of the South for the benefit of their brothers of the East' (Bretherton and Vogler, 2006, p. 211). Such devotion to the African affairs became evident during the 2000 Portuguese EU Presidency that supervised, in conjunction with the Organization for Africa Unity, the first-ever EU–Africa Summit in Cairo. Since then Portuguese foreign policy-makers have repeatedly presented the country as the initiator of the Euro–African dialogue.

In 2007, after the accession of ten central and eastern European states, the Portuguese representatives were determined to promote attention to the southern flank, that is, the Mediterranean, but especially Africa. During the second half of 2007 Portuguese authorities attempted to advance the co-operative efforts under way with the Mediterranean countries through various ministerial meetings, including the first meeting held between the southern Mediterranean partners regarding migration. Africa, meanwhile, was a priority area for an obvious geostrategic reason; a renewed focus on Africa, as opposed to central and eastern Europe, would enable Portugal to gain a more central role within the EU's external relations. Drawing on a comparative advantage springing from its longstanding cultural and historic ties with Africa, as well as privileged relations with the lusophone states, Portugal could present itself as a constructive bridge-builder between the two continents. This would enable it to improve its standing in the eyes of both its European partners and the international community.

Portuguese authorities were able to construct a cogent justification for reinforcing the political dialogue with Africa as part of a common European strategic interest, with major implications for the EU's efforts to define its international *persona* and posture in a globalized multilateral world. That seven years had elapsed since the organization of the first EU–Africa Summit, was an indication of the European apathy *vis-à-vis* the region (Antunes, 2007), and was considered a strategic 'error for Europe'[5] as it had created a

---

[5] Sócrates quoted in *Financial Times*, 2 July 2007; *El Mundo*, 27 October 2007, p. 9.

vacuum of European presence on the continent which was being filled by non-European actors, notably China.

There was a deep conviction within the Portuguese politico-diplomatic establishment that the second EU–Africa Summit would mark the beginning of an EU policy towards Africa and would inaugurate a structured political dialogue with the whole African continent based on a longer-term perspective and a sounder political underpinning. The Portuguese government did not want to miss such a unique opportunity to reaffirm the country's engagement in the strengthening of the EU's rapport with Africa.

A central problem confronting the EU–African Summit was British Prime Minister Gordon Brown's determination not to attend in case Zimbabwean President Robert Mugabe attended. Mugabe's attendance raised widespread criticism over human rights violations and economic mismanagement in Zimbabwe, with Denmark, Germany, the Netherlands and Sweden, being particularly vocal. Counting on the institutional support of the Commission, notably President José Manuel Barroso, the Portuguese government showed unremitting resolve in letting neither the 'pseudo-moralist doctrine' and 'demagogical' criticisms (Antunes, 2008, p. 9) against dialogue with the African dictator at the negotiations table, nor the eventual boycott of the summit by some Member States weaken its determination to co-ordinate an intricate politico-diplomatic process conducive to an agreement on a new EU–Africa joint strategy. The Portuguese inclusive approach was coloured more by *Realpolitik* considerations than by ethical preoccupations (Oliveira, 2008). Portugal argued that urgent joint action was required for a range of issues, from trade and development to illegal migration and climate change. Moreover, it was seen as imperative to counter the growing investments and influence of China in the continent. Eventually, almost all of the other EU Member States came round to this view, with Britain isolated in its opposition.

As a result of intense negotiations and extensive preparatory work involving regular joint meetings between the European and African representatives in the EU–Africa Ministerial Troika, Portugal managed to nail down the texts to be presented at the second EU–Africa Summit and to organize effectively the event. On 8–9 December around 80 African statesmen and European leaders gathered in Lisbon to endorse formally the *Africa–EU Strategic Partnership*, which included a *Joint Africa–EU Strategy* and an *Action Plan* for its implementation. The *Africa–EU Strategic Partnership* conveyed a paradigm shift in the relationship between the EU and Africa: a joint strategy *for* Africa was due to be replaced by a European strategy *with* Africa based on a 'partnership between equals'.

In the end Britain's empty chair policy, the absence of national leaders from some European and African states[6] and divergent views over the human rights record in Zimbabwe and the desirability of Economic Partnership Agreements between the EU and African states (see Allen and Smith, this volume) did not overshadow the significance of this long-awaited gathering of high strategic importance for the EU. Indeed, with Portugal playing the role of the 'perfect bridge between Europe and Africa', this inter-regional summit was considered an achievement in itself (Sócrates, 2007b).

V. Strengthening the Image of a Global Europe

In addition to its steadfast commitment to upgrading EU–African relations, the global outlook underpinning the Portuguese Presidency's strategy was also reflected in its endeavours to oversee high level summits with all of the emerging powers: Brazil, Russia, India and China (BRICs). Among these, the summit with Brazil deserves special mention, because the summits with Russia, China and India occurred in conjunction with established bilateral commitments. The EU had never established an institutionalized relationship involving regular bilateral summits with Brazil. Indeed, it was strongly felt in Lisbon that Brazil was neglected by the EU, in contrast to its efforts to develop relations with the other BRICs.[7] The Portuguese government actively sought to overcome this neglect in view of the role played by Brazil not only in Latin American, but also within the multilateral trade negotiations (see Allen and Smith, this volume).

As Portugal's largest former colony, Brazil has been a continual priority in national foreign policy. In Portuguese rhetoric, it often features as a 'brotherly-country'; and a key partner within the widely disbursed Portuguese-speaking community. Brazil is perceived, for that very reason as a critical ally in preserving the Portuguese as a language with international visibility, which represents a historical asset that enables Portugal to punch above its weight both in geographical and demographic terms. Moreover, Portugal has a plethora of economic and trade opportunities with Brazil.

The Portuguese government perceived its EU Presidency as an important platform on which to capitalize its role as mediator between the EU and Brazil and to launch an institutionalized relationship between EU and Brazil. The intent was to enable the deepening of mutual understanding and closer

---

[6] Besides Britain, the member states that were not represented at the highest political level were: Czech Republic, Cyprus, Slovakia, Hungary, Poland and Lithuania. On the African front, these were the following: Kenya, Democratic Republic of Congo, Gambia, Madagascar, Sierra Leone and Tanzania (Ministry of Foreign Affairs, February 2008, p. 96).
[7] *Financial Times*, 14 May 2007.

co-operation in areas of common interest (e.g. security and defence; climate change, the struggle against poverty and new energies sources). Consequently, the first foreign policy action undertaken under the aegis of the Portuguese Presidency was the organization of the first-ever EU–Brazil Summit on 4 July in Lisbon. The outcome of this landmark meeting was the launching of a 'comprehensive strategic partnership' (Presidency, 2007) along the lines of what had been proposed by the Commission in May 2007. Such bilateral partnership featured itself as a means to reinforce the EU's political dialogue and economic ties with Brazil while reinforcing the existing EU–Latin America relations. An Action Plan aimed at making this strategic partnership operational was due to be carved out with the next Summit in view.

Besides the EU summits with Brazil and Africa, Portugal oversaw the summits with Russia, Ukraine, India and China. This unprecedented concentration of EU summits in a single Presidency was a challenge, as Portugal had to cope with limited administrative and diplomatic resources (Antunes, 2008, p. 5).

For some with inside knowledge, the organization of such an extraordinary number of bilateral summits matched the European leaders' purpose of instilling a global *élan* into the EU's foreign policy.[8] This purpose was linked to their political willingness to see the EU leading and shaping the globalization agenda on the basis of its common interests and values. The desire to send a clear political signal in that direction gained strength immediately after the final agreement on the Reform Treaty and was the main catalyst behind the European Council's adoption of the 'EU Declaration on Globalization'[9] on 14 December. That this was the last EU foreign policy deliberation prepared and endorsed under Lisbon's supervision was an additional indication of the 'think-big-think-global' formula which underpinned the Portuguese tenure.

V. Constructive Bridge-Building as a Response to the Challenge of a Small State's Foreign Policy

During the second half of 2007, Portugal faced the challenging task of concluding a new treaty, thereby instilling the EU with a gulp of fresh air after the gloomy interlude marked by the institutional stalemate. While the credit

---

[8] This idea was stressed by Maria João Rodrigues, Special Advisor to the Portuguese Prime Minister for the EU Presidency, during a conference on the Portuguese EU Presidency held at the Institute of Strategic and International Studies (IEEI), Lisbon, 26 February 2008.
[9] Annex in the Presidency Conclusion of the Brussels European Council, 14 December 2007. Available at «http://www.consilium.europa.eu/ueDocs/cms_Data/docs/pressData/en/ec/97669.pdf»

for shaping the treaty should fall to Germany for securing the approval of the blueprint for the new treaty, the Portuguese should take the laurels for sustaining resolutely the momentum of political consensus around the delineated legal framework and for securing a successful outcome. The speedy agreement of the Lisbon Treaty in the sequence of the shortest IGC in the EU's annals stood out unquestionably as the major achievement of Portugal's Presidency.

At the same time, the Portuguese government succeeded in 'uploading' certain specificities of national foreign policy to the European level. The second EU–Africa Summit and the first EU–Brazil Summit stand out as stark examples of this. As a result, Portugal had a tangible impact upon the extension of strategic partnerships and thereby strengthened the country's imprint on the EU's international relations. The forceful engagement of a 'global Portugal'[10] thus added a layer to the EU's endeavours in building its influence on the international stage as an increasingly independent political and strategic actor. Portugal was also able to demonstrate that its pluri-continental outlook could be put into the service of the EU's goal of shaping the future of globalization.

On balance, the Portuguese Presidency appears competent, inspirational and thorough with a number of extremely important achievements to its credit. By projecting a modern and European image and global orientation of the country, the presidency could enhance Portugal's credibility and influence within the EU. By the same token, the Portuguese Presidency's successful management of key advances in European integration improved its international status; a status that might be capitalized upon with new international ambitions in view, notably the election of Portugal as a non-permanent member of the United Nations Security Council during 2011–12.

References

Amado, L. (2007) 'Estratégia, Perspectivas e Expectativas'. *Europa: Novas Fronteiras*, No. 21, pp. 25–9.

Antunes, M.L. (2007) Presentation by the Secretary of State of European Affairs of the Priorities of the Portuguese Presidency to the Foreign Press, Brussels, 28 June.

Antunes, M.L. (2008) 'Presidência em Balanço'. *Relações Internacionais*, No. 17, pp. 5–10.

Barroso, J.M. (2007) 'Presidência Portuguesa: uma oportunidade histórica'. *Europa: Novas Fronteiras*, No. 21, pp. 21–4.

[10] The expression 'global Portugal' draws on an article by Portuguese Minister of Foreign Affairs Luís Amado (2007, p. 29).

Bretherton, C. and Vogler, J. (2006) *The European Union as a Global Actor* (London: Routledge), pp. 189–214.

Edwards, G. and Wiessala, G. (2001) 'Conscientious Resolve: The Portuguese Presidency of 2000'. *JCMS*, Vol. 39, s1, pp. 43–6.

Presidency of the EU (2007) Joint Statement at the EU–Brazil Summit. Available at «http://www.eu2007.pt/UE/vEN/Noticias_Documentos/20070704BRSUM.htm».

Ministry for Foreign Affairs (2008) *Balanço da Presidência Portuguesa do Conselho da União Europeia*, 11 February. Available at «http://www.eu2007.pt/UE/vPT/Noticias_Documentos/20080211bilan.htm».

Oliveira, R.S. de (2008) 'A Cimeira União Europeia-África'. *Relações Internacionais*, No. 17, pp. 33–7.

Sócrates, J. (2007a) 'Uma União mais forte para um mundo melhor'. *Europa: Novas Fronteira*, No. 21, pp. 9–14.

Sócrates, J. (2007b) Speech by the Prime Minister of Portugal and President of the European Council, José Sócrates, at the Closing Session of the EU–Africa Summit. Available at «http://www.eu2007.pt/UE/vEN/Noticias_Documentos/20071209Noticia_discursoPMnasessaodeencerramentodacimeira.htm, accessed 15 April 2008».

Governance and Institutional Developments: Ending the Constitutional Impasse

DESMOND DINAN
George Mason University

Introduction

Resolving the constitutional impasse was the most consequential development affecting European Union (EU) governance and institutions in 2007. Having invested considerable time and political capital in drafting and defending the Constitutional Treaty, most EU leaders – in national governments, the Commission, the European Parliament (EP) and other positions of authority – wanted to salvage as much of it as possible. The 18 national governments whose countries had ratified the treaty were irate about the document's demise and especially about the way in which eurosceptic elements in other Member States had apparently hijacked the reform agenda.

On one point, at least, there was near unanimity. The use of the word 'constitutional' in the treaty's title had been a misjudgment. In his famous speech at Humboldt University, in May 2000, which launched the far-reaching debate on the Future of Europe, Joschka Fischer, then Germany's foreign minister, had called unequivocally for a new 'constituent treaty' and a 'European constitution' (Fischer, 2000). The European Council's Laeken Declaration of December 2001, which endorsed the idea of fundamental treaty reform, was more circumspect. It used the words 'constitution' and 'constitutional' only once each: 'The question ultimately arises as to whether this simplification and reorganization [of the treaties] might not lead in the long run to the adoption of a constitutional text in the Union. What might the basic features of such a constitution be?' (European Council, 2001). The Laeken

Declaration also called for a Convention to prepare the treaty changes, whose chairman, Valéry Giscard d'Estaing, promptly dubbed the new body the 'Constitutional Convention,' making no secret of his preference for a European Constitution.

The possible use of 'constitution' or 'constitutional' in the title and text of the proposed treaty triggered considerable discussion during the Convention and the Intergovernmental Conference (IGC) that followed, but sparked surprisingly little concern about the likely impact on public opinion of doing so. The British government, more sensitive than most to negative opinion on EU issues, eventually acquiesced in the use of 'constitution' and 'constitutional', playing down the significance of the word and emphasizing its pragmatic rather than political connotation. It was a decision that the British and other governments soon came to regret. Although French and Dutch voters rejected the Constitutional Treaty for various reasons, many of them unrelated to the treaty itself (see Taggart, 2006), the use of such a politically charged word in the title and text was a gift to eurosceptics and a goad to others concerned about the apparent erosion of national authority and identity by the relentless process of European integration. Most leaders got the point. The adjective 'constitutional' would not be used in the title of the alternative treaty.

The irony, of course, is that the existing treaties are constitutional texts, as the European Court of Justice (ECJ) has often affirmed. As is the case with 'federal' and 'federation', however, 'constitutional' and 'constitution' are politically anathema in the EU. One of the lessons of the treaty debacle, which politicians ought already to have learned, is that words matter in the discourse on European integration. In many cases, politically charged words have different meanings on the European and national stages, meanings that vary depending on the linguistic and cultural contexts.

Symbols other than words matter as well. That explains the eventual agreement by national governments to drop the clause in the Constitutional Treaty on 'European symbols' – the flag, anthem and celebration of Schuman Day. The irony, once again, is that such symbols have long been used, without arousing much public response, throughout the EU. Yet their inclusion in the treaty stoked public concerns about the EU's self-image and ambition. The EU may not have the wherewithal to become a state, let alone a super-state – even if EU leaders so desired – but symbols such as a flag, anthem and founder's day are quintessentially state-like. The flap about symbols nevertheless raised pertinent questions about the attachment to such traditional trappings of statehood on the part of those politicians and officials who portray the EU as a post-modern political entity.

One group of European politicians – members of the European Parliament (MEPs) – seemed blissfully indifferent to public concerns about the symbols and significance of the Constitutional Treaty. MEPs are a large (currently 785) and extremely diverse group, ranging from ardent euro-federalists to equally ardent eurosceptics. Accordingly, opinion within the EP on constitutional questions covers a wide spectrum. Yet the majority opinion, reflected in official EP resolutions, is far more favourably disposed toward formal constitutionalization and federalization of the EU than is opinion in almost every national and sub-national (regional) parliament.

A striking aspect of the discussions in 2007 on salvaging the Constitutional Treaty was the extent to which the EP was out of tune with the rest of the European establishment. Even the Commission, an unelected body that might not need to be too sensitive to public opinion, was well aware of the highly controversial nature of the Constitutional Treaty. As the 'motor of European integration' with a predisposition towards euro-federalism, the Commission would be expected to try to salvage the Constitutional Treaty with as few changes as possible. Yet precisely because it is unelected and its legitimacy constantly questioned, the Commission is ultra-sensitive to the perception that it is out of touch with or unresponsive to public opinion – hence its cautious approach to the constitutional question in 2007.

By contrast, the EP *is* an elected body. A majority of its members might therefore be expected to refrain from extravagant statements in support of the Constitutional Treaty and its resolutions to be more restrained on the jettisoning of constitutional trappings in the proposed alternative treaty. Yet the rhetoric of some MEPs, especially those in leadership positions, and the language of relevant EP resolutions were unabashed in their support of the Constitutional Treaty and condemnation of the purportedly retrograde reform treaty (European Parliament, 2007a, 2007b). This stance suggests that the EP is not in tune with public opinion. More precisely, it suggests that most MEPs need not take public opinion into account to the same extent that their counterparts in national and sub-national parliaments must. This is one of the consequences of the consistently declining turn-out in elections to the EP which, in turn, is a consequence of public under-appreciation of the role of the EP and indifference to the work of its members. Extravagant statements and resolutions in the EP in support of the Constitutional Treaty generally went unreported in the national media. Even if reported and noticed by 'ordinary' Europeans, such declarations most likely would merely have confirmed the widespread impression that MEPs are divorced from reality.

These observations about the EP highlight another irony in the effort to end the constitutional impasse. The timetable announced by the European Council in June 2007 – agreement on a reform treaty by the end of the year, ratification in 2008, and implementation in early 2009 – aimed to have the entire operation wrapped up before the next EP elections. The idea was to prevent the constitutional impasse from intruding into the election campaigns, thereby further damaging the image of the EU and further reducing voter turnout. Put positively, the European Council hoped that a reform treaty palatable to public opinion, finally coming into effect in the run-up to the elections, would encourage a larger turnout than last time (2004). The irony is that the European Council strove to reach agreement on the Constitutional Treaty by June 2004 lest the IGC again break down or else drag on inconclusively, thereby negatively affecting turnout in that year's elections. By contrast, the European Council hoped that concluding the IGC promptly and successfully might even encourage a larger turnout than in previous elections. In the event, the IGC and the Constitutional Treaty had little if any effect on voter turnout in 2004, just as the Lisbon Treaty, whether ratified or not, is unlikely to have any effect on voter turnout in 2009.

I. A Novel Intergovernmental Conference

Treaty reform was rare before the IGC of 1985–86 that resulted in the Single European Act, after which it became ubiquitous. An IGC in 1990–91 resulted in the Maastricht Treaty; in 1996–97 the Amsterdam Treaty; in 2000 the Nice Treaty; and in 2003–04 the Constitutional Treaty. In each case the IGC originated in a desire to extend the EU's policy scope and/or to improve the efficiency and democratic accountability of institutional structures and decision-making. The pre-Nice IGC and the pre-Constitutional Treaty IGC focused exclusively on institutional arrangements. Although not intended to be the last word in treaty reform, the Constitutional Treaty was intended at least to obviate the need for such reform, and therefore for another IGC, for many years to come. Instead, failure to ratify the Constitutional Treaty and the decision to salvage as much as possible of it meant that another IGC became necessary in 2007.

Procedurally, IGCs are routine for the EU. They take place at the level of national officials, foreign ministers, and the heads of state and government, who usually conclude the negotiations at either a specially-convened or a regularly-scheduled summit. The Commission participates at all levels, but may not exercise a veto and block agreement from being reached. Increasingly, the EP participates at all levels as well, but in a more restricted way. For instance, as well as not having a right to veto, the president of the EP does not attend regular summits (meetings of the European Council).

The inclusion of policy and institutional issues in an IGC provides ample scope for trade-offs between national governments. Sometimes a trade-off is written into a protocol or declaration attached to the treaty, at other times it is implicit and plays out in subsequent EU business. The narrow, institutional agenda of the pre-Nice and pre-Constitutional Treaty IGCs restricted the scope for obvious trade-offs. Moreover, the intensity of feelings on institutional questions, especially relating to the modalities of qualified-majority voting (QMV), introduced a sharp edge to the proceedings.

National leaders agreed at their regular 'Spring Summit' in March 2007 that they wanted the negotiations on revising the Constitutional Treaty to be as short and swift as possible. To that end, the German Council presidency, in the first half of 2007, decided, in effect, to negotiate the IGC before it would officially begin, in the second half of the year (see Maurer, this volume). That suited Portugal, the succeeding presidency country, which felt that it lacked the diplomatic clout and resources to conduct the kind of intensive preparatory work that Germany envisioned. In the event, Portugal did a creditable job chairing the IGC proper (see Ferreira-Pereira, this volume).

Negotiating the IGC Mandate

Apart from diplomatic heft, the keys to Germany's success in early 2007 were secrecy and speed (see also Maurer, this volume). Chancellor Angela Merkel appointed two 'sherpas' to sound out opinion in other national capitals and circulated a questionnaire to ascertain the limits of each country's negotiating position. Other governments appointed their own sherpas, or 'focal points' in EU-speak, who began to meet bilaterally with their German counterparts in April. The first all-EU sherpas' meeting took place in Berlin in May. Merkel herself began a round of bilaterals with fellow heads of government in mid-May, which culminated in the regularly-scheduled, end-of-presidency summit in June, where the negotiations were to end in the form of a mandate for the IGC. The mandate was intended to resolve all of the contentious political questions, leaving the IGC to wrap up the technical details. In addition to the sherpas' and Chancellor's meetings, there was a flurry of bilaterals and plurilaterals, at all levels, among various configurations of Member States. Commissioners, MEPs and officials in both institutions were active on the pre-IGC circuit as well.

Many MEPs and other advocates of greater openness criticized the German government for adopting the 'Sherpa method' to draft the Berlin Declaration of March 2007, on the 50th anniversary of the Rome Treaty, and to prepare the mandate for the IGC. In their view, the Sherpa method was excessively secretive and inherently undemocratic; it was the antithesis of the preferred Convention method. Merkel was unapologetic. Governments were democratically elected and acted in the interests of their electorates, she reportedly told the EP in January 2007. Politically sensitive declarations and treaties could not be negotiated by 450 million people (Agence Europe, 2007a).

The difficulty of reaching agreement among 27 countries on the text of the hortatory Berlin Declaration hinted at the difficulty that Merkel would face in reaching agreement on the mandate for a revised treaty. The declaration itself contained only an indirect reference to the immediate task ahead: 'we must always renew the political shape of Europe in keeping with the times. That is why today [. . .] we are united in our aim of placing the European Union on a renewed common basis before the [EP] elections in 2009' (Berlin Declaration, 2007). In her post-signing press conference, Merkel indicated a wish to preserve most of the substance of the Constitutional Treaty in the revised version, which she hoped that EU leaders would sign by the end of 2007 at the latest (Merkel, 2007).

An informal summit of EU leaders – the last summit of Jacques Chirac's long tenure as President of France – took place around the signing of the Berlin Declaration and gave Merkel another opportunity to sound out opinion on the constitutional question. Despite the festive nature of the event, all was not sweetness and light. Polish President Lech Kaczyński called the proposed timetable for revising the Constitutional Treaty 'unrealistic', while Czech President Václav Klaus, an avowed eurosceptic, had earlier disputed the necessity for either the Constitutional Treaty or a successor treaty (EurActiv, 2007a).

Despite Klaus's preference for allowing the constitutional debate to languish and die, no national government, including the Czech Republic's, refused to re-launch the negotiations on treaty reform. Yet a large gulf separated the governments' positions. In support of retaining the agreed treaty were the 'Friends of the Constitution', consisting of the 18 countries that had already ratified the Constitutional Treaty, plus Portugal and Ireland, which were well-disposed towards it. On the initiative of Luxembourg and Spain, the only countries that had ratified the Constitutional Treaty by referendum, the Friends of the Constitution met in Madrid on 26 January to stress the merits of the treaty which, in their view, reflected 'delicate balances bringing together diverse political, social, economic and legal interests [in the EU]' (Friends of the Constitution, 2007). They were irritated by the attention being lavished on governments that either opposed the treaty or faced formidable ratification hurdles. The German presidency, which merely observed the proceedings in Madrid, would have preferred that the meeting not have taken place, but took a phlegmatic view of its outcome, hoping that the Friends of the Constitution, having publicly made their point, would accept the political reality of needing to trim the Constitutional Treaty in order to meet the domestic concerns of the other governments.

Of those governments, the British, Dutch and French were in a delicate position. Although inherently in favour of deeper integration – certainly in the Dutch and French cases – they were tightly constrained by actual or anticipated referendum results on the Constitutional Treaty. In view of the referendum results of 2005, the Dutch and French governments were determined to amend the Constitutional Treaty in order to avoid having another referendum. The new Dutch coalition government that came to power in February 2007, with the same Prime Minister (Jan Peter Balkenende), stressed that a new treaty would have to differ markedly from the rejected Constitutional Treaty. Moreover, the Dutch wanted to strengthen elements of the Constitutional Treaty that improved democratic accountability, notably the role of national parliaments in applying the subsidiarity principle (Balkenende, 2007).

Like the Dutch, the British wanted any alternative to the Constitutional Treaty to look sufficiently different in order to obviate the need for a referendum. At a meeting in London in April 2007 to co-ordinate their governments' positions, Balkenende and British Prime Minister Tony Blair hinted at a solution which eventually came to pass: instead of revising the Constitutional Treaty, national governments should amend the existing treaties, albeit on the basis of most of the changes introduced in the Constitutional Treaty. Blair had promised a referendum in Britain on a *new* EU treaty; there would be no need for a referendum to approve revisions to the *existing* treaties, as such revisions had happened in the past without recourse to a referendum (Blair, 2007).

Given the virulence of euroscepticism in the UK, Blair felt it necessary before the June summit to declare a number of 'red lines,' or unalterable demands in the treaty negotiations. These included removing the Charter of Fundamental Rights from the treaty text; dropping the title 'Foreign Minister' from the new position of standing president of the External Relations Council and Vice-President of the Commission; purging the assertion of the primacy of Community law; and retaining national control of foreign policy, defence policy, social security and civil law. In general, Britain wanted the revised treaties to give the EU as un-constitutional and un-state-like an appearance as possible.

France was in an unusual position because the presidential election campaign coincided with the beginning of the informal treaty re-negotiations. Nevertheless French officials and politicians participated fully in the relevant meetings. Nicolas Sarkozy, the leading contender in the presidential race, had declared already in 2006 that, if elected, he would not put a revised treaty to a second referendum. During the election campaign he indicated a willingness to accept an alternative to the Constitutional Treaty that bore a striking resemblance to what eventually emerged at the Lisbon summit in October

2007. Sarkozy made his most forthright statement on the constitutional impasse and, more generally, on the future of the EU in a rousing speech in Strasbourg in February 2007 (Sarkozy, 2007a).

By contrast Ségolène Royal, Sarkozy's main rival for the French presidency, promised a referendum in France on a revised treaty, but she seemed to waver on this point as the campaign came to a close. Given his determination not to hold a referendum, Sarkozy's victory in the election in May 2007 must have been a relief to most EU leaders. Signalling a vigorous approach to the constitutional question and to a variety of policy issues, Sarkozy declared in his first speech as president-elect that 'France is back in Europe' (Sarkozy, 2007b). As soon as he became president, he made a point of visiting Merkel in Berlin and Commission President José Manuel Barroso in Brussels.

In contrast to the Friends of the Constitution, on the one hand, and the referendum-averse British, French, and Dutch, on the other, stood Poland and the Czech Republic, whose avowedly eurosceptical governments would have preferred the constitutional question simply to go away. Accepting that it would have to be resolved, they wanted to change the Constitutional Treaty in ways that the other governments found highly objectionable. Based on principle and pragmatism, the Polish government insisted on reopening the 'double majority' formula (55 per cent of the Member States and 65 per cent of population) for QMV contained in the Constitutional Treaty. Understandably, Poland wanted to retain the status quo – the Nice arrangement whereby Poland's share of the total number of Council votes almost equalled Germany's.

Yet the Polish government was not intransigent on the voting issue. As an alternative to the Nice formula, it proposed an arrangement based on the square root of each Member State's population. With the exception of the Czech Republic, which loyally supported Poland, the other governments adamantly refused to countenance substantive changes to the double majority formula. That led Prime Minister Jarosław Kaczyński and his brother, President Lech Kaczyński, to warn in the run-up to the June summit that Poland might well veto agreement on a revised treaty.

Subsidiarity was the Czech Republic's pet peeve, but not subsidiarity as understood by most other Member States. According to the Czech Republic, subsidiarity meant giving national governments the ability to curtail the Commission's exclusive right of legislative initiative. As in the case of Poland's rejection of double majority voting, this effort to curb one of the Commission's traditional prerogatives was unacceptable to almost all other governments.

The position of the Polish government on the modalities of QMV did not augur well for the success of the June summit. President Kaczyński remained obdurate during a bilateral meeting with Sarkozy in Warsaw a week before the summit and did not budge either when he met Merkel some days later. Insisting that the question of QMV would not be allowed to become part of the IGC proper, which would deal only with legal tidying up, Merkel warned that the summit would likely extend beyond the allotted dates of 21–22 June.

Extensive preparatory work allowed the German presidency to circulate a working paper, covering all the proposed changes, days before the summit opened. The remaining 'open questions' included symbols, terminology, and titles; acknowledgement of the primacy of EC law; where to put the Charter of Fundamental Rights; precise language on the delimitation of competences; and the exact role of national parliaments. The presidency set the question of QMV to one side as a particularly tricky issue. As expected, the presidency also proposed replacing the Constitutional Treaty with a new treaty that would include amendments to the existing treaties – the Treaty on the European Union and the Treaty Establishing the European Community, which would be renamed the Treaty on the Functioning of the European Union. This would help ratification prospects and go some way toward easing public concerns about the nature of the Constitutional Treaty.

Tony Blair's last EU summit was a duly fractious affair (European Policy Centre, 2007). The Friends of the Constitution tried to hold the line as much as possible; the referendum-constrained countries pushed for cosmetic more than substantive changes; and Poland stuck to its guns on majority voting. The Friends of the Constitution made many concessions to accommodate the demands of the other Member States, including protecting Britain's red lines with a number of formal opt-outs. By the end of the second day, only the issue of majority voting remained unresolved. An exasperated Merkel threatened to convene the IGC even if President Kaczyński opposed it, just as Italy had called for an IGC in 1985 even though Prime Minister Margaret Thatcher opposed it. A series of intensive bilaterals involving Merkel, Kaczyński, Blair, Sarkozy, Balkenende, Luxembourg's Prime Minister Jean-Claude Juncker (the longest-serving national leader and traditionally a mediator at EU summits) and Spanish Prime Minister José Luis Rodriguez Zapatero (representing the Friends of the Constitution) gradually narrowed the differences. Under intense pressure from almost every national leader, the Kaczyńskis finally dropped their insistence on the square root formula. In return, they obtained a delay until 2014 in the entry into force of the double majority system, with the possibility thereafter of invoking a safeguard, based on the Ioannina compromise of 1994, for countries coming close to but not quite forming a blocking minority under the new formula.

The presidency conclusions contained the mandate for the ICG, which EU leaders agreed would begin in late July and end in October, at a special summit in Lisbon, capital of the incoming presidency country (European Council, 2007a). The mandate was nothing less than a detailed description of the changes to be made in the existing treaties, based almost entirely on the defunct Constitutional Treaty. Comprehension of the changes required not only a wide-ranging knowledge of the EU, but also recourse to the texts of the Brussels presidency conclusions, the Constitutional Treaty, the Treaty on the European Union, and the Treaty Establishing the European Community. No wonder that Juncker was widely quoted for calling the outcome 'a simplified treaty that is very complicated' (Spiegel Online International, 2007). Inevitably, EU leaders had sacrificed clarity for the sake of compromise. Such is the history of European integration.

EU leaders were hugely relieved with the outcome of the summit. It seemed as if all the contentious questions had been resolved and that the IGC would entail merely producing a legally clean text. With such a limited, highly technical IGC underway, EU leaders could revel in the resolution of the constitutional impasse. Other than in Ireland, whose constitution mandates a referendum on EU treaty change, referendums on the reform treaty seemed unlikely to happen. Although ratification in Ireland or elsewhere could not be guaranteed, EU leaders were confident of success. The supposed constitutional crisis was over. Immediately after the June summit, Merkel and Sarkozy spoke of an end to institutional paralysis in the EU, despite the fact that the EU's institutions were functioning quite well under the existing Nice arrangements (Agence Europe, 2007b).

The IGC Proper

Procedurally, the 2007 IGC appeared to resemble any other. Foreign ministers launched the proceedings on 23 July. They reviewed progress at their semi-annual informal meeting in September and again just before the Lisbon summit in October. The EP was more involved in this IGC than in previous ones, with three rather than the usual two MEPs participating at foreign ministers' level. In addition, the Council president invited the president of the EP to attend the October summit.

Yet the main procedural difference was not a greater role for the EP but the fact that the work of the IGC fell mostly on the shoulders of a technical group of legal experts. This reflected the novelty of the 2007 IGC, which was not a negotiation but an exercise in redrafting the Constitutional Treaty according to the mandate concluded at the June summit. Accordingly, in a series of lengthy meetings in late July and again from late August until early October, the legal experts went through the presidency's draft treaty article by article, line by line, eventually producing a definitive version. Their work was uncontroversial but highly complicated, especially because of the need to accommodate various opt-outs and opt-ins, primarily in relation to the Schengen agreement and the Charter of Fundamental Rights.

Nevertheless the Lisbon summit of 18–19 October was not without political drama. A number of touchy issues had arisen since the previous summit, some directly pertaining to the ICG, others linked to it. First and foremost, no sooner was the June summit over than the Polish government began asking for clarification of the recently-agreed provisions on majority voting. Specifically, the government wanted the Ioannina Compromise to be fully integrated into the treaty rather than appear as a political statement accompanying the text. Second, only weeks before the October summit, Poland raised a new concern about the Advocates General in the ECJ. Currently there are eight Advocates General; one each from Britain, France, Germany, Italy and Spain, and three from the smaller Member States, based on a rotation system. As a 'big' Member States, Poland not unreasonably – but unreasonably late in the treaty re-negotiations – demanded the right to appoint an Advocate General.

Other issues, of varying political importance, arose as well. The Czech Republic again demanded that national governments be allowed to limit the Commission's right of legislative initiative. Bulgaria asked to be allowed to use '*ebpo*' for the euro in Bulgarian language versions of official documents – as it is used in Bulgaria's accession treaty but not as the European Central Bank wants euro written in Bulgarian ('*eypo*') – in order to conform to a common, EU-wide pronunciation. Austria linked agreement on the Lisbon Treaty to resolution of a long-standing dispute with the Commission over limits on the number of Austrian university places available to foreigners, something which the Commission claimed was contrary to Community law and Austria claimed was essential to prevent medical faculties from being overrun by Germans. The EP wanted to be fully involved in the appointment of the High Representative of the Union for Foreign Affairs and Security (the new title for what was to have been called 'Foreign Minister'), as that person would also be a Vice-President of the Commission which, institutionally, is accountable to Parliament. The possible appointment in early 2009 of the first post-Lisbon High Representative gave rise to complaints by MEPs that the EP could be excluded from the process, given that the next Commission was not due to take office until November 2009.

Another issue, related to the Lisbon Treaty but not requiring an immediate solution, concerned the composition of the next directly-elected EP. With the arrival of MEPs from Bulgaria and Romania in January 2007, the number of MEPs had risen to 785. This was a temporary arrangement, as the Nice Treaty mandated only 732 MEPs, a ceiling that would have to be respected during the next elections, in June 2009. However, the Constitutional Treaty lifted the ceiling to 750 MEPs, a number that national governments carried over into the Lisbon Treaty. Rather than haggle among themselves on the allocation of seats per Member State, in June 2007 the European Council called on the EP to propose an allocation on the basis of 'degressive proportionality', whereby less populous countries would fare proportionately better than more populous ones. Although the larger number of seats did not have to be allocated among Member States until early in 2009, at the latest, the European Council wanted to settle the issue at the same time that it concluded the Lisbon Treaty. The EP duly drafted and, a week before the Lisbon summit, approved a report on the reallocation of seats. The EP had no discretion in setting the size of the largest and smallest delegations (Germany's and Malta's), which were mandated by the terms of the Constitutional Treaty and carried over into the Lisbon Treaty. In no case did the EP recommend fewer seats for any Member State than provided for in the Nice Treaty and, in the case of Spain, recommended an additional four seats (see Table 1).

Because a large majority of MEPs favoured the new arrangement, the European Council seemed likely to rubber stamp it at the Lisbon summit. In the run-up to the summit, however, Italy – not Poland, which received an extra seat – objected strenuously to the proposed reallocation. Under the new system, Italy would no longer be on a par with Britain and France, which would gain one and two seats, respectively. Italy justified its case for at least one additional MEP by arguing that the distribution of seats should be calculated on the basis of the number of citizens of each Member State, not the number of inhabitants. The issue became explosive in the Italian media, embarrassed Prime Minister Romano Prodi (a former Commission President who claimed to be above such trifling matters) and required considerable dexterity to defuse. The clever solution was to keep the overall number of MEPs at 750, as stipulated in the draft Lisbon Treaty, but to add the office of president to the total. Thus, in practice, the EP would have 751 members, with the extra seat going to Italy, which would then have 73 seats, the same number as Britain but one fewer than France. The European Council formally adopted this arrangement in December, based on a new proposal from the EP (European Council, 2007b).

The Austrian problem was resolved just before the summit began, when the Commission announced its willingness temporarily to suspend infringement proceedings against Austria for disregarding a 2005 ECJ ruling on university quotas. This was a striking example of the impact of politics on the Commission's role as guardian of the treaties. The Commission was sensitive to the likely negative impact on Austrian public opinion of infringement proceedings and, more to the point, the possibility that the dispute with Austria might derail the Lisbon Treaty. Discretion being the better part of

Table 1: Reallocation of Seats in the European Parliament

Member State	Population (in millions)[a]	% of EU-27 population	Seats until 2009	Nice 2009–14	EP Report 2009–14	Change
Germany	82.438	16.73	99	99	96	−3
France	62.886	12.76	78	72	74	2
United Kingdom	60.422	12.26	78	72	73	1
Italy	58.752	11.92	78	72	72[b]	
Spain	43.758	8.88	54	50	54	4
Poland	38.157	7.74	54	50	51	1
Romania	21.61	4.38	35	33	33	
Netherlands	16.334	3.31	27	25	26	1
Greece	11.125	2.26	24	22	22	
Portugal	10.57	2.14	24	22	22	
Belgium	10.511	2.13	24	22	22	
Czech Rep.	10.251	2.08	24	22	22	
Hungary	10.077	2.04	24	22	22	
Sweden	9.048	1.84	19	18	20	2
Austria	8.266	1.68	18	17	19	2
Bulgaria	7.719	1.57	18	17	18	1
Denmark	5.428	1.10	14	13	13	
Slovakia	5.389	1.09	14	13	13	
Finland	5.256	1.07	14	13	13	
Ireland	4.209	0.85	13	12	12	
Lithuania	3.403	0.69	13	12	12	
Latvia	2.295	0.47	9	8	9	1
Slovenia	2.003	0.41	7	7	8	1
Estonia	1.344	0.27	6	6	6	
Cyprus	0.766	0.16	6	6	6	
Luxembourg	0.46	0.09	6	6	6	
Malta	0.404	0.08	5	5	6	1
EU-27	492.881	100.00	785	736	750	

Source: Adapted from European Parliament (2007c).
Notes: [a] Population figures as officially established on 7 November 2006 by the Commission in Doc. 15124/06 on the basis of Eurostat figures. [b] Increased to 73 seats by agreement of the European Council in December 2007.

valour, the Commission offered a five-year moratorium on taking legal action, hoping in the meantime to reach an acceptable agreement on the substance of the case itself.

Of the remaining political demands, Bulgaria's, the Czech Republic's and the EP's were easily dealt with. The European Council agreed without much dissent to allow the use of '*ebpo*' in official documents. How could it not, given the EU's emphasis on multilingualism? The vast majority of national leaders refused to accede to the Czech Republic's effort to curb the Commission's right of initiative, but all agreed to a seemingly innocuous statement, annexed to the treaty, promising that the Commission would pay 'particular attention' to a request by the Council to withdraw a legislative proposal. A similar statement promised that the European Council would consult the EP if indeed it chose the new High Representative before nominating the next Commission.

Once again, Poland's demands were the most contentious. The demand for a Polish Advocate General was straightforward. Pressed also by other new Member States, the European Council agreed to ask the ECJ to increase the number of Advocates General from eight to 11 – a request that the Court was more than likely to accede to. In that event, one of the Advocates General would always be Polish, and other new Member States would have a better chance of occasionally appointing an Advocate General. Although Advocates General do not act along national lines and presumably share common European values, the discussion at the Lisbon summit of their number and nationality demonstrated the extreme sensitivity, for reasons of legitimacy, influence and prestige, surrounding the appointment of senior EU officials.

As for the thorny question of the Ioannina Compromise, the Polish government uncharacteristically relented without much of a struggle, gaining only minor modifications to the arrangement on double-majority voting already agreed to in June. Instead of giving it the force of Community law, the European Council decided that the new iteration of the Ioannina Compromise could be amended only by unanimous agreement in the European Council, thereby giving Poland (or any other Member State) a veto over its reform. In practice, the Ioannina Compromise is unlikely ever to obstruct EU business. As in 1994, when it emerged in response to British and Spanish complaints about changes in the arithmetic of QMV in anticipation of Austrian, Finnish, and Swedish accession, in 2007 the revised Ioannina Compromise was a means to appease a Member State concerned more about the political than the policy consequences of being outvoted in the Council.

With an election scheduled for the weekend of the summit, and public opinion turning strongly against the antics and euroscepticism of the Kaczyński brothers, the Polish government was disinclined to put up a fight.

Fundamentally, Poland was and would likely remain deeply attached to the EU. The resounding victory in the October election of the opposition Civic Platform, which stood largely on a pro-EU platform, bears out that point (see Henderson and Sitter, this volume). Nor were savvy citizens and mainstream politicians unaware of the material damage that the Kaczyńskis were likely to cause their country. 'Solidarity', a word with special resonance in Polish history, became a code-word used by EU politicians and officials to alert Warsaw to the danger of alienating other Member States. For instance, only days before the June summit, referring to Poland's request for support in its dealings with Russia, Barroso warned Poland that solidarity is a two-way street (EurActiv, 2007b). A Christian Democratic Union member of the Bundestag was more explicit. Just days before the decisive summit, he warned that, in the event of a breakdown, 'Germany will not be giving anything away when it is time for Europe's funding to be re-examined' (Agence Europe, 2007c). These increasingly unsubtle messages did not go unnoticed in Poland in the prelude to the October elections.

II. Significance of the Lisbon Treaty and the Treaty-Reform Process

Signed by national leaders in Lisbon on 13 December, the new treaty included most of the institutional and other innovations originally contained in the Constitutional Treaty. Although the founding treaties, as amended by the Lisbon Treaty, are long, complicated, and difficult to read, the EU that they describe is, in many respects, more coherent and comprehensible than the existing EU. The pillar structure is gone, but different decision-making procedures remain for foreign and security policy. The confusing distinction in the existing treaties between Union and Community is abolished, with the word 'Union' replacing 'Community' throughout the new text. The EU finally acquires legal personality, and the categorization of competences (exclusive; shared; supporting, and co-ordinating or complementary) together with the enumeration of policies within each category is a useful clarification.

Overall, the Lisbon Treaty strikes a better balance between institutional efficiency and democratic legitimacy in the EU. The new method of Council voting – the double majority system – is more equitable than the existing method of QMV based on a relatively arbitrary allocation of votes per Member State. The EP, the EU's only directly-elected body, will have additional budgetary authority and a greater legislative role, thanks to the wider applicability of the co-decision procedure. A smaller Commission should be more manageable and effective than the current college of 27 members, although having fewer Commissioners than there are Member States could weaken the

institution's already fragile legitimacy, regardless of the system chosen for
their selection. The opportunity for national parliaments to object to Commission proposals in defence of the subsidiarity principle further encourages the
Commission to legislate less, if not better. Its usefulness is debatable, however,
because national parliaments cannot tie the Commission's hands – it would be
unreasonable to allow them to do so – and because there is a huge variation in
the interest and ability of national parliaments to evaluate Commission proposals or otherwise involve themselves in EU affairs.

The Lisbon Treaty recasts the balance between the main decision-making
institutions, with the European Council clearly ascendant. In addition to being
given responsibility for decision-making in specific, politically-sensitive
areas other than law-making, the creation of the new office of standing
president, elected by the heads of state and government for a term of up to five
years, is particularly significant for the future of the European Council.
Although the treaty says little about the powers or prerogatives of the new
office, experience suggests that the elected European Council presidency will
evolve into a politically important post. More than likely, it will overshadow
the Commission presidency, to the detriment of the Commission as a whole.
Nor does the dual institutional position of the High Representative for
Foreign Affairs and Security – in the Council and the Commission – augur
well for a more assertive and independent Commission involvement in the
area of external relations. As has been the case in successive treaty changes
beginning with the Single European Act, the EP gains institutionally in the
Lisbon Treaty not only in terms of additional legislative and budgetary
authority but also by strengthening its powers of scrutiny, especially of the
Commission. Overall, the Lisbon Treaty maintains and reinforces the recent
trend within the EU toward the emergence of a commanding European
Council, a confident Council and Parliament sharing legislative responsibility
in a competitive but not excessively contentious relationship, and a politically
circumscribed Commission, defensive in its dealings with the Council and the
Parliament and having a president, regardless of his or her personal abilities,
institutionally incapable of leading the EU.

Valuable though many of the changes in the Lisbon Treaty may be, they
have come at the cost of further souring public sentiment on the EU. It seems
fair to ask, if impossible to answer, whether the Constitutional Treaty and its
successor were worth the trials and tribulations of the prolonged constitutional debate, beginning with Fischer's speech in May 2000 and ending with
implementation of the Lisbon Treaty – if ratified – in early 2009. What did the
Convention contribute? Undoubtedly it provided a wider diversity of views
and greater institutional representation than is the case with IGCs. Yet the
content of the Constitutional Treaty could perhaps have been negotiated as

easily and more expeditiously in an IGC of the kind that resulted in the Single European Act, the Maastricht Treaty, and the Amsterdam Treaty. Had a wholesale replacement of the existing treaties been negotiated in 2002–03 exclusively in an IGC rather than first discussed in the Convention, national governments might never have included in their version of a new, post-Nice treaty the words and symbols that many Europeans found so objectionable in the Constitutional Treaty.

Regardless of what might have been, the narrowness and inadequacy of the Amsterdam Treaty and, especially, the Nice Treaty had undermined the credibility of the IGC process. As a result, it would have been difficult, if not impossible, to convene yet another 'regular' IGC so soon after the Nice debacle. An IGC was both legally required (under the terms of the existing treaties) and politically necessary in order to conclude a new treaty, but extensive preparation by means of the Convention method could not have been avoided.

It is debatable whether the Convention provided more legitimacy for the treaty reform process (Risse and Kleine, 2007). Undoubtedly, it failed to arouse public interest or generate support for the Constitutional Treaty. The negative results in the French and Dutch referendums in 2005 exposed deep-seated public dissatisfaction with the EU's political direction and threatened to nullify the work of the Constitutional Convention and the ensuing IGC. Reaction to the Constitutional Treaty confirmed the impression that the permissive consensus in public attitudes toward the EU was long gone. When asked about European integration in opinion polls, Europeans were generally indifferent or, at best, mildly supportive. If given an opportunity to vote in a referendum on treaty change, opponents of deeper integration could easily exploit public unease to derail the proposed amendments, as happened in France and the Netherlands in 2005 and could happen in Ireland in 2008, with potentially disastrous consequences for the fate of the Lisbon Treaty.

Inevitably, few members of the public were aware of, or interested in, the 2007 negotiations leading to the Lisbon Treaty. Had they been able or willing to follow the negotiations closely, people would have seen the Commission playing a weak hand weakly, the EP advancing its institutional interests in the name of greater democratic legitimacy, and national governments gamely fighting their corners. Once stripped of rhetorical or idealistic cover, a government's primary interest is, quite simply, to remain in power and to do everything possible to win the next election. Despite numerous elections in the EU throughout 2007, only in Britain (where an election was not held, but where a change of leadership took place) and in Poland (where the EU became a major issue in the October election) did the fate of the Constitutional Treaty resonate domestically. In each case the government sought to balance principle and political calculation; the British government managed to do so; the Polish government did not. Other national governments were not as sensitive to, and therefore constrained by, domestic opinion on EU issues. Nevertheless each government assessed the proposed treaty changes on the basis of their likely impact on domestic politics; national influence, power, and prestige; and the legitimacy and efficiency of the EU. The outcome (the Lisbon Treaty) had to be positive sum – beneficial for the EU as well as for each Member State. At the very least it had to be presented, by the EU and its Member States, as mutually beneficial.

Whatever else, the tortuous treaty text, including the numerous protocols, declarations, and statements attached to it, testifies to the extremely convoluted nature of European integration. Every step in the process of building the European Community and, later, the European Union has required concessions and compromises on the part of national governments responsive to domestic pressures and eager to nudge the European project in a preferred direction. The framers of the Lisbon Treaty and the Constitutional Treaty before it could not begin from scratch, on a blank sheet of paper. Like a sedimentary rock gradually forming over time, the Lisbon Treaty incorporates elements of previous treaties, each of which improved to some extent or other upon the ones that went before it. Like every preceding treaty, the Lisbon Treaty is not optimal but reflects the art of the possible at a particular moment in EU history. If ratified, it is likely to last for a long time, national governments having lost their appetites and European publics having lost their patience for further institutionalized reform. If it is not ratified, the existing treaties may have to do, with minor modifications on the margins.

Key Readings

Gornitzka and Sverdrup (2007) is an excellent examination of a key component of everyday EU governance – the committees and experts groups organized by the European Commission. Kurpas *et al.* (2007) provide a valuable assessment of the stresses and strains likely to emerge with implementation of the Lisbon Treaty's many provisions for institutional reform. Beach and Christiansen (2007) explore how various institutions and actors, ranging beyond the usual suspects of Commission, Parliament, and Council, have affected the current round of treaty change. Blavoukos *et al.* (2007) address a question that is uppermost on the minds of EU observers as the Lisbon Treaty moves toward ratification and implementation: how influential will the new position of European Council President really be?

References

Agence Europe (2007a) 'European Parliament Debates Working Programme of the German Presidency with Angela Merkel', 18 January.

Agence Europe (2007b) 'EU/European Council', 24 June.

Agence Europe (2007c) 'A Look Behind the News', 19 June.

Balkenende, J.P. (2007) Speech to the European Parliament, Strasbourg, 23 May. Available at «http://www.minaz.nl/English/News/Speeches/2007/May/Speech_by_the_Prime_Minister_Jan_Peter_Balkenende_to_the_European_Parliament_Strasbourg_23_May_2007».

Beach, D. and Christiansen, T. (eds) (2007) 'Political Agency in the Constitutional Politics of the European Union'. *Journal of European Public Policy*, special issue, Vol. 14, No. 8.

Berlin Declaration (2007) 'Declaration on the Occasion of the Fiftieth Anniversary of the Signature of the Treaties of Rome'. Available at «http://www.eu2007.de/de/News/download_docs/Maerz/0324-RAA/English.pdf».

Blair, T. (2007) Press Conference with Dutch Prime Minister Jan-Peter Balkenende, 16 April. Available at «http://www.number-10.gov.uk/output/Page11479.asp».

Blavoukos, S., Bourantonis, D. and Pagoulatos, G. (2007) 'A President for the European Union: A New Actor in Town?' *JCMS*, Vol. 45, No. 2, pp. 231–52.

EurActiv (2007a) 'EU Leaders Set 2009 Deadline for Institutional Reform', 30 March. Available at «http://www.euractiv.com/en/future-eu/eu-leaders-set-2009-deadline-institutional-reform/article-162740».

EurActiv (2007b) 'Barroso Warns Poland and UK on Risks of Blocking EU Treaty', 20 June. Available at «http://www.euractiv.com/en/future-eu/barroso-warns-poland-uk-risks-blocking-eu-treaty/article-164750».

European Council (2001) 'Presidency Conclusions', Laeken European Council, 14–15 December, Annex 1, Laeken Declaration on the Future of Europe. Available at «http://www.consilium.europa.eu/ueDocs/cms_Data/docs/pressData/en/ec/68827.pdf».

European Council (2007a) 'Presidency Conclusions', Brussels European Council, 21–22 June. Available at «http://www.consilium.europa.eu/ueDocs/cms_Data/docs/pressData/en/ec/94932.pdf».

European Council (2007b) 'Presidency Conclusions', Brussels European Council, 14 December. Available at «http://www.consilium.europa.eu/ueDocs/cms_Data/docs/pressData/en/ec/97669.pdf».

European Parliament (2007a) 'Resolution of A6-0197/2007 of 7 June 2007 on the Roadmap for the Union's Constitutional Process'. Available at «http://www.europarl.europa.eu/sides/getDoc.do?pubRef=-//EP//TEXT+TA+P6-TA-2007-0234+0+DOC+XML+V0//EN».

European Parliament (2007b) 'Resolution A6-0279/2007 of 11 July 2007 on the Convening of the Intergovernmental Conference (IGC): The European Parliament's Opinion'. Available at «http://www.europarl.europa.eu/sides/getDoc.

do?pubRef=-//EP//NONSGML+REPORT+A6-2007-0279+0+DOC+PDF+V0//
EN».

European Parliament (2007c) 'Composition of the European Parliament after European Elections in June 2009'. Available at «http://www.europarl.europa.eu/news/exper/infopress_page/008-11449-283-10-41-901-20071008IPR11353-10-10-2007-2007-false/default_en.htm».

European Policy Centre (2007) 'Post-Summit Analysis: A Midsummer Night's Treaty', 24 June. Available at «http://www.epc.eu/en/pub.asp?TYP=ER&LV=294&see=y&t=15&PG=ER/EN/detail&l=&AI=721».

Fischer, J. (2000) 'From Confederacy to Federation: Thoughts on the Finality of European Integration'. Speech at Humboldt University, 12 May.

Friends of the Constitution (2007) 'For a Better Europe'. Ministerial Meeting of Friends of the Constitution. Available at «http://www.svez.gov.si/fileadmin/svez.gov.si/pageuploads/docs/novice/Madridska_izjava__prijateljev_evropske_ustavne_pogodbe_.doc».

Gornitzka, Å. and Sverdrup, U. (2007) 'Who Consults? Expert Groups in the European Union'. *ARENA Working Paper* 12/2007.

Kurpas, S., Crum, B., de Schoutheete, P., Keller, J., Dehousse, F., Andoura, S., Missiroli, A., Hagemann, S. and Bribosia, H. (2007) *The Treaty of Lisbon: Implementing the Institutional Innovations* (Brussels: CEPS).

Merkel, A. (2007) Press Conference, 23 March. Available at «http://www.eu2007.de/en/News/Press_Releases/March/0325BPAFestakt.html».

Risse, T. and Kleine, M. (2007) 'Assessing the Legitimacy of the EU's Treaty Revision Methods'. *JCMS*, Vol. 45, No. 1, pp. 69–80.

Sarkozy, N. (2007a) 'Je veux que l'Europe change', Strasbourg, 21 February 2007. Available at «http://www.u-m-p.org/site/index.php/ump/s_informer/discours/je_veux_que_l_europe_change».

Sarkozy, N. (2007b) 'Je serai le Président de tous les Français', Paris, 6 May 2007. Available at «http://www.u-m-p.org/site/index.php/ump/s_informer/discours/je_serai_le_president_de_tous_les_francais».

Spiegel Online International (2007) ' "Constitution in Drag" or "Great Step Forward?" '. Spiegel Online 25 June. Available at «http://www.spiegel.de/international/europe/0,1518,490589,00.html».

Taggart, P. (2006), 'Questions of Europe – The Domestic Politics of the 2005 French and Dutch Referendums and their Challenge for the Study of European Integration'. *JCMS*, Vol. 44, s1, pp. 7–25.

Internal Policies: The Commission Defends the EU Consumer

DAVID HOWARTH
University of Edinburgh

Introduction

2007 witnessed several examples of the European Commission invoking the defence of consumer rights in its single market policy proposals and competition policy decisions. The Commission placed emphasis on other themes – business friendly 'better' regulation, competitiveness, innovation and helping small- and medium-sized enterprises (SMEs). A consumer-oriented discourse, however, took centre stage in the Single Market Review and was the leading element in the Commission's justification for a range of single market and competition policy decisions throughout the year. Several observers have argued that consumer interests have traditionally been poorly represented in European Union (EU) policy-making (Grant, 1993; Greenwood, 2003) and that neither the EU nor any of the EU Member States has the kind of consumer lobby or consumer advocates that exist in the US. Nonetheless, the presence and influence of the consumer lobby and interests has increased over the past decade (Young and Wallace, 2000; Greenwood, 2003). Moreover, since the 1990s, the Commission has placed increasing emphasis on consumer interests in its strategy and discourse on single market and competition policies. Multi-annual consumer policy action plans have a two-decade history and consumer policy was officially mainstreamed through the 1997 Amsterdam Treaty (Article 153). In its 2001 report on the 'Action Plan for Consumer Policy 1999–2001', however, the Commission accepted that efforts in consumer policy were ad hoc and focused primarily on product safety. The Commission set about reinforcing the consumer orientation of its policies, recognizing in its 2001 report that its efforts were rather belated but also arguing that consumer policy had become a 'central element of overall EU policy development' (Commission, 2001, p. 21).

While this shift principally reflected Commission concerns with regard to dealing with high profile food safety issues, the consumer-oriented strategy was also applied to market integration and competition policy. The consumer policy strategy for 2002–06 was the Commission's most ambitious to date and included a proposal to find a mechanism to attach legal implications for failure to observe company self-regulatory codes and provide a general framework directive on fair trading practices. The strategy created considerable stir in the Confederation of European Business (UNICE, now known as BUSINESSEUROPE), but was keenly supported by the main EU consumer lobby, BEUC.

The heightened emphasis on consumer interests reflects the deliberate aim of increasing EU citizen (as consumer) interest in and support for the single market. The Commission's turn to the consumer can be seen as an effort to legitimize market integration in the face of powerful forces, both governments and economic interests, that have hindered progress and succeeded in watering down recent pieces of single market legislation, including the Services Directive adopted in 2006 (see Howarth, 2007).

This chapter outlines some of the main developments in the single market and competition policy areas in 2007 and draws out the consumerist focus in Commission policy documents, decisions and discourse on these developments.

I. Towards a New and Improved Single Market?

2007 saw the completion of a major review of the Single Market, the outcome of which was the Commission communication 'A Single Market for 21st Century Europe' published on 20 November (Commission, 2007k). The Review calls for further investigation into new approaches to make the single market more impact-driven, result-oriented and network-based and to enhance its effectiveness, decentralization, accessibility and responsiveness to the global context. It spells out how the single market can do more to take advantage of globalization, improve opportunities for small businesses, and stimulate innovation, all the while maintaining high social and environmental standards. 'A Single Market that puts consumers and small business first' is the Commission's official slogan for the review and the emphasis upon 'empowering consumers' is repeated directly in three (and indirectly in two) of the six core review themes, which are to:

- help consumers to exercise their contractual rights and obtain redress across borders;
- help consumers to benefit to a greater extent from the opening-up of financial markets;
- provide better information for consumers and small businesses;
- respond to weaknesses in sectors where the single market should deliver more;
- propose a 'small business act' and introduce a 'researcher passport';
- specify how Community rules are to apply to services and social services of general interest and promote the quality of social services across the EU.

The Review sets out a new approach to the single market, explicitly avoiding a 'classic legislative action programme' (Commission, 2007k, p. 4). The aim of the Review 'is rather to foster flexibility and adaptability while maintaining the legal and regulatory certainty necessary to preserve a well-functioning single market' (p. 4). The Review provides various illustrative actions and is accompanied by documents that clarify the Commission's preferred approaches to market monitoring, single market instruments, trade instruments and, more specifically, on the application of these approaches to the retail financial services sector. The Review dedicates considerable attention to the goal of improving the day-to-day management of the single market with increased focus on Commission assistance for senior national officials to identify the best ways to help Member States implement and enforce EU policies, notably through the creation of national 'Single Market Centres'. The Review outlines a modification of the annual single market scoreboard, which will from 2008 monitor the overall performance of the single market, rather than focus on transposition delays and infringement cases, and will include a new 'consumer scoreboard' on the performance of consumer markets. Amongst other proposed initiatives, the Commission announced that it would propose a small business act in 2008 that would seek to cut red tape, reduce obstacles to cross-border activity, increase SME access to European programme funding, and increase their share of public procurement contracts.

The Commission's new reform proposals for EU telecommunications rules were presented as a flagship of the new single market (Commission, 2007h, 2007i). Presented on 13 November, two proposed directives aim to complete the single market in telecom services and enable consumers to benefit from better-quality communications services at lower prices. The new legislation aims to address the problem of the telecom sector being largely fragmented upon national lines, with very few operators present throughout the EU market and even fewer offering pan-European services. The proposals involve improving regulation in the telecoms sector by removing regulations in 11 of the 18 markets in the sector where it is no longer necessary because competition has been achieved and by focusing new regulatory action in those markets where the dominance of incumbents has been least challenged. The Commission also proposed a regulation calling for the creation of a European Electronic Communications Market Agency (Commission, 2007j) that will assist the Commission and the national regulatory authorities to ensure the uniform and consistent application of market rules and consumer protection throughout the EU. Protecting the financial interests, security and privacy of consumers was a central element of the Commission's reform proposals. The Commission called for new obligations to be imposed on operators to publish information on prices and to facilitate transfer of customers from one service provider to another so that they can effectively take advantage of improved transparency on prices and conditions.

Wanting to avoid accusations of prioritizing market integration and liberalization over social progress, the 20 November communication includes a section covering social, environmental and cohesion dimensions. Moreover, on the same day, the Commission published an additional communication (Commission, 2007l) on services of general interest, including social services of general interest and a paper which outlined a 'new social vision' for the EU (Commission, 2007n).

The single market review was the subject of considerable discussion and debate throughout the year that involved several EU institutions including the European Economic and Social Committee, Committee of the Regions, European Parliament (EP), Council and European Council. The Commission presented its interim report on the single market to the March European Council (Commission, 2007c). In its response, the European Council stressed the need to improve still further the way the single market worked so it could adapt to new economic developments. The EP's 4 September resolution on the single market review placed emphasis on making the single market work better by improving the implementation and enforcement of existing rules.

The Commission's single market review represents a shift in the strategy to advance European market integration at a time when integration has stalled in a range of sectors, most notably financial services. Much in the review is not new: it reflects the move away from legislative devices that has been taking place over the past decade as a pragmatic response to the powerful opposition to further integration in a range of sectors and the glacial speed of the EU legislative process. The shift also reflects a broader intellectual change and a business-centred agenda. Moreover, the traditional model of market integration involving legislation to approximate national rules is better suited to removing barriers to trade in goods than services and has largely run its course. At the very least legislation needs to be complemented by alternative mechanisms. Services account for over 70 per cent of EU-15 gross domestic product (GDP) and 67 per cent of employment, but only 20 per cent of intra-EU-15 trade. This is because numerous administrative, tax, regulatory and supervisory factors restrict the free movement of services. Thus there is significant scope for cross-border growth of trade in a range of services and major efficiency gains and lower costs for consumers from increased competition. The 2006 Services Directive (2006/123/EC), while achieving some progress in this area, failed to eliminate many barriers. The directive does not apply to a range of sectors, including services of general interest (SGI), social services of general interest (SSGI) and services of general economic interest (SGEI) – including health care, audiovisual services, transport (including taxis), energy and telecommunications – financial services, notaries, temporary work agencies, as well as casinos and other gambling venues (see Howarth, 2007).

Moreover, there are several long-standing criticisms of the EU legislative method: slow transposition to national law, incorrect application and inadequate enforcement (for the EU-25 in May 2007 there were over 1628 instances of a Member State not having yet transposed a directive into national law).[1] The tendency to opt for legislative action in the past resulted in a failure to consider non-legislative alternatives. EU rules have also been criticized by many EU-based firms for undermining their competitiveness by imposing high (and uneven) regulatory burdens on producers. Moreover, attempts to legislate in sensitive areas of economic and social activity, such as services of a general interest, have triggered political opposition.

The difficulties of making progress using the traditional model of integration helps to explain the drive for 'better', less, and more flexible regulation. The 'better' regulation/market-oriented approach is also very much part of the Lisbon Agenda – the galvanizing reform programme intended to transform the EU into the 'most dynamic knowledge-based economy in the world by 2010'. This emphasis on non-legislative mechanisms – such as co-regulation, standardization and self-regulation – to achieve progress in market integration was picked up in the single market review.

Free Movement of Goods

In addition to the push towards new mechanisms to advance market integration, the Commission also dedicated considerable attention in 2007 to the free

---

[1] 'Internal Market Scoreboard: Member States need to focus on correctly applying Internal Market rules', Commission, Press release, IP/07/991, 2 July 2007.

movement of goods, which should have been attained long ago, but where many less evident obstacles remain. On 14 February, the Commission outlined an important package of legislative measures to be adopted on the development of the single market, the principal element of which was the communication 'The Internal Market for Goods: A Cornerstone of Europe's Competitiveness' (Commission, 2007b). The package comprises four initiatives that seek to streamline freedom of movement of goods and to simplify and modernize the rules and principles governing the single market. The Commission proposed two regulations, a decision and an interpretative communication. The first regulation seeks to establish procedures relating to the application of certain national technical rules to products marketed in another Member State; the second seeks to set out requirements for accreditation and market surveillance relating to the marketing of products. The decision seeks to create a common framework for the marketing of products, while the communication seeks to clarify existing procedures for the registration of motor vehicles originating in another Member State. The Commission also insisted that it would recommend measures to reinforce existing rules on product safety.

Freedom to Provide Services and Freedom of Establishment

Financial services have been the focus of renewed attention since the beginning of 2007. On 27 February, the Council adopted conclusions on the clearing and settlement of securities transactions, a key component of financial integration within the EU where significant progress is needed to improve the efficiency and the reliability of post-trading services, such as clearing and settlement. On 19 March the Commission presented an interpretative communication (Commission, 2007d) on the respective powers retained by the home Member State and the host Member State in the marketing of undertakings for collective investment in transferable securities (UCITS) – which include managed, mutual and other funds that allow an individual to invest with others in a wider range of investments than may be feasible for the individual. The communication seeks to correct diverging interpretations of the existing UCITS directive (Directive 85/611/EEC) in order to improve the way it works. The directive was adopted to allow collective investment schemes to operate freely throughout the EU on the basis of a single authorization (UCITS status) from one Member State.[2] However, the imposition of additional regulatory requirements by several Member States – usually with the effect of protecting local asset

---

[2] In 2005, approximately €5 trillion were invested in collective investments, of which 70 per cent were UCITS ('Collective investment fund regulation (UCITS Directive))' in EurActiv.com, 15 July 2005, «http://www.euractiv.com/en/financial-services/collective-investment-fund-regulation-ucits-directive/article-142577», accessed 20 March 2008.

managers – has blocked free operation. The Commission placed emphasis on the importance of progress in the construction of a single market for transferable securities for consumers in that economies of scale reduce costs for investment managers which can be passed on.

In April, the Commission adopted a report (Commission, 2007e) on the continued appropriateness of the requirements for professional indemnity insurance imposed on intermediaries under Community law and a Green Paper (Commission, 2007f) on retail financial services in the single market. In its report, the Commission argued that major efforts are needed in both these areas if consumers are to reap the benefit of a genuine single market in financial services. On 8 May, the Economic and Financial Affairs (Ecofin) Council welcomed the Commission's 2006 White Paper on enhancing the single market framework for investment funds (Commission, 2006a). On 18 December the Commission adopted a White Paper (Commission, 2007n) that outlined its comprehensive review of the level of integration of mortgage credit markets and identified a package of measures designed to improve their competitiveness and the efficiency, which will benefit consumers, lenders and investors. The Commission also adopted a communication 'Financial Education' (Commission, 2007o) that set out non-binding principles to guide the Member States and other concerned parties when drawing up and implementing financial education schemes for the general public. Moreover, in its communication of 21 December, the Commission put forward measures intended to increase cross-border investments by venture capital funds (Commission, 2007p). During 2007 work also continued within the various EU institutions on the directive seeking to complete the single market in postal services (amending Directive 97/67/EC). On 1 October, EU transport ministers agreed to support a plan to open up postal services to full competition ending national monopolies on the delivery of lightweight letters and postcards in 2011, two years later than originally planned – a delay due to opposition primarily from France and Italy.

The Payment Services Directive

In another direct plug to consumer interests, on 27 March, the Council agreed to a draft of the payment services directive that was drawn up to streamline and unify the EU's national payment regimes in order to eliminate the cost of cross-border transactions and allow banks, credit card companies and other payment providers to compete more freely across the EU. The directive was a core element of the Commission's long-standing campaign to create a single market for financial services and improve competition in a sector that has operated largely along national lines. Under an EU law from 2001, cross-border credit and card transfers cannot cost anymore than domestic payments. Consumer groups, led by BEUC, have long criticized banks for exploiting the lack of harmonised rules to overcharge customers.[3] The status quo affects citizens who have to make regular cross-border transfers – for example because they own a second home in another country and thus are almost always required to open a bank account in the country where the bills fall due. Beyond the costs and hassle for consumers, the Commission estimated that the annual cost of making payments between the various national systems amounts to 2 to 3 per cent of EU GDP. While the directive will not eliminate all barriers to free movement, it aims to facilitate the use of credit and debit cards in other EU Member States, encourage cross-border money transfers and new forms of payment services, including money transmitters such as Western Union and mobile phones, which will further intensify competition in the sector. In addition, by 2012 providers will be expected to process all cross-border credit and debit transfers within one working day. Moreover, the directive sets out common rules on the information that companies must provide to their customers and on liability. The adoption of the payment directive, by providing a legal framework, was a crucial step in the development of the Single Euro Payment Area (SEPA) to begin in 2008. SEPA, an industry initiative supported by the Commission and the European Central Bank, aims to facilitate and cut the cost of cross-border payments through a pan-European payment infrastructure. On 13 November, the EP and the Council adopted the final version of the payment services directive (2007/64/EC).

The 'Roaming' Fee Debate

In 2006 the Commission proposed a regulation to lower international mobile call ('roaming') fees, pushing for cuts of up to 70 per cent by mid-2007. The Commission's campaign to cut roaming fees has been one of its highest-profile initiatives in favour of the consumer in the history of European integration. Viviane Reding, the Commissioner for Information Society and Media, argued that roaming fees were unjustifiably high for the EU's 478 million mobile phone subscribers and had been warning operators since 2005 to cut their fees voluntarily or face possible legislation. Moreover, the Commission had in 2004 and 2005 begun anti-trust investigations against Vodafone (UK and Germany), O2 (UK) and T-Mobile (Germany) for abusing their dominant market positions by demanding 'unfair and excessive' roaming fees. In particular, the Commission challenged the level of wholesale rates that the companies charged one another for network use in the UK and Germany. The adoption of maximum roaming charge fees was strongly

[3] *Financial Times*, 28 March 2007.

opposed by Europe's mobile phone companies, which made an estimated €8.5 billion a year from roaming services. They argued that it was inappropriate for the EU to engage in price regulation.

On 12 April, the EP's Industry Committee gave strong support to the introduction of tough limits on roaming fees. It approved a cap of €0.40 a minute to make a call and €0.15 to receive one and stipulated that caps apply automatically to users unless they rejected them for another price scheme. The mobile phone industry body, the GSMA, said these tariffs would force them to operate below cost and Vodafone claimed that the proposed prices were extreme and far lower than any others that had been suggested.[4] There were significant divisions in the EP between those MEPs who supported the position of the Industry Committee and those who – siding with industry – supported significantly higher maximum fee caps.

The cuts in roaming fees were also the subject of considerable debate among the Member States which threatened to derail the Commission's plan for the cuts to come into effect in time for the 2007 summer tourist season. Britain, France and Spain (home to Vodafone, France Telecom and Telefonica respectively) and some other Member States opposed cuts to roaming fees and opposed the maximum fee caps adopted by the EP Industry Committee. Most of the smaller Member States, including Denmark and the Netherlands, favoured sharply lower fees as their citizens were likely to travel to these popular tourist destination countries for foreign holidays.

Negotiations collapsed in early May and the EP vote scheduled for 9 May was postponed until later in the month to allow more time to reach an agreement. On 16 May, the Member States industry ministers reached an agreement to cuts to a maximum of €0.49 a minute for outgoing calls while in another EU country. Charges to receive a call while abroad would be capped at €0.24 a minute. The maximum charges (the 'eurotariff') was to fall further in 2008 and 2009 when it would reach €0.43 for outgoing and €0.19 for incoming calls. While higher than the EP's Industry Committee's proposed figures, these amounts were still a substantial decline from the previous average roaming rates on calls between two EU countries of €1.10 and €0.58 respectively. As only maximum rates were set, several mobile operators could continue to offer lower rates and roaming fees would continue to vary widely across the EU. The automaticity of the maximum rate preferred by the EP's Industry Committee, however, was blocked; phone users who had signed up to mobile operators' overseas price plans would have to request the lower price for it to apply to them. On 23 May, the EP agreed to compromise. Thanks to the new regulation, prices started dropping in July, and the

[4] *Financial Times*, 13 April 2007.

Commission reported that by October EU mobile users were able to save up to 60 per cent on calls made or received in another Member State.

On 18 July, the Commission closed its long-running investigations into three big mobile phone companies that were accused of charging excessive roaming charges. The decision to close the case was unusual in that the Commission rarely stops anti-trust investigations without either securing a settlement or imposing a fine. The Commission argued that the new law addressed the issues raised in the anti-trust proceedings. It was also suspected, however, that the Commission was offering a goodwill gesture to the operators.[5]

On 16 September, however, the Commission challenged the mobile phone operators again. Commissioner Reding announced the need for rules to harmonize the rates that mobile phone operators could charge for connecting calls to their networks. The rates are known as wholesale charges because they are paid by telecommunications companies rather than consumers. The amounts involved were substantial: in the UK, in 2007, the charges represented about 15 per cent of mobile operators' revenues, amounting to approximately £2.5 billion.[6] Charges varied considerably across Member States and most mobile phone operators were opposed to convergence. Some individual Member State telecommunications regulators – as in France – were already attempting to impose cuts in the charges. However, those Member States with low charges and the Commission argued in favour of EU regulation to bring about greater harmonization and price cuts. 2007 ended with the hanging threat of EU legislation.

II. Competition Policy

DG Competition as a World Leader

In a major survey published in early June,[7] the Commission was crowned one of the three best antitrust enforcement agencies in the world out of 38 agencies examined, along with the UK's Competition Commission and the US's Federal Trade Commission. Although these three agencies often pursue different policies and cases, the range of anti-trust experts interviewed for the survey found little difference in the analytical skills of the three bodies. The results provided a rare boost to the Commission, which has often been criticized for being more interventionist than its US counterpart, showing a greater willingness to place companies under investigation. Since the

[5] *Financial Times*, 19 July 2007.
[6] *Financial Times*, 16 September 2007.
[7] *Global Competition Review*, 9 June 2007.

appointment of Neelie Kroes as Competition Commissioner in 2004, the Commission has intensified its crackdown on companies operating price-fixing cartels. In 2006 the Commission imposed record-breaking fines of €1.8 billion, more than all of the other agencies in the *Global Competition Review* (9 June 2007) survey combined. The *Global Competition Review* also praised the Commission's role on merger control and its use of sweeping sector inquiries in industries such as energy and financial services. The principal negative evaluation of the Commission's activities was the slow pace of its cartel investigations, which averaged 35 months, making it one of the slowest to be examined. Some of the anti-trust experts surveyed also criticised the inadequate economic reasoning of the Directorate General for Competition in some cases.

Legislative Developments

The Commission's major legislative initiative in competition policy consisted of a two-part proposal for a new block exemption regulation for state aids. The proposal, of 24 April and 8 September, was the Commission's response to several Member States' criticism of the operation of EU state aid policy. The German government has led the charge in favour of softening the hard line adopted by the Commission against governments that grant state aid to private sector companies. The German government consistently provides more state aid than any other Member State (€20 billion out of €64 billion in total in 2005). The Germans argued that many non-EU companies enjoyed subsidies which placed them at a competitive advantage in relation to EU-based firms.[8] In April, the German government circulated a paper to Member State industry ministers calling for the relaxation of EU state aid rules in individual cases to allow Member States governments to 'match' financial enticements offered by governments outside the EU. The German discussion paper also placed emphasis on the need for an 'efficient, rapid and predictable' Commission procedure for reviewing state aid plans.

As a partial response to these kinds of objections to the existing state aid regime, the proposed Commission regulation was designed to simplify and consolidate into one text the four existing block exemptions for aid to SMEs, including aid for research and development, employment, training and regional development. The new regulation would also allow the block exemption of two additional types of aid – environmental aid and aid in the form of risk capital – as well as an expanded definition of allowable research and development aid, including to large companies. On 12 December the Commission amended regulations from 1999 and 2004 that set out the rules for the

[8] *Financial Times*, 25 April 2007.

application of Article 93 of the EC Treaty, including new details on the notification procedure and new forms for notifying aid in the areas of venture capital and research.

Battling the Cartels; Defending the Consumer

2007 was also noteworthy for the record level of fines levied by the Commission and some high profile Commission decisions and supportive judicial decisions. In its own documentation about these cases, the Commission argued that 2007 was a particularly successful year for the EU's competition policy in safeguarding consumer interests. 'The EU's robust competition policy is there to ensure that dominant companies cannot use their market power to restrict competition. The focus is on consumer choice and on maintaining a level playing field for companies throughout the EU single market' (Commission, 2007q). The rise in the level of fines was in large part due to the new fining guidelines adopted by the Commission in 2006, which made it easier to impose maximum penalties, equivalent to 10 per cent of a company's annual global turnover. In January the Commission imposed a record fine of €751 million on 11 firms involved in a long-running price-fixing cartel in the gas insulated switchgear sector, including a record single fine of €397 million on the German company Siemens for its leading role in the cartel. Commissioner Kroes announced that 'the Commission [had] put an end to a cartel that [had] cheated public utility companies and consumers for more than 16 years'.[9] In February, the Commission issued another record anti-trust fine (€992 million) on five companies that manufacture elevators, including the German engineering group ThyssenKrupp, which received a new record fine for a single company of €479.7 million. Kroes said the lift and escalator cartel had behaved 'outrageously', while a Commission spokesman said taxpayers, public authorities and other customers had been 'ripped off big time'.[10] The Commission also urged customers of the companies involved in the agreement to renegotiate their contracts and said they might have the right to sue for damages. On 4 July, the Commission levied a fine of €151 million on Telefónica for abuse of a dominant position imposing unfair prices on the Spanish broadband market over a period of five years. All told, in 2007 the Commission imposed fines totalling €3.33 billion.

Sectoral Investigations: Challenging Banks and Credit Card Companies

Starting in 2006, the Commission undertook major investigations into several sectors of the EU economy in which there were significant obstacles to both

[9] *Financial Times*, 24 January 2007.
[10] *Financial Times*, 22 February 2007.

competition and cross-border trade. In January 2007, the Commission published the results of two inquiries into the European gas and electricity sectors (10 January) and retail banking markets (31 January) (Commission, 2006b, 2007a) and stressed that it was vital to apply both competition and regulatory-based remedies to barriers in these sectors. On 25 September, the Commission presented the results of its inquiry into business insurance and recommended a series of measures to intensify competition (Commission, 2007h). Although the Commission's sector-wide investigations were not directed at any specific companies and thus did not trigger antitrust fines, the Commission let it be known that its investigations would allow it better to pursue individual infringements in the future.

In its 31 January report, the Commission criticized retail banks and credit card companies for charging artificially high fees (and 'ripping off customers') and a lack of cross-border competition.[11] The Commission argued that 'in some Member States the combination of high profits, a high level of concentration and the existence of barriers to market entry is worrying, with the banks being able to abuse their market power towards consumers and small businesses'.[12] The Commission was particularly critical of the high level of market concentration among savings banks and co-operative banks in several Member States, including France, Germany, Italy and Spain, and their failure to compete with each other in local markets. The Commission highlighted the barriers that discourage consumers from switching banks, such as fees for closing an account.

The Commission also challenged cross-border 'interchange fees,' the charges paid between banks' servicing retailers and those servicing cardholders – which raise competition concerns and result in higher costs to consumers. The problem is long-standing; associations representing retailers presented complaints about these fees to the Commission a decade previously and the Commission began investigations into various aspects of the credit card industry in June 2000, the day after American authorities launched anti-trust cases against Visa and MasterCard activities. Visa and MasterCard and other major credit card companies argued that the elimination of interchange fees would create chaos in the EU's payment card system.[13] In 2002, Visa avoided Commission action by lowering its fees. In 2007, MasterCard was still waiting for a Commission decision on whether its fee structure violated competition rules. In its 31 January report, the Commission noted its preference for self-regulation by banks and credit card companies, but also

[11] *Financial Times*, 1 February 2007.
[12] *Financial Times*, 1 February 2007.
[13] *Financial Times*, 30 January 2007.

threatened action if the situation did not improve. The Commission, however, stopped short of calling for the abolition of fees or of specifying reductions.

In spite of the apparently soft position of the Commission on interchange fees in its 31 January report, by the end of the year, it adopted a tough stance on MasterCard. On 19 December, the Commission told the company that it would face daily fines of $316,000 unless it eliminated within six months its cross-border interchange fees for cross-border payment card transactions with MasterCard- and Maestro-branded debit and consumer credit cards which, the Commission argued, violated EC Treaty rules on restrictive business practices. The Commission stressed that, while interchange fees were not inherently illegal, they were only compatible with EU competition rules if they contributed to technical and economic progress and benefited consumers. The Commission argued that MasterCard's fees did not meet these criteria. MasterCard said it would launch a legal challenge to the ruling (and was eventually to do so on 2 March 2008). The Commission's 2002 deal with Visa also expired on 31 December and the company was then required to eliminate its fees altogether or face fines.

Microsoft's Defeat before the Court

On 17 September, the Court of First Instance (CFI) confirmed most elements of the Commission's decision of March 2004 that found Microsoft guilty of abusing its quasi-monopoly position in the market for PC operating systems and media players. The Commission fined Microsoft €497 million for infringing the EC Treaty rules on abuse of dominant market position (Article 82).[14] In its battle with Microsoft the Commission placed considerable emphasis on the negative effects of the company's practices on both innovation and consumer choice. The Commission found that Microsoft acted illegally by preventing data exchange with competing operating systems and by bundling products together, thereby limiting consumer choice. The Commission found that Microsoft prevented innovative server products from being brought to the market and distorted competition in the streaming media player market. The CFI court largely upheld this decision. A Commission statement on the CFI ruling said that the court has underlined that computer users are 'entitled to benefit from choice, more innovative products and more competitive prices' (Commission, 2007r).

The Commission's victory against Microsoft was not total, however. While the CFI confirmed the Commission's assessment as to the appropriate

---

[14] Directorate General Competition, Commission, 'Anti-trust cases: Microsoft case', available at «http://ec.europa.eu/comm/competition/antitrust/cases/microsoft/».

legal tests to be applied, in addition to the evidence needed to satisfy those tests, it annulled aspects of the Commission's decision that ordered Microsoft to submit a proposal for the appointment of a monitoring trustee with the power to have access, independently of the Commission, to Microsoft's assistance, information, documents, premises and employees and to the source code of the relevant Microsoft products. The Commission had also wanted Microsoft to bear all the costs associated with that monitoring trustee.

Conclusion: Defending the Citizen Consumer

During 2007 the Commission extensively justified its advocacy of market integration and assertive application of EU competition policy in terms of protecting consumer rights. The Commission's intention appears to be to increase EU citizen interest in, and support for, the single market following the stumbling progress of recent years in integrating services markets. The shift in strategy and discourse should also be seen in terms of the decreasing relevance of the traditional model of advancing economic integration through legislation and the corresponding increased focus on alternative mechanisms to achieve progress. There is an element of populism in the Commission's consumerist discourse. Presenting its single market review, the Commission sniped at 'vested interests with disproportionate market power' 'creaming off' the benefits of globalization and promised to 'take action where markets do not deliver for consumers'.[15] The Commission appears to respond to widespread public concern about the economic and social effects of liberalization and globalization. This kind of message seems to target an audience that has not traditionally looked to European market integration for salvation. While the message should meet with a favourable (but sceptical) hearing in the UK, in some Member States with different socio-economic cultures (notably France) one wonders if addressing citizen-consumers will have the same kind of appeal.

Key Readings

Commission (2007l) sets out the Commission's new approach to the single market, deliberately avoiding a 'classic legislative action programme'. House of Lords (2008) provides the best critical account to date of the European Commission's Single Market review.

---

[15] 'Commission unveils its vision for a modern single market for all', Press release, available at «http:// europa.eu/rapid/pressReleasesAction.do?reference=IP/07/1728».

References

Commission of the European Communities (2001) 'Action Plan for Consumer Policy 1999–2001 and on the General Framework for Community Activities in Favour of Consumers 1999–2003'. COM(2001)486.

Commission of the European Communities (2006a) 'White Paper: Enhancing the Single Market Framework for Investment Funds'. COM(2006)686.

Commission of the European Communities (2006b) 'Communication: Inquiry Pursuant to Article 17 of Regulation (EC) No. 1/2003 into the European Gas and Electricity Sectors (Final Report)'. COM(2006)851, 10 January.

Commission of the European Communities (2007a) 'Communication: Sector Inquiry under Article 17 of Regulation (EC) No. 1/2003 on Retail Banking (Final Report)'. COM(2007)33, 31 January.

Commission of the European Communities (2007b) 'Communication: The Internal Market for Goods: a Cornerstone of Europe's Competitiveness'. COM(2007)35, 14 February.

Commission of the European Communities (2007c) 'Communication: A Single Market for Citizens – Interim Report to the 2007 Spring European Council'. COM(2007)6, 22 February.

Commission of the European Communities (2007d) 'Interpretative Communication: Respective Powers Retained by the Home Member State and the Host Member State in the Marketing of UCITS Pursuant to Section VIII of the UCITS Directive'. COM(2007)112, 19 March.

Commission of the European Communities (2007e) 'Report from the Commission to the European Parliament and the Council: The Continued Appropriateness of the Requirements for Professional Indemnity Insurance Imposed on Intermediaries under Community Law'. COM(2007)178, April.

Commission of the European Communities (2007f) 'Green Paper: Retail Financial Services in the Single Market'. COM(2007)226, April.

Commission of the European Communities (2007g) 'Communication: Sector Inquiry under Article 17 of Regulation (EC) No 1/2003 on Business Insurance (Final Report)'. COM(2007)556, 25 September.

Commission of the European Communities (2007h) 'Proposal for a Directive of the European Parliament and of the Council amending Directives 2002/21/EC on a Common Regulatory Framework for Electronic Communications Networks and Services, 2002/19/EC on Access to, and Interconnection of, Electronic Communications Networks and Services, and 2002/20/EC on the Authorization of Electronic Communications Networks and Services'. COM(2007)697, 2007/0247/ COD.

Commission of the European Communities (2007i) 'Proposal for a Directive of the European Parliament and of the Council Amending Directive 2002/22/EC on Universal Service and Users' Rights Relating to Electronic Communications Networks, Directive 2002/58/EC Concerning the Processing of Personal Data and the Protection of Privacy in the Electronic Communications Sector and

Regulation (EC) No. 2006/2004 on Consumer Protection Co-operation'. COM(2007)698, 2007/0248/COD.

Commission of the European Communities (2007j) 'Proposal for a Regulation of the European Parliament and of the Council Establishing the European Electronic Communications Market Authority'. COM(2007)699, 2007/0249/COD.

Commission of the European Communities (2007k) 'Communication: A Single Market for 21st Century Europe'. COM(2007)725, 20 November.

Commission of the European Communities (2007l) 'Communication: Accompanying the Communication on "A single market for 21st century Europe" – Services of General Interest, including Social Services of General Interest: a New European Commitment'. COM(2007)725, 20 November.

Commission of the European Communities (2007m) 'Communication: Opportunities, Access and Solidarity: Towards a New Social Vision for 21st Century Europe'. COM(2007)726, 20 November.

Commission of the European Communities (2007n) 'White Paper: Integration of EU Mortgage Credit Markets'. COM(2007)807, 18 December.

Commission of the European Communities (2007o) 'Communication: Financial Education'. COM(2007)808, 18 December.

Commission of the European Communities (2007p) 'Communication: Removing Obstacles to Cross-Border Investments by Venture Capital Funds'. COM(2007)853, 21 December.

Commission of the European Communities (2007q) 'Europe and EU in 2007: A Snapshot of EU Achievements: Dominant Companies Cannot Limit Consumer Choice'. Available at http://ec.europa.eu/snapshot2007/consumer/consumer_en. htm. Accessed 16 April 2008.

Commission of the European Communities (2007r) 'Antitrust: Commission Welcomes CFI Ruling Upholding Commission's Decision on Microsoft's Abuse of Dominant Market Position'. Press release, MEMO/07/359, 17/09/2007. Available at «http://europa.eu/rapid/pressReleasesAction.do?reference=MEMO/07/359&format=HTML&aged=0&language=EN&guiLanguage=en».

Grant, W. (1993) 'Pressure Groups and the European Community: An Overview'. In Mazey, S. and Richardson, J. (eds) *Lobbying in the European Community* (Oxford: Oxford University Press), pp. 27–46.

Greenwood, J. (2003) *Interest Representation in the European Union* (Basingstoke: Palgrave), pp. 197–209.

House of Lords (2008) 'The Single Market: Wallflower or Dancing Partner? Inquiry into the European Commission's Review of the Single Market'. 5th Report of Session 2007–08: House of Lords Papers 36-I, European Union Committee, TSO (London: The Stationery Office), 8 February.

Howarth, D. (2007) 'Internal Policies: Reinforcing the New Lisbon Message of Competitiveness and Innovation'. *JCMS*, Vol. 45, s1, pp. 89–106.

Young, A.R. and Wallace, H. (2000) *Regulatory Politics in the Enlarging European Union: Weighing Civic and Producer Interests* (Manchester: Manchester University Press).

Justice and Home Affairs

JÖRG MONAR
Université Robert Schuman de Strasbourg

Introduction

For the Justice and Home Affairs (JHA) Council the year 2007 brought a record: the 164 texts adopted were not only an increase of nearly 40 per cent compared to 2006, but also the highest number of texts ever adopted during a single year.[1] This increase was due mainly to the accelerated implementation of parts of the Hague Programme (which had been subject to serious delays the year before); the extension of external relations activity in the JHA domain (mainly in the form of readmission and visa agreements); and the putting into place of the new 2007–13 financial framework and of the Schengen Information System (SIS) II. The Commission also injected new impetus in the migration policy developments. The well-managed German Presidency secured agreement on the incorporation into the EU of most of the police co-operation and data-exchange provisions of the Prüm Convention, which had still divided Member States the year before, and the Portuguese Presidency contributed much to the extension of the Schengen border control zone to the new Member States in December.

At the end of the year, however, the impressive numerical increase in output could not hide the fact that substantive progress was overall more modest. The adoption of the 'Rome I' Regulation on non-contractual obligations, for instance, contrasted with the Member States' failure to agree on the

[1] Lists of texts provided by the General Secretariat of the Council and own calculations.

© 2008 The Author(s)
Journal compilation © 2008 Blackwell Publishing Ltd, 9600 Garsington Road, Oxford OX4 2DQ, UK and 350 Main Street, Malden, MA 02148, USA

long overdue Framework Decision on procedural rights in criminal proceedings. Several important legislative acts also continued to be delayed because of the unanimity requirement and national parliamentary scrutiny reserves. Against this background, the quite extensive reforms in the Treaty of Lisbon for the 'area of freedom, security and justice' (AFSJ) appeared all the more important, although the new perspectives thus opened came with an enhanced potential for further differentiation in the JHA domain.

I. Developments in Individual Policy Areas

Refugee Policy

With the Hague Programme providing for the introduction of a Common European Asylum System (CEAS) by 2010, the pressure on the EU to start decision-making on the necessary 'second stage' legislative instruments increased. According to the Programme, the new instruments should be introduced on the basis of a comprehensive evaluation of the functioning of the 'first stage' instruments, which had provided for minimal harmonization of national legal frameworks. Yet as the completion of the 'first stage' instruments had been delayed until the end of 2005, when the so-called 'Procedures Directive' was adopted, the data available on the implementation of these instruments and its problems were still far from sufficient for a substantial evaluation in 2007. Concerned about the 2010 deadline, the Commission nevertheless launched a 'Green Paper on the future Common European Asylum System' on 6 June (Commission, 2007a), which started the 'second stage' process. In this Green Paper, the Commission identified a range of issues which would need to be tackled in order to ensure that the CEAS could become, as intended, a single protection area for refugees. These issues included a fuller harmonization of the eligibility criteria for refugee status; the introduction of one uniform status for refugees and another for beneficiaries of subsidiary protection (for those not qualifying for asylum status); the reduction of existing divergences with regard to asylum seekers' access to the labour market and other reception conditions; limiting the flexibility of the current legal framework regarding the content and duration of the rights to be granted as well as for the possibility of mutual recognition of national asylum decisions; the possibility of transfer of protection responsibilities; and co-operation with third countries on protection and resettlement measures. The Commission raised an ambitious set of questions in relation to each of theses issues. The Member States gave a cautious and rather mixed response, which did not augur well for rapid progress across a broad front that the 2010 deadline would require.

How far the EU still is from a uniform support and protection system was highlighted in November when the Commission issued its final report on the application of the 2003 directive on minimum standards for the reception of asylum seekers (Commission, 2007b). It indicated major differences between support standards (in six Member States financial support appeared too low to cover subsistence); the right to free movement (with problematic detention practices in some Member States); and access to employment.

A more positive picture emerged with regard to the functioning of the 'Dublin system' with its rules on determining which Member State is responsible for examining an asylum application and resulting transfers of asylum seekers between Member States. A Commission Report issued in June (Commission, 2007c) provided clear evidence that contrary to the widespread supposition that the majority of transfers are directed towards the Member States located at external borders – which had caused political tensions over the issue – the overall allocation between border and non-border Member States was actually rather balanced. In 2005 a total of 3,055 transfers went to EU external border Member States and 5,161 transfers to non-border Member States. Yet the report also indicated that multiple asylum applications continued to be a significant problem (16 per cent of total applications) and that only around 30 per cent of requested transfers were actually carried out, which underlined the need for a further reform of the Dublin system as part of the future CEAS.

Migration Policy

On the internal side of EU migration policy the most significant development was the Commission's proposal of 23 October for a directive on the conditions of entry and residence of third-country nationals for the purposes of highly qualified employment, which under the label of the 'Blue Card proposal' attracted widespread attention and some controversy. The proposal (Commission, 2007d) foresees a fast-track procedure for the admission of highly qualified third-country workers, based on a common definition and criteria, which include a valid work contract of at least one year, professional qualifications and a salary above a minimum level to be defined by each Member State. Workers admitted would be issued a residence permit that allows them to work ('EU Blue Card') and provides them and their families with a series of rights, including favourable conditions for family reunification. Access to the Member State of residence's labour market would be restricted for the first two years to the framework of the initial work contract, but after that period the person concerned would enjoy equal treatment with nationals as regards access to highly qualified employment. The proposal also includes the possibility for a 'Blue Card' holder to move for work to another Member State under certain conditions after two years of legal residence in the first Member State. In order to also attract younger highly qualified workers, lower access conditions to the Card – especially as regards the salary level – are foreseen for third-country nationals under the age of 30.

The Blue Card proposal appeared as the first major bid of the EU as such to increase its share in the global competition for highly skilled third-country workers. The EU's share of such third-country nationals in its total work force is only 1.72 per cent (Commission, 2007e) seriously lagging behind Australia (9.9 per cent), Canada (7.3 per cent), the US (3.2 per cent) and Switzerland (5.3 per cent). Being all too aware of the Member States' determination to retain full control over admission for work purposes the Commission downsized its initial ambitions about EU-wide job-seeking possibilities, left the admission procedure in its proposal under the control of the 27 national immigration systems and set the relatively high admission condition of a one-year work-contract signed before application. Yet in spite of these concessions, several Member States almost immediately raised objections. Germany is concerned about the scheme interfering with national competences in the labour immigration field. France and the United Kingdom prefer their own currently evolving national skill selective immigration schemes to the proposed system. Several of the new Member States consider the proposal as inappropriate so long as the transitional post-accession arrangements limiting the labour mobility of their citizens within the EU are still in place (EUobserver, 2007a). The proposal also failed to address a number of important 'technical' issues – such as the recognition of qualifications from outside of the EU – and other mobility barriers – such as the restrictions on the portability of social security contributions.

Another major migration policy initiative – the proposal for a directive on sanctions against employers of illegally staying third-country nationals (Commission, 2007f) – was able to build on an in principle stronger political consensus, as the Council had repeatedly acknowledged that illegal employment belongs to the primary pull factors of illegal immigration. Yet here the Commission encountered objections because of its provision for criminal sanctions in serious cases (repeated infringements, four or more illegally employed third-country nationals, particularly exploitative working conditions). Only 19 Member States currently provide for such sanctions in case of illegal employment and many Member States continue to be reluctant to accept criminal law measures based on Community, rather than (intergovernmental) 'third pillar' criminal law, competences.

In parallel to the debates and negotiations on the above issues, the EU continued its efforts in the integration policy sphere with the adoption of the second edition of the EU 'Handbook on Integration for Policy-Makers

(Commission, 2007g) and Practitioners' in June; the integration during the year of all Member States in the network of 'National Contact Points' on integration issues; a new emphasis placed by the Council on intercultural dialogue; and the announcement of new Commission initiatives in this respect (Commission, 2007h).

On the external side, the EU made some progress with the implementation of its new 'Global Approach' formulated in December 2005, which tries to combine migration measures, external relations and development policy instruments in an integrated and comprehensive way in close co-operation with countries of origin and transit. The primary focus during 2007 was on co-operation with African and Mediterranean countries which involved the reinforcement of the migration policy dialogue both at the multilateral level (especially with the African Union and the Economic Community of West African States) and the bilateral level (especially with Algeria and Morocco). Several projects were started or continued to improve the capacity of public authorities in the partner countries to manage labour migration, to promote co-operation in matching labour supply and demand, and to carry out information campaigns. On the repressive side, significant EU-funding went into projects aimed at helping the partner countries to strengthen border management capacities; fostering co-operation among law enforcement agencies in the prevention of illegal migration (especially by sea along the coasts of West Africa); building capacity in migration management and border control; improving the response of the police and criminal justice system to trafficking; and promoting co-operation in border management (Commission, 2007i). Building on the initial experiences of the application of the 'Global Approach' to Africa and the Mediterranean, the Commission proposed on 16 May to apply a broadly similar approach to the EU's Eastern and South-Eastern neighbouring regions, albeit with a strong degree of differentiation between the individual neighbourhood partners and taking into account the countries of transit and origin in the Middle East, Central Asia and Asia (Commission, 2007j). In December the European Council approved these adapted strategic guidelines for the EU's external migration policy.

The Member States gave a more cautious welcome to a related Commission initiative – presented on 16 May – regarding 'circular migration' and 'mobility partnerships' with third countries (Commission, 2007k). Presenting circular migration as a way of helping Member States to address their labour needs while responding at the same time to the needs of sending countries as regards skills transfers and the reduction of brain drain effects, the Commission developed a range of ideas on the legal form of 'mobility partnerships'. The proposed obligations for the EU should include improved opportunities for temporary legal immigration, financial assistance and return incentives.

Proposed obligations for the countries of origin are the readmission of the persons concerned and co-operation with the EU against illegal immigration, trafficking in human beings and on document security. As some Member States fear that a common EU approach could interfere with their existing bilateral arrangements with third-countries, the conclusions of the JHA Council on the subject on 7 December went no further than to support the basic principles, subject to a strict respect of national competences and existing arrangements and to the give a green light to exploratory talks about pilot mobility partnership projects with Cape Verde and Moldova (Council, 2007a).

The EU's readmission policy – an essential element of both asylum and migration policy – made substantial progress with the signing of readmission agreements with Ukraine (June), Bosnia-Herzegovina, the Former Yugoslav Republic of Macedonia, Montenegro, and Serbia (September), as well as Moldova (October). Yet Ukraine's initial rejection of the EU readmission demands in 2006 and the ongoing delays in negotiating such agreements with Algeria and Morocco showed again that this remains one of the most difficult external instruments of the JHA domain.

Border and Visa Policy

The seriously delayed preparations for the 'second generation' Schengen Information System (SIS II), a central element of the Schengen border control system, took a step forward with the adoption on 12 June of the 'third pillar' Council Decision regulating the law enforcement functionalities of the new system (Council, 2007b). The 'pillar division' of the JHA domain made it necessary to agree a separate 'third pillar' legal act (dealing with police and judicial co-operation matters, such as alerts regarding persons wanted for arrest, for surrender or extradition purposes) to complement the 'first pillar' SIS II Regulation (dealing with the immigration and border control issues which had already be adopted the year before). Yet this element of progress was overshadowed by the failure of the Member States to agree on the Framework Decision on the protection of personal data processed in the framework of police and judicial co-operation in criminal matters, which is widely seen as crucial for ensuring adequate personal data protection under the new SIS II and should already have been adopted at the end of 2006. On 9 November the JHA Council agreed on a 'general approach' regarding the 'third pillar' data protection directive (Council, 2007c). However, this agreement provided for substantially lower protection standards than foreseen in the original Commission proposal; it did not address all of the concerns of the European Data Protection Supervisor, and remained subject to several parliamentary scrutiny reservations at the end of the year. In view of the unsatisfactory personal data protection context it was in a sense just as well that technical tests conducted during the year also revealed a number of problems regarding the stability of the system and the security of its data, which made Council and Commission push back its likely operational start well into 2009.

The protracted difficulties with the introduction of the SIS II could have caused a political crisis in the EU if – as originally intended – the abolition of internal border controls between the old and the new (2004 accession) Schengen members had been made conditional upon its entry into operation. But this risk was avoided by the full operational integration in December of the new Schengen members into the 'SISone4ALL' (surely one of the most creative EU acronyms so far). This intermediate version between the old SIS and the SIS II extends the technical accommodation capacity of the existing SIS without the new functionalities of the SIS II. This considerable success of the Portuguese Presidency was made possible by a 'cloning' of the Portuguese national system in favour of the new Member States. A Council Decision of 6 December (Council, 2007d) abolished controls on persons at the internal borders for all of the 2004 accession countries with the exception of Cyprus (because of problems relating to the partition of the island) at land and sea borders on 21 December 2007 and at air borders on 31 March 2008. The common Schengen border control zone – which in many respects also forms a common internal security zone – thus expanded to a total size of 3.6 million km^2. Although the evalutions of the state of preparedness of the new members had still indicated a few points of concern, the overall progress achieved was widely considered as satisfactory and the political pressure exercised by the new members would have made a further postponement politically very difficult. As of the end of 2007 the 'Schengen associates' Switzerland and Liechenstein were expected to join the system by November 2008, but Bulgaria and Romania not before 2011.

2007 saw significant developments also in the sphere of external border protection which was one of the priorities of the German Presidency of the first half of the year. On 11 July Council and Parliament adopted Regulation (EC) No. 863/2007 (European Parliament/Council, 2007a) establishing a mechanism for the creation of Rapid Border Intervention Teams (RABITs). The RABITs were introduced as a means of providing rapid operational assistance for a limited period to a requesting Member State facing a situation of 'urgent and exceptional pressure' at external borders, especially as regards the arrival of large numbers of third-country nationals trying to enter the territory of the Member State illegally. The mechanism is to be managed by the FRONTEX border management agency. Its Management Board, on a proposal by the FRONTEX Director, will decide by a three-quarters majority on the profile and number of border guards to be made available for the teams (so-called 'Rapid Pool'). If a Member State requests a RABIT intervention because of one of the above-mentioned emergency situations, FRONTEX has to decide within five days. In case of a positive decision the FRONTEX Director and the Member State requesting support has to establish a joint operational plan, which will, however, leave operational instructions during deployment to the receiving Member State. Within a maximum of five days after adoption of the operational plan, upon the request of FRONTEX, the border guards forming part of the pool then have to be deployed by the other Member States in one or more RABITs.

The RABITs can be seen as an important new solidarity instrument as regards the management of migratory pressures at external borders – and a further step towards creating integrated border control and surveillance capabilities. The Regulation allows the border guard officers from the other Member States to wear their uniforms ('with a blue armband with the insignia of the European Union') and to carry their service weapons. The principle of full national control in matters of borders is reaffirmed by the provision that RABIT members may only perform tasks and exercise powers under instructions from, and in the presence of, border guards of the host Member State. A first RABIT exercise aimed at testing the new mechanism for deployment in real circumstances took place in Porto in November, involving border guards from 16 Member States helping Portuguese authorities to avert a simulated illegal immigration threat from a fictional Central American island (Frontex, 2007a).

The RABIT Regulation showed the continuous rise of the role of FRONTEX whose budget – always an indication of political salience – was successively increased from €19 million in 2006, to €42 million in 2007 and a prospective €70 million in 2008. During 2007, the agency further developed the 'FRONTEX Risk Analysis Network' (FRAN), composed of the analytical units of Member States' border guard services and established a system for regular exchange of information within FRAN. The Agency also set up the 'Central Record of Available Technical Equipment' (CRATE) for joint operations which is to be adapted on a regular basis to new or changing situations regarding the control and surveillance of the external borders of Member States. FRONTEX also set up a 'European Patrol Network' (EPN) for Mediterranean and Atlantic coastal waters. It became operational on 24 May and will serve as co-ordination and burden-sharing framework for maritime patrolling activities of Member States. On the external side FRONTEX established contacts with the regional EU's Immigration Liaison Officer (ILO) networks in Africa to improve the flow of information.

During 2007 several joint operations were carried out at land, sea and air borders. Both the size and the success of these operations were variable. For instance, the 'Poseidon 2007' operation in the Eastern Mediterranean involved staff from nine Member States and several patrol vessels, land patrol cars, aircrafts and fixed and mobile radar units. It led to the interception of nearly 1600 illegal immigrants, the arrest of 27 facilitators and the confiscation of over 400 forged or falsified documents (Frontex, 2007b). By contrast, the much smaller operation 'Gordius', aimed at tackling illegal immigration of Moldovan nationals at the Austrian, Hungarian, Slovakian and Romanian borders, resulted in the identification of only 109 illegal border crossings (Frontex, 2007c). As the operation deployed 31 officers from 14 Member States over two weeks, this result was far from setting a new record for efficiency in the joint deployment of resources.

The EU's visa policy took a step forward with the political agreement reached in the Council on 12 June on the Visa Information System (VIS) Regulation and the related VIS Decision governing access to the VIS for law enforcement authorities (Council, 2007e). The VIS Decision had caused tensions between the Council and the European Parliament (EP). The latter wanted to ensure higher data protection standards and to limit the access of law enforcement authorities to the system to cases involving serious crime. The Parliament was able to obtain some concessions from the Council regarding the VIS Decision because of its co-decision powers regarding the VIS Regulation. The VIS will store data of up to an estimated 70 million third-country nationals applying for entry or transit visa which – because of the inclusion of fingerprints and photographs – could well make it the biggest biometric data-base in the world (EUobserver, 2007b). Both the Regulation and the Decision still remained subject to national parliamentary scrutiny reserves at the end of the year.

On the external side, visa facilitation agreements were concluded with Ukraine, Bosnia-Herzegovina, the Former Yugoslav Republic of Macedonia, Montenegro, Serbia and Moldova (on the occasion of the signing of the above-mentioned readmission agreements with these countries) as well as with Albania, with whom a readmission agreement had already been signed in 2005. In all these cases the visa facilitation arrangements granted by the EU – such as a reduction of visa issuing fees, simplified procedures for business-men, journalists and students – were part of the incentives offered to the partner countries to ensure the conclusion of the respective readmission agreements. While the EU was able to maintain a united position on this part of its external visa policy, the visa reciprocity conflict with the United States and Canada continued to cause tensions within the Council. At the end of the year, signs were increasing that some of the new Member States to which the two countries continued to refuse visa free travel might seek a bilateral deal at least with the US, thereby undermining both the common visa regime and the EU's common international negotiating position on this issue.

Judicial Co-operation

In the sphere of judicial co-operation in civil matters, a substantial step forward was taken with the adoption on 11 July of the so-called 'Rome II'-Regulation (EC) No. 864/2007) on the law applicable to non-contractual obligations (European Parliament/Council, 2007b). This regulation establishes uniform rules on the determination of the applicable law in situations of conflicts of laws regarding non-contractual obligations in civil and commercial matters. It covers not only cross-border tort litigation (in product liability, unfair competition and infringement of intellectual property rights, for instance). It also covers non-contractual obligations in relation with unjustified enrichment (including payment of amounts wrongly received) and obligations arising out of an act performed without due authority or dealings prior to the conclusion of a contract. The regulation establishes as a general rule that the law applicable to a non-contractual obligation arising out of a tort shall be that of the country in which the damage occurs. But it also provides that where the person claimed to be liable and the person sustaining damage both have their habitual residence in the same country at the time when the damage occurs, the law of that country shall apply. Although highly technical, the 'Rome-II'-Regulation is of major importance for enhanced legal certainty both to individuals (in cases of tourists victims of traffic accidents in another Member State, for instance) and companies (in cases of unfair competition, for instance). The negotiations had been very complex. Some Member States had no rules for conflicts of laws regarding non-contractual obligations at all; others only partial rules; and existing rules in one Member State often diverged with those in another. It also needed no less than six inter-institutional 'trialogues' between Council, EP and Commission to overcome differences between the Council and the Parliament. The EP fought in vain to have defamation included in the scope of the Regulation, but won a compromise on the compensation to be awarded in the case of road traffic accidents.

Parallel negotiations on the 'Rome I'-Regulation on contractual obligations aimed to convert and revise the 1980 Rome Convention on the law applicable to contractual obligations (consumer contracts, property purchase contracts, etc.) into an EC Regulation. The negotiations focused on issues relating to the extension of the rights of consumers, where again substantial differences existed between the positions of Parliament and Council. They were overshadowed by an 'opt-out' of the United Kingdom arising from concerns about how potential legal uncertainty regarding high-value financial contracts could affect the City of London. The Council and Parliament nevertheless reached agreement at the first reading, which remained to be finalized at the end of the year. The accordingly amended draft Regulation was based on the principle of party autonomy, i.e. the parties being free to choose the law governing their contract. However, it also provided rules to determine the law applicable in the absence of choice, and conflict-of-law rules for specific cases, such as consumer contracts, contracts of carriage, and individual employment contracts (Council, 2007f).

Judicial co-operation in criminal matters developed at a slower pace, although here the Member States did not have to struggle with the EP, but only among themselves. In June the Council agreed on a general approach on the proposed Framework Decision on the organization and content of the exchange of information extracted from criminal records between Member States. It is to facilitate the exchange of information on criminal convictions in both criminal and non-criminal proceedings and also addresses the sensitive issue of information exchange regarding convictions for sexual offences committed against children. Rather than establishing a central EU criminal records register, it was agreed that national criminal records will be the base of the improved information exchange. The Member States will hold centrally all information relating to convictions regarding their own nationals (including convictions pronounced against their nationals in other Member States) and will only make criminal record information available to the requesting authorities of other Member States within ten days. At the end of the year this instrument was still being finalized, but 12 Member States were already involved in a pilot scheme for the electronic exchange of criminal record information, the 'Network of Judicial Registers' (NJR).

In December the Council also agreed a general approach on a draft Framework Decision on the recognition and supervision of suspended sentences, alternative sanctions and conditional sentences. The Decision is aimed at defining common rules under which a Member State, other than the one in which a person has been sentenced, can supervise within its own territory under a European Supervision Order (ESO) the probation measures or alternative sanctions provided for by a criminal conviction. The Portuguese Presidency achieved rapid progress on this Framework Decision which was regarded as a means to fostering social reintegration of sentenced persons and preventing recidivism. However, several Member States and the Commission expressed disappointment that it had been impossible to go further with the abolition of double criminality verification. Some progress was also made on a Framework Decision on the application of the principle of mutual recognition to supervision orders in pre-trial procedures. This measure is aimed, *inter alia*, at ensuring that in terms of pre-trial detention a suspect not residing in the trial state is not treated any differently from a suspect who is a resident and at promoting the harmonization of national non-custodial pre-trial regimes. The measure is important for the equal treatment of EU citizens to the extent that non-residents are currently still much more likely to be detained before their trial, because of the perceived risk that they might flee to their home country.

At the JHA Council meeting on 13 June, the German Presidency finally had to conclude that the Council was unable to reach agreement on the Framework Decision on certain procedural rights in criminal proceedings. The Decision attempted to define certain rights of persons arrested in connection with, or charged with, a criminal offence in order to safeguard the fairness of criminal proceedings throughout the EU. This 'third pillar' instrument was one of the few on the Council's agenda that promoted the rights of the individual, rather than co-operation on the repressive side. Its non-adoption thus reconfirmed the imbalance between action on security and on individual rights within the AFSJ. After the negotiations had already reduced the rights to information, legal assistance, interpretation and translation of documents of the procedure, a compromise on such a thinned-out instrument appeared at first possible. However, a final (and terminal) divide appeared over the issue whether the EU was competent to legislate also on purely domestic proceedings – which 21 Member States seemed willing to accept – or whether the legislation should be devoted solely to cross-border cases (Council, 2007e). This failure could be regarded as the most important of the Council in 2007. It highlighted both the sensitivity of even very limited attempts at harmonizing criminal procedural law and the difficulties of moving forward under a unanimity requirement.

The yearly balance-sheet for the criminal law field was not improved by the continued delay of the adoption of the Framework Decisions on the European Evidence Warrant and on the taking account of convictions in the Member States in the course of new criminal proceedings. In both cases political agreement had been reached on the texts well before the end of 2006, and the delays highlight the problem of ineffective national parliamentary scrutiny procedures that have difficulties to cope with the increasing volume of JHA legislation.

Police Co-operation and the Fight against Terrorism

The German Presidency achieved a major breakthrough regarding the application of the principle of availability of information for police co-operation purposes on the basis of the principles agreed by seven of the Member States in the context of the 2005 Prüm Treaty, although quite a few details of implementation were still under negotiation at the end of the year. As the Prüm provisions had already entered into force between Germany and Austria, the German Presidency could point to encouraging first experiences with the automated exchange of DNA profiles between Austria and Germany. By February matches had been made in 1,500 cases and Germany was pursuing 700 cases involving suspects believed to be known to the Austrian authorities. In June the Council reached political agreement on a 'Decision on the stepping up of cross-border co-operation, particularly in combating terrorism and cross-border crime'. The Decision took over essential parts of the Prüm Treaty and established the rules for the automated access to and transfer of DNA profiles, electronic fingerprinting data and certain national vehicle registration data, as well as for the supply of data in connection with major events with a cross-border dimension (such as sporting events and European Council meetings) and the prevention of terrorist offences. It will also provide rules for stepping-up cross-border police co-operation through joint patrols and other joint operations. The draft text remained subject to several parliamentary scrutiny reserves at the end of the year (Council, 2007g). The political agreement reached on the main principles of the enhanced level of law enforcement data-sharing also involved a host of technical questions that required a separate implementing Council Decision, proposed by Germany. Its technical annex regarding the exchange of the different data categories on its own amounted to 89 densely printed pages (Council, 2007h). Its length led the Council to take the unusual step of asking the EP – which had to be consulted on the Decision – to start preparing its Opinion on the basis of the English version of the technical annex, as a translation into all official languages would take too long. In addition, the European Data Protection Supervisor – who, interestingly, had not been consulted by the Council – delivered an own initiative opinion on 19 December that raised a number of critical questions and recommended that the Prüm Decisions should not enter into force before the implementation of the delayed Framework Decision on the protection of personal data (European Data Protection Supervisor, 2007). As of the end of 2007 negotiations on the technical details were still ongoing.

Progress was also achieved in the negotiations on the replacement of the Europol Convention by a 'third pillar' Decision. The decision would be much easier to amend than the Convention (for which national ratification procedures are needed) and would contribute to greater legal coherence, as Europol would then become an EU agency with the same status as Eurojust. The Member States are keen to bring this status change to completion before the entry into force of the Treaty of Lisbon in 2009, which might force them to use a Regulation that is subject to co-decision powers of the EP. The Member States were able to agree on some important principles, such as the future funding of Europol by the EC budget (not any longer through national contributions) and the lifting of the immunity of Europol officials when participating in operational activities. Yet at the end of the year, the Council was still struggling over the details of ensuring the 'budget neutrality' of Europol's funding basis, the principle of staff rotation, and the lifting of immunity of Europol officers when participating in Joint Investigation Teams.

Advances in the fight against terrorism were rather uneven (Council 2007i, 2007j). On the prevention side, some steps forward were taken with the 'check the web' initiative to tackle terrorist incitement on the internet and with a greater involvement of Europol and the European Police College regarding the fight against radicalization and recruitment. Yet in other fields of preventive action – such as EU co-operation with regard to the prevention of radicalization at educational institutions, training for religious leaders and community polic-ing – there was little more than enhanced information exchange and a prolif-eration of proposals. As regards protection, the Council was able to adopt a Decision on an improved Community Civil Protection Mechanism regarding preparedness, mutual assistance and co-ordination in the response to terrorist attacks and disasters (Council, 2007k), which will enhance interoperability among EU teams. Yet the negotiation of a Council directive on the identifica-tion and designation of European Critical Infrastructures and their protection was slowed down because of the reluctance of some Member States, which preferred to impose legal obligations for the owners/operators of critical infrastructures (such as vital water or information technology suppliers) to establish operator security plans and to identify security liaison officers.

The Prüm breakthrough was also of importance for (and indeed partially driven by) counter-terrorism objectives, but the widely differing national practices allowed little progress regarding the abuse of the non-profit sector by terrorist financers. International co-operation developed mainly through the implementation of counter-terrorism assistance measures regarding Algeria, Morocco and Indonesia and the conclusion in June of the (controversial) EU–US Agreement on the processing and transfer of passenger name record (PNR) data by air carriers to the US department of Homeland Security (Council, 2007l). Some external initiatives were affected by the lack of appropriate EU funding and problems with using the Common Foreign and Security Policy (CFSP) budget in this context. A positive development was the appointment on 19 September of Gilles de Kerchove, a senior Council official with extensive JHA experience and international contacts, to the post of the EU's Counterterrorism Co-ordinator which had been vacant since March.

A new counter-terrorism package proposed by the Commission on 6 November included a proposal for a European PNR system, which was met with fierce criticisms in the EP. The proposal not only failed to justify properly each individual category of passenger data but also demonstrated a curious understanding of 'stakeholders' as the stakeholders consulted prior to the initiative included Member States and associations of airline companies,

but not a single entity representing passengers or civil rights activists
(Commission, 2007k).

II. New Development Perspectives

The Treaty of Lisbon signed in December highlighted the increasing importance of the AFSJ in the overall EU context. The domain attracted the highest
number of new treaty changes and was also moved up in the list of the
fundamental treaty objectives (new Article 3 TEU) to the second position
before fundamental objectives such as economic and monetary union (EMU),
the internal market and the CFSP. The Lisbon Treaty maintained most of the
Constitutional Treaty reforms of the AFSJ, including the abolition of the
'pillar division', enhanced competences (especially in the field of criminal
justice co-operation), the strengthening of the role of the Parliament and the
ECJ and the extension of qualified majority voting and co-decision to most of
the current 'third pillar' issues of police and judicial co-operation in criminal
matters. Yet this agreement had to be bought at a price. It both extended the
opt-outs of the United Kingdom and Ireland to the current 'third pillar'
matters and made it easier for potential pioneer groups (of at least nine
Member States) to pursue enhanced co-operation on substantial issues in
these fields, thereby increasing the risks of further differentiation within the
JHA domain.

The prospect that in 2009 both the current Hague Programme will come to
an end and a (most likely) new enhanced treaty framework will come into
force provided a strong impetus for an early start of negotiations on the new
2010 to 2014 'Post-Hague Programme'. In February the ministers of interior
endorsed a proposal from German interior minister Wolfgang Schäuble and
Commission Vice-President Franco Frattini to establish a ministerial-level
advisory group under the name of 'Future Group' to identify and debate
possible key targets for the new programme in view of a final report in June
2008. The establishment of this Group – which met several times during 2007
– was an innovate step as it involved only the Ministers of Interior (not those
of Justice!) from only the outgoing and incoming Presidencies of Germany,
Portugal, Slovenia, France, the Czech Republic, Sweden, Spain, Belgium and
Hungary, as well as Frattini himself. The declared aim was to create a 'centre
of gravity' for the later formal Council negotiations which would not be
subject to the constraints of seeking consensus between 27 Member States.
The Group started to work around six priority areas: the preservation of
internal security, the management of asylum, immigration and external
borders, civil protection, the use of new technologies and information

networks and the implementation of the external JHA dimension. At the end of the year it remained to be seen how substantial the outcome of this process would be; whether it would cause tension with those not participating and what would be the consequences of dissociating the 'interior' agenda from the 'justice' agenda.

Key Readings

For a fairly comprehensive and critical survey of major issues and problems of EU asylum and immigration policy, see Baldaccini, Guild and Toner (2007). A very good analysis of the state of development of EU civil and criminal justice co-operation is provided by Barbe (2007). The major impact of national preferences on the development of European law enforcement co-operation is analysed in Friedrichs (2007).

References

Baldaccini, A., Guild, E. and Toner, H. (eds) (2007) *Whose Freedom, Security and Justice? EU Immigration and Asylum Law and Policy* (London: Hart).

Barbe, E. (2007), *L'espace judiciaire européen* (Paris: La documentation française).

Commission of the European Communities (2007a) 'Green Paper on the Future Common European Asylum System'. COM(2007)301, 6 June.

Commission of the European Communities (2007b) 'Report [. . .] on the Application of Directive 2003/9/EC of 27 January 2003 Laying Down Minimum Standards for the Reception of Asylum Seekers'. COM(2007)745, 26 November.

Commission of the European Communities (2007c) 'Report [. . .] on the Evaluation of the Dublin System'. COM(2007)299, 6 June.

Commission of the European Communities (2007d) 'Proposal for a Council Directive on the Conditions of Entry and Residence of Third-Country Nationals for the Purposes of Highly Qualified Employment'. COM(2007)637, 23 October.

Commission of the European Communities (2007e) 'Proposal for a Council Directive on the Conditions of Entry and Residence of Third-Country Nationals for the Purposes of Highly Qualified Employment: Summary of Impact Assessment'. SEC(2007)1382, 23 October.

Commission of the European Communities (2007f) 'Proposal for a Directive [. . .] Providing for Sanctions Against Employers of Illegally Staying Third-Country Nationals'. COM(2007)249, 16 May.

Commission of the European Communities (2007g) Directorate-General Justice, Freedom and Security: 'Handbook on Integration for Policy-makers and Practitioners', 2nd edn.

Commission of the European Communities (2007h) 'Communication [. . .] Third Annual Report on Migration and Integration'. COM(2007)512, 11 September.

Commission of the European Communities (2007i) 'Interim Progress Report on the Global Approach to Migration'. SEC(2007)1632, 5 December.

Commission of the European Communities (2007j) 'Communication [. . .] Applying the Global Approach to Migration to the Eastern and South-Eastern Regions Neighbouring the European Union'. COM(2007)247, 16 May.

Commission of the European Communities (2007k) 'Communication on Circular Migration and Mobility Partnerships between the European Union and Third Countries'. COM(2007)248, 16 May.

Commission of the European Communities (2007l) 'Proposal for a Council Framework Decision on the Use of Passenger Name Record (PNR) for Law Enforcement Purposes'. COM(2007)654, 6 November.

Council of the European Union (2007a) '2838th Council Meeting, Justice and Home Affairs'. Brussels, 6–7 December, Press Release, 15966/07.

Council of the European Union (2007b) 'Council Decision 2007/533/JHA of 12 June 2007 on the Establishment, Operation and Use of the Second Generation Schengen Information System (SIS II)'. OJ L 205, 8 August.

Council of the European Union (2007c), '2827th Council Meeting, Justice and Home Affairs'. Brussels, 6–7 December, Press Release, 14617/07.

Council of the European Union (2007d) 'Council Decision of 6 December 2007 on the Full Application of the Provisions of the Schengen *acquis* in the Czech Republic, the Republic of Estonia, the Republic of Latvia, the Republic of Lithuania, the Republic of Hungary, the Republic of Malta, the Republic of Poland, the Republic of Slovenia and the Slovak Republic'. OJ L 323, 8 December.

Council of the European Union (2007e) '2807th Council Meeting, Justice and Home Affairs'. Brussels, 12–13 June, Press Release, 10267/07.

Council of the European Union (2007f) 'Interinstitutional File 2005/0261 (COD): Proposal for a Regulation of the European Parliament and the Council on the Law Applicable to Contractual Obligations (Rome I), Outcome of the European Parliament's First Reading'. 3 December, 15832/07.

Council of the European Union (2007g) 'Council Decision on the Stepping up of Cross-Border Co-operation, Particularly in Combating Terrorism and Cross-Border Crime'. 17 September, 11896/07.

Council of the European Union (2007h) 'Draft Council Decision on the Implementation of Decision 2007/ [. . .] /JHA on the Stepping Up of Cross-Border Co-operation, Particularly in Combating Terrorism and Cross-Border Crime'. 18 October, 11045/07.

Council of the European Union (2007i) 'Implementation of the Strategy and Action Plan to Combat Terrorism'. 23 November, 15411/07.

Council of the European Union (2007j) 'The EU Strategy for Combating Radicalization and Recruitment – Implementation Report'. 23 November, 15443/07.

Council of the European Union (2007k) 'Council Decision of 8 November 2007 Establishing a Community Civil Protection Mechanism (recast) 2007/780/EC'. OJ L 314, 1 December.

Council of the European Union (2007l) 'Agreement Between the European Union and the United States of America on the Processing and Transfer of Passenger Name Record (PNR) Data by Air Carriers to the United States Department of Homeland Security'. OJ L 2004, 4 August.

EUobserver (2007a) 'EU Work Permit "Blue Card" Faces Opposition'. 7 December.

EUobserver (2007b) 'EU to Create World's Biggest Bio-data Poll'. 13 June.

European Data Protection Supervisor (2007) 'Opinion on the Initiative of the Federal Republic of Germany, with a View to Adopting a Council Decision on the Implementation of Decision 2007/. . . /JHA on the Stepping up of Cross-Border Co-operation, Particularly in Combating Terrorism and Cross-Border Crime'. 19 December.

European Parliament and Council (2007a) 'Regulation (EC) No. 863/2007 [. . .] of 11 July 2007 Establishing a Mechanism for the Creation of Rapid Border Intervention Teams'. OJ L199, 31 July.

European Parliament and Council (2007b) 'Regulation (EC) No. 864/2007 [. . .] of 11 July 2007 on the Law Applicable to Non-Contractual Obligations (Rome II)'. OJ L199, 31 July.

Friedrichs, J. (2007) *Fighting Terrorism and Drugs: Europe and International Police Co-operation* (London: Routledge).

Frontex (2007a) 'Rapid Border Intervention Teams First Time in Action'. Warsaw, News Release, 6 November.

Frontex (2007b) 'Eastern Mediterranean – Poseidon'. Warsaw, News Release, 16 September.

Frontex (2007c) 'Illegal Migration of Moldovan Nationals Targeted – Operation Gordius'. Warsaw, News Release, 16 September.

Legal Developments

MICHAEL DOUGAN
Liverpool Law School, University of Liverpool

Introduction

The main event of 2007 was, of course, the negotiation and signing of the Treaty of Lisbon.[1] But despite the new Treaty's treasure trove of legal innovations and interpretive problems, this chapter will retain its traditional focus on the rulings of the Community courts, which are hardly less rich in their diversity and interest: for example, concerning the legality of the framework decision introducing the European Arrest Warrant;[2] judicial review of common positions adopted under the Third Pillar;[3] Member State liability in damages in respect of public statements made by their own officials;[4] the impact of the free movement of goods on Sweden's restrictive laws on the importation and sale of alcohol;[5] the power of Member States to object to the public disclosure of documents of the Community institutions;[6] the conditions under which the United Kingdom and Ireland may participate in measures building on the Schengen *acquis*;[7] and the long-awaited ruling in the

---

[1] [2007] OJ C 306. See Dougan, M. (2008) 'The Treaty of Lisbon 2007: Winning Minds not Hearts'. *Common Market Law Review*, Vol. 45, p. 617.
[2] Case C-303/05 *Advocaten voor de Wereld* (3 May 2007).
[3] Case C-355/04 *Segi* (27 February 2007).
[4] Case C-470/03 *AGM-COS.MET* (17 April 2007).
[5] Case C-170/04 *Rosengren* (5 June 2007).
[6] Case C-64/05 *Sweden v Commission* (18 December 2007).
[7] Case C-77/05 *UK v Council* and Case C-137/05 *UK v Council* (18 December 2007).

Microsoft litigation concerning the multinational's compliance with Community competition rules (see Howarth, this volume).[8]

This chapter focuses on just a handful of the other major rulings delivered by the Community courts during 2007, selected on the basis of their likely general interest to EU lawyers.

I. Free Movement, Social Dumping and Collective Labour Action

Viking Line and *Laval un Partneri* attained a public profile and notoriety matched by few other rulings by the European Court of Justice (ECJ).[9] Both cases involved collective action by trade/s unions against undertakings seeking to take advantage of the less costly terms and conditions of employment afforded to workers in the Member States which acceded to the EU in 2004. The Court was thereby called upon to clarify the balance struck under Community law between the exercise of economic freedoms and the threat of social dumping leading to a 'race to the bottom' within the enlarged EU. Not only that: in *Viking Line* and *Laval un Partneri*, those tensions arose in the context of private rather than Member State action, thus provoking further difficult questions: how far do barriers to movement arising from the exercise of private autonomy fall within the scope of the Treaty and what limits does Community law impose upon the freedom of trade/s unions to engage in collective action for the protection of labour interests?

Freedom of Establishment

Viking Line concerned an employer seeking to exercise its freedom of establishment under Article 43 EC so as to transfer permanently certain economic activities from an old Member State to a new Member State.

Viking, a ferry company incorporated under Finnish Law, operated the *Rosella* under the Finnish flag on the route between Helsinki and Tallinn. In accordance with its collective agreement with the Finnish Seamen's Union (FSU), Viking was obliged to pay the *Rosella*'s crew at Finnish wage levels. In order to compete more effectively against Estonian ships serving the same route and paying their crews the (substantially lower) Estonian wage, however, Viking proposed reflagging the *Rosella* in Estonia with a view to entering into a new collective agreement with the relevant Estonian trade union. The FSU notified this plan to the London-based International Transport Workers' Federation (ITF). The latter operates a 'flag of convenience policy' designed to ensure that a genuine link exists between a vessel's flag

---

[8] Case T-201/04 *Microsoft v Commission* (17 September 2007).
[9] Case C-438/05 *Viking Line* (11 December 2007); Case C-341/05 *Laval un Partneri* (18 December 2007).

and its owner's nationality, according to which only unions established in the vessel's state of actual ownership may conclude collective agreements. The ITF therefore sent a circular to its affiliated national unions calling for co-ordinated solidarity action, by refraining from entering into any negotiations with Viking. For its part, the FSU demanded that Viking agree to respect the *Rosella* workers' existing terms and conditions of employment, failing which the FSU intended to commence strike action. Viking subsequently sought a declaration from the English courts that the ITF and FSU were acting contrary to its freedom of establishment under Article 43 EC.

In its preliminary ruling, the ECJ first addressed the issue of whether collective action by a trade/s union is excluded *per se* from the scope of Article 43 EC. In this regard, the Court recalled its well-established caselaw that the Treaty provisions on the free movement of persons apply not only to the actions of public authorities, but also to other rules adopted by associations or organizations not governed by public law, which are nevertheless aimed at regulating economic activities in a collective manner. For these purposes, it is not necessary that the relevant organization or association is exercising regulatory tasks or quasi-legislative powers entrusted to or conferred upon it by the state; it is sufficient that the relevant body is exercising the legal autonomy accorded to it under national law. Article 43 EC could therefore in principle be relied upon against a trade/s union taking collective action in accordance with domestic law. That finding is not called into question by the fact that the rights of association and to strike are recognized in the EU Charter of Fundamental Rights, and indeed, form part of the (legally binding) general principles of Community law. Rulings such as *Schmidberger* and *Omega* demonstrate that the correct approach is to reconcile exercise of the right to strike against respect for the freedom of establishment.[10]

The next issue was whether collective action such as that proposed by the ITF and FSU did actually restrict Viking's freedom of establishment under Article 43 EC. In that regard, the Court recalled that Article 43 EC applies not only to the treatment of migrant Community nationals by their host state, but also to acts adopted within the home state aimed at deterring a claimant from exercising its freedom of establishment abroad, including strike and solidarity action of the sort pursued by the FSU and ITF. Nevertheless, the right to take collective action for the protection of workers is a legitimate public interest capable of justifying an infringement of the Treaty. Indeed, since the Community pursues not only an economic but also a social purpose, the internal market freedoms must be balanced against social policy objectives. While the final assessment in this case fell to the national judges, the ECJ offered some

---

[10] Case C-112/00 *Schmidberger* [2003] ECR I-5659; Case C-36/02 *Omega* [2004] ECR I-9609.

assistance in striking the correct balance. As regards the FSU's proposed strike, it would be necessary to establish that the jobs or employment conditions of workers on the *Rosella* were actually under serious threat; moreover, the national court should ascertain whether the FSU had exhausted any less drastic means at its disposal for bringing its negotiations with Viking to a successful conclusion. As regards the ITF solidarity action, to the extent that its policy was simply aimed at preventing 'flags of convenience', rather than protecting and improving seafarers' terms and conditions of employment, it could not be objectively justified. In fact, it appeared that the ITF initiates solidarity action at the request of an affiliated national union, irrespective of whether the proposed reflagging might detrimentally affect the relevant workers.

As a matter of legal principle, the notion that collective action capable of erecting barriers to movement falls within the scope of the Treaty is hardly revolutionary, since it constitutes merely a logical fulfilment of previous caselaw under the free movement provisions. Nor is there much controversy in the idea that the right to take collective action is not unlimited, but must be exercised in accordance with conditions established by law, having regard to the competing interests of other interested actors. The importance of the ruling in *Viking Line* stems rather from the novel combination of those two propositions. As in so many other fields, the deceptively simple step of bringing a measure within the scope of the free movement provisions triggers the full transformative potential of Community law, i.e. its capacity to reshape the entire policy and decision-making system applicable to exercise of the right to take collective action. Choices about the regulatory framework governing collective labour rights are no longer left alone to the Member State to determine, according to its own framework of economic and social values, negotiated through its own democratic political processes. Nor are decisions about when and how far to exercise the collective labour rights offered to them under national law the simple prerogative of the competent trade/s unions and their members. National regulatory choices and autonomous labour decisions alike are now exposed to the additional layer of scrutiny imposed by Community law – and must thus comply with the framework of values judged legitimate under the Treaty, as regards which the final decision rests ultimately with the judges.

That transformation has constitutional and conceptual importance, but it also raises crucial substantive questions, precisely about which framework of values and balance of interests Community law in general, and the ECJ in particular, will now promote in this field. On its face, the Court strikes a conciliatory note: the Treaty's objectives are social as well as economic; the right to collective action, including the right to strike, is a fundamental freedom recognized as such under Community law. But the proof of the pudding is in the eating – or rather, in the principle of proportionality. Given the sensitivities involved, one might have expected the ruling in *Viking Line* to recognize that trade/s unions enjoy a wide margin of autonomy when exercising their right to take collective action. In fact, the Court was surprisingly interventionist: collective action must be aimed at protecting workers, the threat to workers' interests must be actual and serious and striking must be used only as a last resort. From the perspective of a Member State whose legal order offers trade/s unions a considerable degree of market power, *Viking Line* might thus appear relatively intrusive.

In any case, future rulings will have to clarify how Article 43 EC might apply in other factual situations: for example, where the employer proposes closing its operations within the home state and transferring (rather than merely re-registering) its activities abroad, so that collective action is aimed at preventing job losses (as opposed to protecting existing terms and conditions of employment);[11] or where an undertaking claims that trade union activities within the host state amount to a restriction on its establishment there, even in cases where the collective action is not in any way related to the undertaking's exercise of its free movement rights.[12] Having established the principle of amenability to scrutiny under Community law, one suspects that the ECJ will eventually be compelled to acknowledge the intimate relationship between collective action and the particular economic, social and regulatory context of each Member State, and the consequent impossibility of identifying anything like a common approach across the EU.

Freedom to Provide Services

Many of the policy issues at stake in *Viking Line* also underlie the ruling in *Laval un Partneri*. However, the latter dispute arose in a quite different legal context, since it concerned an undertaking based in a new Member State that sought to exercise its freedom to provide services under Article 49 EC so as to carry out temporary economic activities within the territory of an old Member State.

Laval, a Latvian construction company, posted some of its workers to a building site in Sweden. The local branch (Byggettan) of the Swedish building and public works trade union (Byggnads) opened negotiations with Laval with a view to securing its compliance with two demands. First, Laval should sign the applicable Swedish collective agreement for the building sector,

---

[11] Consider, e.g. Nokia's decision in January 2008 to close a major factory in Germany, with the loss of several thousand jobs, in order to relocate production to lower-cost states such as Romania.
[12] By analogy with the principle established in Case C-55/94 *Gebhard* [1995] ECR I-4165.

whose terms on issues such as working time and annual leave were more generous than those applicable under ordinary Swedish law, and which would also have required Laval to pay certain financial contributions to Byggettan. Secondly, even though Swedish law does not lay down any statutory minimum wage *per se*, Laval should guarantee its posted workers a particular hourly wage of approximately €16. Since Laval did not agree to all those demands, Byggettan requested Byggnads to initiate collective action against Laval: the building site was blockaded and the Latvian workers prevented from entering; other Swedish unions launched solidarity action by boycotting Laval's operations. Laval sought a declaration from the Swedish courts that the blockade and boycotts were unlawful, and claimed compensation from Byggettan and Byggnads for the losses it had incurred.

In its preliminary ruling, the ECJ's first task was to decide how far the dispute fell within the scope of the Posted Workers Directive 96/71.[13] That measure obliges the Member State to ensure that workers temporarily posted to its territory by an undertaking established in another Member State, within the context of a cross-border service provision, benefit from a minimum core of employment terms and conditions within the host country. However, those terms and conditions cover only a fixed list of matters, such as working time, annual leave and minimum wages. Moreover, they must be laid down by law, or in collective agreements/arbitration awards universally applicable to the construction sector. As regards Byggettan's demand that Laval's posted workers be paid a specific hourly wage, the Court noted that this derived neither from Swedish law itself, nor from any universally applicable collective agreement. Such case-by-case negotiations between management and labour to determine the wages paid to construction workers fell outside the scope of Directive 96/71. As regards Byggettan's demand that Laval respect the provisions of the collective agreement for the building sector concerning working time and annual leave, the Court observed that those provisions went beyond the standards set by ordinary Swedish law and could not therefore be considered part of the mandatory core set out in Directive 96/71. Finally, as regards Byggettan's demand that Laval pay certain financial contributions, again pursuant to the terms of the collective agreement for the building sector, the Court noted that such obligations were not listed as part of the mandatory core at all. Directive 96/71 does permit the host state to extend to posted workers other terms and conditions of employment, provided those can be considered 'public policy provisions', but obviously that cannot apply to private negotiations between management and labour.

---

[13] [1997] OJ L 18/1.

Since none of Byggettan's demands fell within the scope of Directive 96/71, the collective action taken by the Swedish unions had to be assessed directly under Article 49 EC. In this regard, the Court recalled its analysis in *Viking Line* and confirmed that the Treaty provisions on the free movement of services, just as much as those on the freedom of establishment, are capable in principle of being relied upon against a trade/s union taking collective action in accordance with domestic law. Here, the Swedish unions' blockades and boycotts were liable to make it less attractive for Laval to carry out construction work in Sweden and therefore constituted a restriction under Article 49 EC. As regards justification for that restriction, the Court agreed that collective action may in principle be aimed at the protection of workers – either those of the host state against possible social dumping, or the posted workers themselves so as to ensure a certain level of employment conditions. In practice, however, it was not possible to justify Byggettan's demand that Laval comply with the various obligations contained in the collective agreement for the building sector: as a result of the regime contained in Directive 96/71, cross-border service providers are already required to observe a nucleus of mandatory rules for the protection of posted workers within the host state. Byggettan's demand that Laval pay its workers a particular hourly wage also fell foul of Community law: the relevant pay negotiations formed part of a national context totally lacking in provisions which are sufficiently precise and accessible that they do not render it impossible or excessively difficult for an undertaking such as Laval to determine the obligations with which it is required to comply as regards minimum pay.

Laval un Partneri offers useful technical guidance concerning the correct interpretation of Directive 96/71 and its relationship to Article 49 EC. First, as regards the enumerated terms and conditions of employment falling within the Directive's mandatory core, posted workers must be protected in accordance with the minimum rules ordinarily applicable under national law. But neither the Directive nor Article 49 EC permit the host state to insist that posted workers benefit from more favourable labour standards, and the same prohibition applies to trade/s unions acting autonomously. Secondly, as regards terms and conditions of employment falling outside the express list, the host state may only extend these to posted workers where they constitute 'public policy provisions' in accordance with the Directive.[14] However, Community law will prevent trade/s unions from taking collective action with a view to extending any such terms and conditions to posted workers. Thirdly, where the Member State's particular regulatory system for establishing some

[14] A concept whose precise definition remains unclear, though it seems to be more restricted than the ordinary category of imperative requirements, and possibly even than the concept of public policy in the express Treaty derogations.

or all of the enumerated employment rights falls altogether outside the scope of Directive 96/71, the situation must be assessed under Article 49 EC alone. At the very least, the Treaty seems to require, in such cases, a degree of transparency and predictability, when ascertaining the relevant terms and conditions of employment, equivalent to what one would expect in situations actually governed by the Directive. It remains unclear whether, in such cases, Article 49 EC further requires that posted workers benefit only from the degree of employment rights they could have expected had the situation actually been governed by the Directive and its minimum protective core – but that seems the most likely interpretation after *Laval un Partneri*.

On the one hand, putting all of those technical requirements together, *Laval un Partneri* might seem to promote cross-border service provision on the basis of posted labour, limiting the degree to which the national authorities and trade/s unions alike can seek to neutralize the competitive advantages of foreign providers by assimilating the relevant workers to the sectoral labour standards applicable within the host territory. Certainly, the restrictions on collective action imposed pursuant to Directive 96/71 and Article 49 EC exceed those applicable under Article 43 EC as identified in *Viking Line*: even if genuinely intended as a last resort to protect workers against actual and serious threats to their terms and conditions of employment, collective action other than to enforce the mandatory core of protective rights expressly identified in Directive 96/71 now appears strictly circumscribed (and the host state's own freedom for manoeuvre is little wider). Given the wide discrepancies between labour costs between the old and new Member States, and the potential for social dumping or regulatory competition those discrepancies entail, one might wonder whether more of the EU-15 countries should perhaps have negotiated transitional provisions (of the sort secured by Germany and Austria) under the Treaty of Accession 2003, permitting restrictions on the posting of workers by service providers established in central and eastern Europe.

On the other hand, one should not overlook the fact that Directive 96/71 itself remains in place and does equalize for domestic and foreign service providers those core employment costs – on issues such as minimum wages, working time and annual leave – that could otherwise provide the trigger for wide-scale social dumping. Of course, there are some rough edges in this regulatory package and these were essentially what the dispute in *Laval un Partneri* was about: the issue of wages for Laval's posted workers was complicated by Sweden's peculiar regulatory context, which did not fit neatly into the Directive's specific drafting. At heart, however, the regulatory frame-work established by Community law does protect labour standards against rampant market forces. Viewed in that light, perhaps the Court in *Laval un Partneri* felt that the Community legislature had already defined for itself the appropriate conditions for striking the balance between free trade and social dumping, and the primary Treaty provisions on free movement should be interpreted so as to reinforce rather than undermine that choice.

II. More on Union Citizenship and the Export of Social Benefits

The recent caselaw on the free movement of persons might give the impression that the situation as regards the treatment of economically inactive migrants within their host society has become relatively stable, while the legal framework governing the relationship between a Union citizen and his/her country of origin continues to develop apace. In that regard, previous caselaw had already established the principle that a Member State's refusal to pay social benefits to its own nationals, on the grounds that they have exercised their right to free movement in another Member State, constitutes a restriction on the right to move and reside freely across the EU under Article 18 EC, which must be justified by a valid public interest and the principle of proportionality.[15] Two rulings delivered in 2007 tested just how far this caselaw would extend.

Relationship between the Treaty and Community Secondary Legislation

Hendrix[16] concerned a Dutch incapacity benefit for disabled young people which had been designated as a 'special non-contributory benefit' by the Community legislature for the purposes of Regulation 1408/71 on the cross-border co-ordination of national social security systems.[17] As such, the Dutch incapacity benefit was not subject to the ordinary principle of exportation enshrined in Regulation 1408/71, according to which the national authorities must continue the payment of social security benefits even where a claimant moves to another Member State. On the contrary, Regulation 1408/71 states that special non-contributory benefits are to be paid only in the claimant's state of habitual residence. Community legislation itself therefore instructs the national authorities to cease the payment of certain social benefits to their own migrant nationals: how far would the ECJ be prepared to interfere with this regulatory choice on the basis of Article 18 EC? *Hendrix* was a perfect test case for answering this question. The claimant was a disabled Dutch national living and working in the Netherlands whose employer was

---

[15] E.g. Case C-192/05 *Tas-Hagen* [2006] ECR I-10451; Case C-406/04 *De Cuyper* [2006] ECR I-6947.
[16] Case C-287/05 *Hendrix* (11 September 2007).
[17] Last consolidated text published at [1997] OJ L 28/1. The relevant provisions of the new Regulation 883/2004 (due to enter into force shortly) are not materially different: [2004] OJ L 200/1.

permitted to pay him less than the minimum wage; Hendrix was then paid incapacity benefit so as to bring his income up to the standard level. When the claimant moved residence to Belgium, while keeping his job in the Netherlands, the Dutch authorities terminated the payment of his incapacity benefit in accordance with the provisions of Regulation 1408/71.

The ECJ decided at the outset that Hendrix should be treated as a frontier worker for the purposes of Article 39 EC. As such, the residency requirement for entitlement to the disputed incapacity benefit was to be treated as indirectly discriminatory. The mere fact that the benefit was correctly designated as a special non-contributory benefit and the Dutch decision to cease payment was fully congruent with the Community co-ordination regime, did not shield it from scrutiny. Regulation 1408/71 must be interpreted in the light of Article 42 EC, its legal basis under the Treaty, which seeks to promote the greatest possible freedom of movement for migrant workers. Moreover, Article 39(2) EC enshrines the general principle of equal treatment for migrant workers. Thus, any residency requirement for the disputed benefit could only be enforced if it was objectively justified. In that regard, the Court observed that the incapacity benefit was closely linked to the socio-economic situation of the Netherlands, since it was based on the Dutch minimum wage and standard of living. In accordance with the provisions of Regulation 1408/71, the Member State was therefore entitled in principle to impose a residency requirement. However, application of that condition should not entail an infringement of the claimant's free movement rights going beyond what is necessary to achieve the legitimate objective pursued by the national legislation. In particular, the national judge must take into account the fact that the claimant maintained close economic and social links to the Netherlands as his country of origin. Since the case could be satisfactorily resolved on the basis of Article 39 EC and the principle of equal treatment, there was no need to analyse it further under Article 18 EC on Union citizenship and the concept of non-discriminatory barriers to movement – though one can safely assume that the basic thrust of the analysis would have been the same.

There are two very important lessons to be drawn from the ruling in *Hendrix*. First, the Court confirmed that, even where the Community legislature itself seeks to limit the exportation of certain social benefits between Member States, any decision to terminate entitlement in respect of a claimant who has exercised his/her right to free movement within the EU will constitute a *prima facie* breach of the Treaty that must be objectively justified. The primary Treaty provisions on free movement have thus been elevated above all other forms of legal competence, whether domestic or supranational in status, so that neither the Member State nor the Community legislature may enact unjustified restrictions on the Union citizen's migration rights. But as rulings such as *Hendrix* accumulate, the Court exposes itself more and more to the accusation that it is taking away from the political institutions an appreciable part of their power to decide on important questions of public expenditure and social solidarity, on the basis of purely legal tools which may well possess their own internal logic and doctrinal consistency, but are no substitute for fuller and more representative debate about the allocation of welfare rights and responsibilities between citizens and states within the EU.

Secondly, for the purposes of objectively justifying any refusal to export social benefits, the Court seems averse to the use of entirely generalized, abstract and absolute rules or presumptions: for example, that all non-residents are *per se* excluded from the domestic welfare system. It seems to favour an approach whereby the national authorities must take into account the particular circumstances of each individual claimant, to determine whether a refusal to export would cause such a degree of hardship as to outweigh the Member State's own legitimate interest in preserving the territorial boundaries of its welfare system. Admittedly, *Hendrix* is not totally clear on this point. Dutch law expressly provided for waiver of the residency requirement in cases where it would cause an 'unacceptable degree of unfairness', and the Court may well have intended merely to offer guidance to the national judge on how to apply that domestic waiver within the context of this particular dispute. That more conservative interpretation of the judgment is supported by the arguments of Advocate General Kokott: she cautioned against any obligation, under Community law, to undertake individualized assessments of each and every claimant to determine their personal circumstances, arguing that that would be incompatible with the needs of mass administration based on clear criteria and expeditious decision-making.[18]

Exportation of Student Financial Assistance from the Home State

Nevertheless, the proposition that Community law will demand a 'personal circumstances' assessment, before the national authorities can terminate the cross-border payment of benefits, is bolstered by the ruling in *Morgan*.[19] The case concerned German rules governing the award of financial assistance to study at a university in another Member State which provided, *inter alia*, that grants would only be awarded to students who had already completed at least one year of their course in Germany and were now continuing the same training abroad (the 'first stage studies condition'). The claimants were German nationals studying applied genetics in the UK and ergotherapy in the Netherlands (respectively) whose applications for financial assistance were

[18] See the Opinion of 29 March 2007.
[19] Cases C-11/06 and C-12/06 *Morgan* (23 October 2007).

rejected on the grounds that they failed to satisfy the 'first stage studies condition'. In its preliminary ruling, the ECJ recalled that Article 18 EC prohibits rules that place a Member State's own nationals at a disadvantage simply because they have exercised their right to free movement. That consideration is particularly important in the context of migration for educational purposes, having regard to Articles 3 and 149 EC, which refer to the objective of encouraging the mobility of students and teachers. Consequently, where a Member State provides for a system of financial assistance to study at a foreign university, it must ensure that the detailed rules for awarding such assistance do not create unjustified obstacles to movement. Here, the specific obligations imposed by the 'first stage studies condition' gave rise to personal inconvenience, additional costs and possible delays which were liable to discourage Union citizens from exercising their Community law rights.

From the wide range of possible justifications advanced in respect of the 'first stage studies condition', only two deserve explicit mention. First, the Court was prepared to recognize the risk that students claiming financial assistance for studies outside their home state could impose an unreasonable burden capable of having adverse consequences for the overall level of educational assistance that that country could afford – thereby justifying the imposition of qualifying criteria designed to ensure a sufficient degree of integration with the relevant society. However, it was disproportionate for the Member State to enforce a generalized requirement that claimants already complete at least one year of their course in Germany, without taking into consideration the fact that these particular individuals had been raised in Germany and completed their secondary schooling there. Secondly, although concerns were expressed that abolition of the 'first stage studies condition' could, in the absence of any co-ordinating provisions at the Community level, lead to the possible duplication of financial support by home and host states, the Court pointed out that the 'first stage studies condition' took no account of grants received in another country and thus could not help ensure against duplication in any case. The Court concluded that Article 18 EC precludes application of the 'first stage studies condition' to these claimants.

Bearing in mind our previous discussion of *Hendrix*, the ruling in *Morgan* is significant because it supports the argument that, when deciding whether to maintain or set aside a *prima facie* territorial bar on the payment of welfare support, Member States will be obliged *in all cases* to give appropriate weight to the claimant's personal circumstances, including their actual economic and social links with the relevant society. But *Morgan* is also crucially important in its own right as the Court's latest contribution to the complex system of cross-border educational rights within the EU.

On the one hand, the Court's caselaw on Union citizenship,[20] and the Community legislature's new directive on free movement,[21] both recognize that there are inherent limits to how far any host society can be expected to show financial solidarity with foreign students. Under the present compromise, the host state must always offer equal treatment as regards tuition fees for university study within its territory. However, the host state is not obliged to provide equal access to financial support in the form of educational grants and loans, unless the claimant falls under the specific provisions on migrant workers or permanent residents. Moreover, the host state can only be expected to offer limited support from its general social assistance schemes, since economically inactive migrants should not become an unreasonable burden upon the public finances of the host society. On the other hand, the expectation that economically inactive migrant students will basically provide for their own subsistence within the host state has attracted serious criticism: Community law seems to reserve meaningful rights to educational free movement only to those citizens wealthy enough to afford them. To help overcome such criticism, it has been argued that attention should focus more on the obligations of the home state to facilitate the educational mobility of its own nationals. In particular, if the Court were prepared to categorize the home state's refusal to provide financial assistance for studies in another country as a barrier to movement under Article 18 EC, then the burden of justification would shift onto the national authorities, holding out a real prospect of enhancing the practical value of Union citizenship for a broader category of its potential beneficiaries.

That was precisely the opportunity presented to the Court in *Morgan*. At first glance, the ruling does indeed seem to vindicate academic hopes that Article 18 EC will open up a new avenue of financial support – based on the home state rather than the host state – for promoting cross-border educational mobility. However, the judgment cannot be seen as unequivocal. After all, Germany had already accepted the principle of exportation and the Court's primary finding was that the precise conditions laid down under German law were arbitrary in character. In fact, the Court seems to have chosen its words very carefully: *where* a Member State provides educational grants to enable students to pursue studies abroad, the *detailed rules* for awarding such grants must not create unjustified restrictions on the right to free movement. It is unclear how the Court would have approached the case had the Member State imposed an absolute (or near absolute) territorial bar on its system of student finance. Although logically such a bar should also constitute a *prima facie*

---

[20] Especially Case C-184/99 *Grzelczyk* [2001] ECR I-6193; Case C-209/03 *Bidar* [2005] ECR I-2119.
[21] Directive 2004/38 [2004] OJ L 158/77.

breach of Article 18 EC, that cannot be taken for granted, since the Court could still decide that, in the present state of Community law, such decisions fall within the inherent competence of each Member State and would be best dealt with through legislative co-ordination (either by the EU or through the Bologna Process). Even if the Court were to be bold and bring a total/near total refusal to export within the scope of Community law, it would not necessarily conduct the same detailed and rigorous scrutiny as it undertook in *Morgan*, but might rather decide to offer the Member State a wide margin of discretion and thus conduct only a relatively 'light touch' proportionality assessment.

III. The Continuing Evolution of EU Criminal Law

The landmark ruling in *Commission v Council (Environmental Crimes)* established that the Community enjoys a certain degree of competence to adopt measures in the field of criminal law, and that, pursuant to Article 47 TEU, such Community competence is protected against encroachment by the EU taking action pursuant to its Third Pillar powers.[22] The *Environmental Crimes* ruling raised as many questions as it answered: for example, as to whether the Community's powers were limited to the field of environmental law, or could extend to other internal policies such as agriculture, internal market and social protection; concerning the threshold that had to be crossed before the effectiveness of any given Community policy could justify not only the adoption of ordinary administrative sanctions, but also the imposition of criminal law measures; and about the degree of detail the Community could legitimately prescribe when harmonizing national criminal legislation under its First Pillar powers. *Commission v Council (Ship-Source Pollution)* gave the Court an opportunity to clarify these issues.[23]

The Council adopted Framework Decision 2005/667 on strengthening the criminal law framework for the enforcement of the law against ship-source pollution under Title VI TEU.[24] Its aim was to supplement the Ship-Source Pollution Directive 2005/35,[25] a First Pillar act, by requiring the Member States to adopt various criminal law measures with a view to ensuring a high level of safety and environmental protection in relation to maritime transport. To that end, Articles 2, 3 and 5 of Framework Decision 2005/667 established a basic obligation to ensure that certain infringements of Directive 2005/35, whether committed by natural or legal persons, are regarded as criminal offences under national law, punishable by effective, proportionate and

---

[22] Case C-176/03 *Commission v Council* [2005] ECR I-7879.
[23] Case C-440/05 *Commission v Council* (23 October 2007).
[24] [2005] OJ L 255/164.
[25] [2005] OJ L 255/11.

dissuasive penalties. Moreover, Articles 4 and 6 of the Framework Decision set out detailed rules on the types and levels of criminal sanctions to be imposed under national law, according to factors such as the defendant's state of mind and degree of culpability (including specific provisions on the liability of legal persons) and the severity of the damage inflicted on the marine environment (including to animals, plants and persons). The Commission considered that all of the provisions contained in Framework Decision 2005/667 could have been enacted by the Community under Article 80(2) EC, which provides for the adoption of specific measures concerning sea transport within the context of the common transport policy, including measures aimed at improving maritime transport safety and (in accordance with Article 6 EC) promoting environmental protection. Arguing that the Council had therefore infringed Article 47 TEU by adopting those provisions under the Third Pillar, the Commission sought annulment of the Framework Decision.

The ECJ reiterated its finding in the *Environmental Crimes* case that, although criminal law generally falls outside the Community's competence, when the application of effective, proportionate and dissuasive criminal penalties is an essential measure for combating serious environmental offences, the Community legislature may require Member States to introduce such penalties, in order to ensure that the relevant Community rules are fully effective. Here, the provisions laid down in Framework Decision 2005/667 relate to conduct likely to cause particularly serious environmental damage as a result of the infringement of Community rules on maritime safety. Furthermore, the Council had clearly taken the view that criminal penalties were indeed necessary to ensure compliance with those Community rules. Accordingly, Articles 2, 3 and 5 of the Framework Decision, requiring Member States to apply criminal penalties to certain forms of conduct, could have been validly adopted under Article 80(2) EC; to that extent, the Council had infringed Article 47 TEU. By contrast, determination of the type and level of the criminal penalties to be applied does not fall within the Community's sphere of competence. Thus, Articles 4 and 6 of the Framework Decision could not have been adopted by the Community legislature; to that extent, the Council had not infringed Article 47 TEU. Nevertheless, since all of the Framework Decision's provisions were inextricably linked together, such that it was impossible to sever good from bad, the measure had to be annulled in its entirety.

The ruling in *Ship-Source Pollution* does not offer much illumination as regards the potential scope of the Community's criminal law competences. Even though the case involved maritime transport and safety, the Court's reasoning was still closely tied to the objective of environmental protection, which formed an integral part of the Framework Directive's provisions. The Court neither endorsed nor rejected explicitly the Council's contention that the *Environmental Crimes* ruling should be limited to 'essential, transversal and fundamental' Community objectives. At first glance, the Court was similarly unforthcoming about clarifying the threshold of effectiveness that must be crossed before criminal rather than administrative sanctions are justified. Upon closer inspection, however, it is arguable that the ruling does shed some important light on this issue. The ECJ referred simply to the fact that the Council considered criminal penalties to be necessary to ensure compliance with the relevant Community rules. Does *Ship-Source Pollution* thereby suggest that the choice to impose criminal rather than administrative sanctions is essentially a political one, not open to second-guessing by the courts and thus amenable to judicial review only in cases of manifest inappropriateness? In any event, the ruling's most important clarification concerns the actual content of the Community's criminal law competences: the latter are limited to imposing upon Member States a basic obligation to ensure that effective, proportionate and dissuasive criminal sanctions exist under national law; if there is a need for more detailed common rules concerning the actual type and/or level of penalties, that need should be fulfilled through approximation measures adopted pursuant to the Third Pillar.

However, the latter finding may have to be reconsidered should the Treaty of Lisbon 2007 enter into force. In particular, Article 83(2) of the amended Treaty on the Functioning of the European Union (TFEU) provides that, if the approximation of criminal law proves essential to ensure the effective implementation of an EU policy in an area subject to harmonization measures, directives may establish minimum rules with regard to the definition of criminal offences and sanctions in that field. Problems arise because the proper scope of Article 83(2) TFEU is unclear. Should this new legal basis be used for the adoption of *all* post-harmonization criminal measures, even if limited to the imposition of a basic obligation to criminalize certain forms of conduct? If so, that would have the effect of abrogating the implied criminal law competences which arise under specific substantive legal bases as recognized in *Environmental Crimes* and *Ship-Source Pollution*. Or instead, should Article 83(2) TFEU be employed *only* where the Union wishes to set out more detailed rules concerning the level and/or type of criminal penalties? In that case, the implied criminal law competences affirmed in *Environmental Crimes* and *Ship-Source Pollution* would remain in place and this line of jurisprudence could well remain relevant post-Lisbon. After all, even though the revised Treaties contain no equivalent to existing Article 47 TEU, giving preference to First Pillar rather than Third Pillar competences, the potential would still exist for disputes about the correct legal basis for post-harmonization criminal measures: the substantive legal bases are available for certain acts, but Article 83(2) TFEU should be used for others.

Of course, the incentive for engaging in such legal basis disputes would be drastically reduced under the revised Treaties as compared to the existing situation: as regards the available legal instruments and the applicable legislative procedures, the legal bases for substantive Union action (on the one hand) and Article 83(2) TFEU (on the other hand) are virtually identical. However, there may be situations when recourse to the express competence under Article 83(2) TFEU would be appreciably different from exercise of an implied competence to criminalize under the substantive legal bases: after all, legislation under Article 83(2) TFEU can be initiated by Member States as well as the Commission, which generally retains its monopoly to make legislative proposals; the threshold for national parliaments to show a 'yellow card' on the grounds that a legislative proposal breaches the principle of subsidiarity is lower under Article 83(2) TFEU than in other internal policy fields; the UK, Ireland and Denmark all have opt-outs from measures adopted under Article 83(2) TFEU, whereas they would be automatically and fully bound by criminal measures adopted under the substantive legal bases; in situations where Article 83(2) TFEU involves the ordinary legislative procedure, every Member State enjoys the right to apply an 'emergency brake' veto within the Council, which might in turn trigger an extraordinary authorization for other Member States to engage in enhanced co-operation. In short: Article 83(2) TFEU may well change the nature of the debate about the Union's criminal law competences, but that debate is far from settled by the Treaty of Lisbon, which means that cases such as *Environmental Crimes* and *Ship-Source Pollution* cannot yet be considered of purely historical interest.

Concluding Observations

Identifying common themes or trends in the caselaw of the Community courts, especially on the basis of such a small number of rulings, is an inherently dangerous task. However, one interesting observation may apply to several of the judgments analysed in this article. Issues such as the right to collective action, the provision of welfare benefits and the organization of educational policy all fall within fields where EU regulatory power is relatively weak, yet the Member States' duty to respect the obligations imposed directly under the Treaty manages to exert an increasingly profound influence on the exercise of their domestic competences. It is true that the ECJ's caselaw pursues an admirable logic when it refuses to exclude such matters *per se* from the impact of the Treaty. But as the response to rulings such as *Viking Line* and *Laval un Partneri* demonstrates, logic can provide the ECJ with only so much legitimacy. The political and social sensitivities of interfering with national rules on collective action, welfare benefits or educational policy are similar regardless of whether that interference emanates from the Community legislature, or instead from the Community judiciary. Future litigation will continue to test how far the ECJ is prepared to tread in fields of complementary or even non-existent Union regulatory competence – and academic research should continue to question how far the ECJ's response contributes to the constitutional coherence of the Union legal order.

Key Reading

If it is difficult enough to select a handful of rulings which may be of general interest to EU lawyers from the hundreds delivered annually by the Community courts, the task is even more fraught when is comes to academic publications. The following choices are therefore entirely subjective, adding up to nothing more than a few suggestions for some interesting and rewarding reading, across a range of legal topics.

Beveridge, F. (2007) 'Building Against the Past: the Impact of Mainstreaming on EU Gender Law and Policy'. *European Law Review*, Vol. 32, p. 193.

Bronckers, M. (2007) 'The Relationship of the EC Courts with Other International Tribunals: Non-committal, Respectful or Submissive?' *Common Market Law Review*, Vol. 44, p. 601.

De Leeuw, M.E. (2007) 'Openness in the Legislative Process in the European Union'. *European Law Review*, Vol. 32, p. 295.

Lenaerts, K. (2007) 'The Rule of Law and the Coherence of the Judicial System of the European Union'. *Common Market Law Review*, Vol. 44, p. 1625.

Peers, S. (2007) 'Salvation Outside the Church: Judicial Protection in the Third Pillar after the *Pupino* and *Segi* Judgments'. *Common Market Law Review*, Vol. 44, p. 883.

Somek, A. (2007) 'Solidarity Decomposed: Being and Time in European Citizenship'. *European Law Review*, Vol. 32, p. 787.

JCMS 2008 Volume 46 Annual Review pp. 145–164

Relations with the Wider Europe

SANDRA LAVENEX
University of Lucerne, Switzerland
FRANK SCHIMMELFENNIG
ETH Zurich, Switzerland

Events in 2007 amply demonstrated the obstacles to effective political accession conditionality in the European Union's (potential) candidate countries: structural problems of transition and governance, legacies of ethnic conflict and, in the case of Turkey, fundamental opposition to accession by important Member States. After three years of existence, evaluations of the European Neighbourhood Policy (ENP) also provide mixed results. Sectoral co-operation in areas of strategic interest to the EU has progressed faster than ambitions for political change and the differences between countries willing and able to co-operate with the EU and other ENP countries have increased.

I. Enlargement

On 1 January 2007, Bulgaria and Romania joined the EU, bringing the number of Member States up to 27. This step officially concluded the fifth enlargement of the EU. It also moved the focus of attention to the remaining countries with an explicit membership perspective: the Western Balkans and Turkey. Developments in 2006 had been characterized by stagnation and setbacks (Lavenex and Schimmelfennig, 2007). Negotiations with Serbia and Turkey were (partially) suspended; those with most other countries failed to move forward decisively. The main question for 2007 was therefore whether these setbacks were mere bumps on the road to accession or whether the problems that had caused them were more durable. In other words, would the

EU's political accession conditionality be effective in the remaining (potential) candidate countries for membership?

In the past, political accession conditionality proved effective under two main conditions. One, there has to be a credible prospect of membership; that is, candidate countries need to be certain that they will be accepted if they fulfil the accession criteria and that they will not be admitted otherwise. Two, EU conditionality has to fall on fertile domestic ground. In particular, when the political costs of compliance are high for the target government – such as if fulfilling EU conditions would threaten the survival of the government – even credible membership incentives generally prove ineffective.

To varying degrees, the remaining candidate countries possess two commonalities that distinguish them from most of the new Member States. First, they have to cope with, on average, more serious problems of transition and governance. These problems are difficult to overcome with short-term external rewards and punishments, but require longer-term 'compliance management', including extensive assistance to improve the governance capabilities of the target countries. Second, most of these countries have to face the legacies of recent (and partly ongoing) ethno-nationalist conflicts. Political accession criteria that touch upon these legacies are likely to arouse nationalist sentiment and create high domestic political costs of compliance for the governments of the candidate countries. Both commonalities reduce the short-term effectiveness of political accession conditionality. Finally, Turkey faces an additional problem likely to undermine the effectiveness of accession conditionality. Some Member State governments reject the membership perspective for Turkey in principle and favour alternative institutional arrangements regardless of how well Turkey fulfils the political criteria. How were these problems of accession conditionality reflected in the relations of the EU with its prospective Member States in 2007?

Enlargement Strategy and Assistance

The EU's debate on the future strategy of enlargement, which had raged throughout 2006 and revolved around the issue of absorption or integration capacity (Lavenex and Schimmelfennig, 2007), had calmed down markedly in 2007. The Commission's enlargement strategy could therefore refer to a 'renewed consensus defined by the December 2006 European Council', which was 'based on the principles of consolidation of commitments, fair and rigorous conditionality and better communication with the public, combined with the EU's capacity to integrate new members' (2007a, p. 2). It needs to be stressed, however, that this 'consensus' does not signal a substantive convergence of Member State preferences on whether and how far the EU should expand. Rather, it indicates a lull in the conflict about enlargement, in particular with regard to Turkey, as no major enlargement decisions had to be taken in 2007.

The concrete policy priorities of the Commission for the prospective Member States pertain to 'the fundamental issues of state-building, good governance, administrative and judicial reform, rule of law, reconciliation, compliance with the International Criminal Tribunal for the Former Yugoslavia (ICTY) and civil society development' (Commission, 2007a, p. 4). These issues reflect the specific governance and transition problems of the region and appear in the documents on the EU's instruments of assistance as well.

From 2007, the Instrument for Pre-Accession (IPA) has superseded all previous instruments of assistance for candidate and potential candidate states. According to the documents, assistance under this scheme will be clearly accession-oriented and targeted at medium-term goals. The major objectives are the strengthening of democratic institutions and the rule of law, public administration reform, economic reforms, respect for human rights, minority rights and gender equality, development of civil society, regional co-operation, sustainable development and poverty reduction. For non-candidate countries, the focus is on transition assistance and institution-building, whereas candidate countries (currently Croatia, Macedonia, and Turkey) benefit from assistance for regional, rural, and human resources development as well. In sum, the EU has allotted almost €4 billion in assistance to the Western Balkans and Turkey for the period 2007–09. This sum far exceeds EU assistance to other regions, including the ENP region. Whereas the EU's assistance to the Western Balkans ranges from €20 to €45 per capita per year, the countries of the ENP region are allocated between €2.50 and €12 (own calculations from Commission, 2007b, 2007d).

Croatia

Among the candidate countries, Croatia has made the most progress toward membership. At the end of 2007, two negotiating chapters were provisionally closed and 14 opened. What is more, in March 2008, Commission President Barroso presented Croatian Prime Minister Sanader with a timetable for concluding the negotiations. Under the condition that a few thorny issues are settled, the accession negotiations could be concluded by the end of 2009. The signing of the Lisbon Treaty removed the main legal obstacle for the EU to Croatia's membership. Ratification of the treaty by all Member States will put in place the necessary institutional reforms for admitting new members. Croatia, for its part, stopped barring EU fishermen (mainly Italian and Slovenian) from its proclaimed protection zone in the Adriatic Sea. Croatia, however, 'needs to make further progress in judicial and administrative reforms, minority rights and refugee return as well as restructuring in heavy industries' (Commission, 2007a, p. 11). In comparison with the other Western Balkan countries, the governance and transition problems of Croatia are the least severe. There is a stable consensus in favour of reform and EU membership among the major political parties and after the arrest of General Gotovina in 2005, there are no major issues that can rouse nationalist sentiment and potentially block the way to membership.

Turkey

Accession negotiations with Turkey inched ahead during 2007. Three negotiating chapters (enterprise and industry, statistics and financial control) were opened in March and June and two more (on transport and consumer and health protection) in December. Faster progress was blocked by three main factors: Turkey's persistent refusal to extend fully the Customs Union to Cyprus; the ongoing power struggle between the Justice and Development Party (AKP) that forms the government and the Kemalist 'deep state' in the security and judicial establishment; and the continuing conflict within the EU over Turkey's accession perspective.

First, there was no major movement on the Cyprus issue during 2007. The Turkish government continued to insist that Cypriot ships and airplanes would only be allowed to enter Turkey if the embargo on the Turkish-controlled part of the island was lifted. Such a move, however, continued to be resisted by the Republic of Cyprus. Ultimately, Turkish concessions will depend on developments on the island. Under the Greek–Cypriot hardline government of Tassos Papadopoulos, which had rejected the United Nations peace plan in 2004, negotiations about a peace settlement failed. The change in government in the Republic and the election of the new President Dimitris Christofias in February 2008, however, may generate new momentum toward overcoming the division of the island.

Second, Turkey faced a domestic political crisis in 2007. It was triggered by the end of the mandate of President Sezer, who was regarded by the old Kemalist political establishment as a guardian of secularism and the Kemalist state doctrine against the moderately Islamist AKP who controls the parliament and the government. When the AKP announced Foreign Minister Gül as its presidential candidate, the opposition parties boycotted the vote in parliament. The AKP emerged strengthened from the ensuing crisis. It won the parliamentary elections it had proposed, allowing it to continue its single-party government under Prime Minister Erdogan. Abdullah Gül was elected president in August 2007 and a referendum in October confirmed the AKP's plan to have the president elected by popular vote in the future. The clash with the Kemalist 'deep state' in the military and the judiciary is continuing, however.

In their annual reports, the European Parliament (EP) and the Commission praised the outcome of the domestic political crisis in Turkey but – just as in 2006 – deplored a general slowdown in political reform. The Commission singled out the freedom of expression as a major area in need of reform and proposed blocking negotiations on the chapter relating to the judiciary and human rights unless Turkey reforms its Article 301 of the penal code (on insults to Turkish identity) in line with the European Convention on Human Rights and the case law of the European Court of Human Rights. In addition, the Commission emphasized the rights of non-Muslim religious minorities, the fight against corruption, trade union rights, women's and children's rights, the accountability of the public administration and full rights and freedoms for the Kurdish population (Commission, 2007a).

Finally, the deep divergence in preferences among the Member States over the desirability of Turkey's accession persisted unabated in 2007. The Commission and a group of Member States including Italy, Spain, Sweden and the United Kingdom sought to keep the accession process with Turkey alive and to make as much progress as Turkish compliance with EU rules and demands allowed for. By contrast, France under President Nicolas Sarkozy confirmed its position as the leader of the anti-accession coalition. He openly declared that Turkey had no place in the EU and tried to obstruct the negotiations. In June, the French government blocked the opening of a chapter on economic and monetary integration on the grounds that this would bring Turkey too close to membership and, in a more subtle and symbolic move, it insisted on removing the term 'accession' from Council decisions and documents relating to Turkey.[1] On the other hand, the French government submitted a bill to remove compulsory referendums on the accession of new Member States to the EU from the constitution, by making it the President's choice whether to seek ratification by referendum or by a three-fifths majority in the 'congress', comprising the national assembly and the senate.

Albania, Macedonia and Montenegro

Macedonia remained in the antechambers of accession negotiations. An official candidate since 2005, the country still waits for the EU to give the country a starting date for membership talks. *Montenegro's* Stabilization and Association Agreement (SAA) was signed in October 2007. Macedonia, Montenegro and *Albania* form the intermediate tier of Western Balkan countries that

---

[1] *Financial Times*, 11 December 2007.

are associated with the EU, but have not started membership negotiations. The Commission report acknowledged progress in several areas, but criticized the confrontational political climate in Albania and Macedonia, listed problems with democratic consolidation and effective governance, and told them to accelerate the pace of reforms.

Bosnia-Herzegovina

Talks with Bosnia-Herzegovina on an SAA have been going on since the end of 2005. Although the technical talks were completed in 2006, the negotiations could not be concluded because the constitutional reforms that the EU demanded were blocked. In March 2007, Enlargement Commissioner Olli Rehn described the situation in rather undiplomatic language before the EP: '2006 was not a year of success for Bosnia and Herzegovina. As a result of an extended election campaign, the reform agenda stagnated and the political climate turned sour, leading to nationalist rhetoric and tensions. We've had enough of it'.[2] Rehn reiterated that the conclusion of negotiations depended on two conditions: police reform and co-operation with the ICTY.

Police reform remained out of reach for the better part of 2007. The goal of the international community was to overcome the division of police forces along ethnic lines. The EU stipulated three principles for reform: federal legislative and budgetary control over the police, the division of police forces according to functional rather than (ethno-) political lines and operational autonomy of the police. The conflict was mainly over the status of the police forces of the Republika Srpska. Whereas the Serb leadership sought to keep control over its own police and avoid its merger with Croat and Muslim police forces, the Muslim leaders tried to abolish any separate Serb police force. After several failed negotiations, the new High Representative Miroslav Lajcak set a deadline of 30 September and threatened to use his powers to force through legislation. His threat and EU pressure prompted the ethnic groups to reach a compromise at the end of October 2007. It included central funding and management of the police and political non-interference with police operations but preserved a separate (although less autonomous) police force of the Republika Srpska. At the end of November, an action plan for implementing police reform followed.

In the meantime, however, a new conflict had arisen. In order to unblock policy-making, Lajcak announced in October 2007 the introduction of new legislative quorum rules. The rule changes were designed to end the common practice of obstructing decisions unwelcome to one of ethnic groups by failing to attend sessions of the federal institutions. He set 1 December as the

[2] *Euractiv.com*, 15 March 2007.

deadline before he would use his powers to impose the new rules. This plan was met with fierce resistance by the Republika Srpska whose leaders feared that they would be outvoted under the new rules. The increasingly acute showdown ended at the last minute when, on 30 November, Bosnia-Herzegovina's leaders accepted the new rules. According to Bosnian-Serb leader Dodik, 'at this moment in time the most important thing for Bosnia-Herzegovina was the signing and initialling of the Stabilization and Association Agreement, which will direct Bosnia-Herzegovina permanently towards European integration'.[3] The SAA was duly initialled on 4 December but the EU made the formal signing of the agreement dependent on the actual adoption of the reform. In April 2008, the Bosnian parliament paved the way by voting in favour of the police reform.

Serbia and Kosovo

Among the potential candidates for EU membership, Serbia and Kosovo were clearly the focus of attention throughout 2007. Since the start of the year, the big question was whether Serbia would get a government that would be willing to reach a compromise on the independence of Kosovo, improve its co-operation with the ICTY and thus pave the way for resuming association talks.

The politics of Serbia are characterized by a party constellation in which the Democratic Party of Serbia (DSS) holds the key to government formation. The party leader, Vojislav Kostunica, is a democrat but also a Serb nationalist who has long denounced the ICTY as an anti-Serbian and illegitimate court and fiercely resisted any independent statehood for Kosovo. The DSS can either align itself with the liberal democratic forces, mainly the Democratic Party (DS), or with the extreme nationalists of the Radical Party or the Socialist Party of former President Milosevic.

The elections of January 2007 did not change this fundamental political constellation. Although Kostunica's DSS had fewer seats than either the DS or the Radical Party, it remained in a pivotal position and retained both coalition options. In order to provide an incentive to Kostunica, the EU informally offered to drop the extradition of the Bosnian Serb General Ratko Mladic, who was charged with genocide and crimes against humanity by the ICTY, as a prerequisite for reopening association talks if a pro-EU and pro-reform government was formed and if key security positions were filled with people willing to co-operate seriously with The Hague.[4] Nevertheless, coalition talks among the democratic parties dragged on for months and

[3] *RFE/RL Newsline*, 3 December 2007.
[4] *RFE/RL Newsline*, 9 and 13 February 2007.

risked breaking down in early May – precisely because the major parties could not agree on the division of key security posts. After the DSS had briefly joined forces with the Radicals and Socialists to elect a new speaker of the parliament, a coalition between the DSS, the DS and another reform-oriented party (the G17+) was concluded at the last minute before new elections would have had to be called. Under the coalition deal, Kostunica remained prime minister and the DSS kept the Interior Ministry, but had to cede control over the security services – responsible for tracking down Mladic – to President Boris Tadic (DS). In return, Commissioner Rehn promised that SAA negotiations would be resumed once the new government showed evidence of its determination to co-operate with the ICTY. He added further that the SAA would not be signed until Mladic is arrested and extradited. In addition, Serbia was rewarded with a visa facilitation agreement.

Initially, the change in government met the EU's expectations. On 31 May, General Zdravko Tolimir, the third-most-wanted fugitive indictee after Radovan Karadzic and Mladic, was captured. A few days later, the ICTY's chief prosecutor Carla Del Ponte gave a positive assessment of Serbia's co-operation and on 13 June, the SAA negotiations were resumed. After this early success, however, Serbian efforts produced no further tangible results. Del Ponte's assessment in October 2007 was therefore more negative, but she recognized the political will of the Serbian authorities to co-operate. As the EU had bound its own decision on the SAA to Del Ponte's assessment, it found a solution that mirrored her mixed message. On 7 November, the EU initialled but did not sign the SAA.

The political constellation in Serbia also frustrated any hopes that the EU might have harboured about winning Serbian consent to a UN-brokered settlement on the status of Kosovo in exchange for a membership perspective. Kostunica had made it clear early on that he would not agree to the independent statehood of Kosovo under any circumstances, refused to trade Kosovo's independence for EU membership and warned of 'serious consequences' for any state that recognized Kosovo as an independent state.[5] By contrast, his coalition partners from the DS, while also rejecting Kosovan independence, were willing to pursue EU membership nevertheless and asked the EU to clear Serbia's path to membership as a compensation for the loss of the province.[6]

From the beginning of the year, divisions appeared among the EU Member States as well. Cyprus, Greece, Romania, Slovakia, and Spain – mostly countries with national minorities seeking autonomy – feared that the Ahti-saari plan would set a precedent for, and encourage, separatism. At the same

---

[5] *RFE/RL Newsline*, 1 February 2007; *Euractiv.com*, 17 July 2007.
[6] *RFE/RL Newsline*, 28 August 2007, 20 September 2007.

time, there was a consensus that the EU needed to avoid an open split on the issue and should prepare for providing the international civilian presence to supervise Kosovo after independence. In addition, there was discussion within the EU on whether Serbia should get a special deal (such as less rigorous conditionality and a fast-track to membership) in return for agreeing to statehood for Kosovo.

Toward the end of 2007 matters came to a head. In the EU, a solid majority of states, including France, Germany and the UK, formed in favour of recognizing Kosovo's independence in the likely case that no agreement would be reached between Serbia and Kosovo by 10 December. The European Council agreed that in the wake of the anticipated failure of the talks Kosovo would declare its independence after the presidential elections in Serbia scheduled for January 2008, independence would be recognized by a substantial number of Member States, and the EU would dispatch the 1,800-strong EULEX mission of police offers, judges, and administrators to Kosovo to supervise independence.

At the same time, the EU made a vague offer of accelerating Serbia's progress toward membership.[7] Subsequently, this offer revealed splits within the EU as well as within the Serbian government. The Dutch government (backed by Belgium) vetoed the signing of the SAA (against a large majority of the other Member States) if the main condition, the arrest and extradition of Mladic, was not fulfilled. The EU, therefore, ended up offering Serbia an expanded trade and visa liberalization agreement at the end of January 2008 in order to influence the second round of the presidential elections in favour of the incumbent, Boris Tadic. Within Serbia the DS welcomed the EU's offer whereas Prime Minister Kostunica exercised 'reverse conditionality' by insisting that Serbia would not sign any agreement unless the EU refrained from recognizing Kosovo. On 4 February 2008, President Tadic was confirmed in office and on 17 February Kosovo declared its independence, which was subsequently recognized by a large majority of EU Member States. As a result, EU–Serbian negotiations broke down and, finally, the Serbian government collapsed over EU policy differences.

Conclusions

Developments in EU relations with the (potential) candidate countries for membership in 2007 provide ample evidence for the increased problems of enlargement and the decreased effectiveness of accession conditionality. Transition and governance problems are particularly pronounced in countries, such as Albania, Macedonia and Montenegro, that do not intentionally violate

---

[7] *RFE/RL Newsline*, 17 December 2007.

fundamental EU political norms but need a long time and sustained assistance before they are ready for accession negotiations. The legacies of ethnic conflict and the close connection between EU accession criteria and issues of national identity are obviously responsible for the weakness of EU political conditionality in Bosnia-Herzegovina, Serbia and Turkey. Whereas EU conditionality has failed so far in Serbia and Turkey (with regard to Cyprus), the combination of EU incentives with the authority of the High Representative brought about change in Bosnia-Herzegovina.

Finally, the credibility of EU conditionality is being undermined in two ways. One, as in the case of Turkey, is when a group of Member States prefers unconditional exclusion and thereby puts in doubt the credibility of the EU's membership promise. The second, evident in the case of Serbia, is when a majority of the Member States was willing to accept an unconditional fast-track and thereby risked compromising the EU's threat of excluding non-compliant candidates. Events in Serbia have demonstrated, however, that even an unconditional offer of membership would not have changed the nationalist stance of Prime Minister Kostunica.

II. European Neighbourhood Policy

After the ENP had been in place for three years, 2007 was a year of reflection and realignment. Several policy initiatives followed the Commission's December 2006 'Communication on Strengthening the European Neighbourhood Policy' (Commission, 2006; see also Lavenex and Schimmelfennig, 2007) with the aim of revitalizing the policy and increasing EU leverage. The German Council Presidency gave up its original ambitions for a privileged partnership with eastern ENP countries and presented a report that was broadly endorsed by the European Council (Council, 2007a). France's newly elected President Sarkozy re-emphasized the southern dimension with his idea of a 'Mediterranean Union'. The European Parliament (EP) followed this trend towards a stronger regional differentiation within the ENP in a report in which it 'expressed doubt about the meaningfulness of the ENP's geographic scope, as it involves countries which geographically are European together with Mediterranean non-European countries' (European Parliament, 2007, 5ff.). The report recognized in the former group a transition towards democracy and an EU vocation, but criticized the weakness of the EU's democracy and human rights promotion towards the Mediterranean and called for greater use of the instrument of conditionality. The common concern of all these initiatives and reports was how to increase the incentives the ENP has to offer in its attempt to foster political and economic reforms in target countries.

In the meantime, more technical sectoral policy dialogues intensified with most countries, thereby confirming the growing dissociation between the political transformation ambitions of the ENP and its more functionalist, sectoral aspects (Lavenex and Schimmelfennig, 2007). The work of the sectoral sub-committees charged with the implementation of the Action Plans intensified and a total number of 64 formal technical meetings in these formats were held during 2007 (Commission, 2007c). In addition, TAIEX short-term technical assistance and advice on convergence with EU legislation and twinning secondments of Member State officials in partner countries started. By the end of 2007, 146 twinning covenants had been established or were under negotiation.

In sum, sectoral and political progress during 2007 confirmed the growing differentiation of EU external relations under the ENP. Whereas countries such as Ukraine, Moldova, Morocco and Israel were willing and able to move towards some sort of enhanced status, the gap between them and the other ENP countries has widened.

Progress Made and Innovation

During 2007 the contours of a future Enhanced Agreement with Ukraine took shape. For the EU, the agreement is a 'flagship project' to demonstrate the ENP's potential benefits. The credibility of the EU's willingness to reward implementation of Action Plan priorities was also tested in negotiations on an 'advanced status' for Morocco. Meanwhile, Lebanon, Egypt as well as Armenia, Azerbaijan and Georgia started to implement their Action Plans, and the Commission produced a non-paper on Belarus preparing for its eventual participation in the ENP once it had moved towards democracy. The ENP's eastern dimension was boosted by a new regional initiative, the Black Sea Synergy. This EU initiative aims to develop co-operation within the Black Sea region itself and between the region and the EU, and is intended to complete the 'chain' of regional co-operation frameworks in the EU's neighbourhood, adding to the Euro-Mediterranean Partnership and the Northern Dimension. The Black Sea Synergy will build upon ongoing Community sectoral programmes and initiatives. As it involves also Russia and Turkey as well as the eastern ENP partners, one hope is that it will create a better climate for the solution of the 'frozen conflicts' in the region.

At the sectoral level, ENP activities focused on energy and migration. The March European Council adopted the Energy Action Plan (Council, 2007b) that calls for a common approach to external energy policy. To the east, energy relations were deepened through the implementation of the Energy Memoranda of Understanding with Ukraine and Azerbaijan and the launch of the

Black Sea Synergy. To the south, the EU–Africa–Middle East Energy Conference in November 2007 confirmed the plan to launch a Euro–Africa Energy Partnership as well as the promotion of regional integration of the energy markets between African, Middle East and European countries. At the bilateral level, Algeria was offered a strategic energy partnership involving convergence of regulatory frameworks; the development of energy infrastructures of common interest; and technology co-operation and exchange of expertise.

The importance of migration policies was stressed in the Commission's December Communication (Commission, 2007c, p. 5), which stated that the 'ability of people to move and interact with each other is of the utmost importance for many aspects of the ENP', and proposed 'facilitation of legitimate short-term travel as well as more ambitious – longer-term – developments in the area of managed migration, potentially involving the opening of Member States' labour markets.' The financial means of co-operation with third countries were increased with a new programme entitled 'Thematic Co-operation Programme with Third Countries in the Development Aspects of Migration and Asylum' for the years 2007–13.

Finally, the EU took initial steps towards allowing ENP countries to participate in activities of EU agencies and programmes. The Commission began negotiations on such participation with Israel, Morocco and Ukraine – the three partner countries that the Presidency's report of June 2007 identified as being the most likely to benefit from these measures.

Meanwhile, little progress was made with the countries that have not yet adopted ENP Action Plans. Whereas Algeria continued to implement its association agreement, the association agreement with Syria was still pending signature at the end of 2007. Exploratory discussions were initiated on a first framework agreement with Libya, while co-operation with Belarus remained conditional on key improvements in the fields of human rights and respect for fundamental freedoms.

Eastern Europe

The political instability that followed *Ukraine*'s first truly free and fair parliamentary elections in its history in 2006 persisted during most of 2007. The difficult 'cohabitation' between President Viktor Yushchenko and Prime Minister Viktor Yanukovych, his rival in the 2004 presidential elections, created considerable tension. As a result, early parliamentary elections took place in September 2007 – the country's fourth national elections in three years. After the thin victory of pro-Western parties, President Yushchenko and Yulia Tymoshenko announced the establishment of a new 'Orange Coalition' in October, with the latter celebrating a return as prime minister.

In the meantime, endeavours to give Ukraine some sort of privileged status under the ENP continued. In March 2007 the negotiation of a New Enhanced Agreement (NEA) started, and intensified after Ukraine joined the World Trade Organization (WTO) in February 2008.

Energy co-operation was a second focus during 2007. Ukraine is a key energy partner of the EU, notably because some 80 per cent of EU imports of Russian gas pass through Ukrainian pipelines. Under the Memorandum of Understanding on energy co-operation, five Joint Working Groups continued to meet on a regular basis to monitor and guide efforts aiming at the various energy-related objectives of the Action Plan reaching from nuclear safety to integration of electricity and gas markets, energy supply and environmental standards. Furthermore, after obtaining observer status in the Energy Community Treaty (ECT) in 2006, Ukraine applied for full membership in 2007. In order to promote transparency of markets and security of supplies, the Commission allocated €87 million in 2007 for the reform of the Ukrainian energy sector. A list of priority projects in the electricity, gas and oil sectors has been prepared and agreed, and significant funding from international financial institutions has been secured for their implementation.

The third major focus of co-operation was Justice and Home Affairs (JHA) (see also Monar, this volume). The EU–Ukraine Co-operation Council on 18 June endorsed a new JHA Action Plan and signed agreements on visa facilitation and on readmission of illegal immigrants. The two agreements were the result of long and tedious negotiations and may be considered as a package deal offering very limited liberalization of travel to the EU in exchange for Ukraine's willingness to take back irregular migrants from the EU, including Ukranians as well as third country nationals and stateless people. Under the visa agreement, a decision on whether or not to issue a visa has to be taken within ten days and the procedures have been simplified. The agreement also simplifies the criteria for issuing multiple-entry visas for certain groups of people, such as close relatives of the applicant, lorry drivers, people on business, students, journalists and members of official delegations. Moreover, visa fees applied by Schengen Member States are fixed at €35, compared to the usual €60 and they are waived for certain groups (such as those visiting close relatives, students, disabled people, journalists and pensioners). Ukrainian diplomatic-passport holders will be exempt from the visa obligation under the agreement. With regard to readmission, Ukraine succeeded in introducing a transitional period of two years for the readmission of third-country nationals and stateless people. A special accelerated procedure will apply to persons apprehended in common border regions who can be returned within a few days. The Commission committed €35 million in 2007 for the implementation of the EC–Ukraine readmission agreement, to improve

Ukraine's capacity to deal with irregular migration and ensure compliance with Western European best practice and humanitarian standards.

In the area of external border control, the EU agency Frontex and Ukraine concluded a working arrangement preparing for their operational co-operation on border management issues. The EU halted negotiations on a strategic co-operation agreement between Ukraine and Europol, aimed at enhancing the common fight against organized crime, subject to Ukraine's ratification and implementation of the Council of Europe 1981 data protection convention. Ratification and implementation of this convention will also enhance the contacts between Ukraine and Eurojust, the European agency for the promotion of judicial co-operation.

In the transport sector, negotiations on a comprehensive EU–Ukraine aviation agreement started in December 2007. Furthermore, the Ukrainian parliament ratified the Ukraine–EU Co-operation Agreement on Civil Global Navigation Satellite System. While Ukraine and the EU started negotiations on Ukraine's access to EU agencies and programmes, increased use was made of the Community's twinning instrument (24 projects under preparation and six currently underway) and TAIEX assistance to help advance reforms and to share EU know-how and best practices in various areas.

In local elections in *Moldova* during 2007, the Communist Party received the most votes and seats, but their popularity dropped substantially. Analysts suggest that an electoral shift might take place before the 2009 parliamentary elections.[8]

In October 2007, a visa facilitation and readmission agreement similar to that concluded with Ukraine was signed. The EU opened a Common Visa Application Centre in Chisinau in April to facilitate access to Member State consulates after the introduction of visa requirements against Moldovans by Romania upon EU accession. The EU Border Assistance Mission to Moldova and Ukraine (EUBAM) was extended for another two years until November 2009.

South Caucasus

2007 was the first year of implementation for the Action Plans with Armenia, Azerbaijan and Georgia. *Armenia*'s parliamentary elections in May largely conformed with its commitments within the Organization for Security and Co-operation in Europe (OSCE) and other international standards. *Azerbaijan*'s progess in the area of democratic governance was more limited. For instance, the electoral framework has not yet been reformed in line with the recommendations of the OSCE/Office for Democratic Institutions and

---

[8] *RFL/RL News*, 27 June 2007.

Human Rights (ODIHR) and the Council of Europe's Venice Commission, despite presidential elections approaching in autumn 2008. Sectoral co-operation with Azerbaijan mainly focused on energy with the implementation of the Memorandum of Understanding on a strategic energy partnership signed in November 2006.

In *Georgia*, too, democratic consolidation was mixed. Constitutional changes envisaged a delay of parliamentary and presidential elections until the autumn of 2008 and extended the term of the parliament by six months. The changes led to civil unrest in November 2007 and calls for the respect of the normal duration of the legislature and the introduction of a parliamentary political system. The excessive use of force by law enforcement officials, the destruction of the independent TV station Imedi, and the imposition of a state of emergency were condemned in a declaration of the EU's Common Foreign and Security Policy (CFSP) in November 2007. In response to these concerns, President Saakashvili decided to hold Presidential elections as originally planned in January 2008.

Although the EU is not a formal party to the existing processes for the resolution of conflicts in South Ossetia and Abkhazia, a number of conflict-related objectives were included in the ENP Action Plan in order to underline the EU intention to contribute to the settlement of Georgia's internal conflicts. A joint EU Special Representative–European Commission expert mission to Georgia, Abkhazia and South Ossetia took place in January 2007. As the result of this mission the Commission identified a package of confidence building measures, aimed at improving the trust between Tbilisi and the separatist regimes in Abkhazia and South Ossetia. The implementation of this package, which includes embedding police advisors to the UNOMIG and OSCE missions, as well as the appointment of an EU adviser to the Ministry of Conflict Resolution, started in autumn 2007.

Since June 2007, Armenia and Georgia have been invited to align themselves with CFSP declarations on a case-by-case basis, which they did on most occasions. Feasibility studies exploring the possibility of free trade agreements with Georgia and Armenia will be concluded in 2008.

III. Mediterranean Countries

To the south, the third year of the ENP confirmed the increasing differentiation of bilateral relations with the Mediterranean countries, while the situation in the Middle East remained profoundly unstable. New Action Plans were adopted with Lebanon (January) and Egypt (March). The more advanced ENP partners continued to seek closer ties with the EU, e.g. through negotiations on the liberalization of services and the right of establishment as well as on trade in agricultural products. These trade negotiations however also highlighted internal differences within the EU about granting concessions, with the Commission urging the Member States in its December communication to limit the number of products excluded from full liberalization (Commission, 2007c).

Middle East

During most of 2007, relations with the Palestinian Authorities (PA) were stalled due to continuing Israeli occupation and the PA Government's lack of control over the Gaza Strip, where Hamas enforced its own rule. Meanwhile, talks with Israel focused on the possibility of granting it some sort of enhanced status. Having agreed a framework protocol with the EU, Israel was the front-runner for making use of the new possibilities for ENP partner countries' participation in Community programmes. It also sought closer co-operation with EU agencies. In October 2007 Israel agreed to start negotiations on a free trade agreement on the liberalization of services and rules of establishment. It was also invited to align itself with CFSP declarations on a case-by-case basis, but has not yet taken up the offer.

With the PA, the overall security and political context stalled progress in the implementation of the Action Plan during 2006 and the first half of 2007. This changed after the EU resumed normal relations in June 2007 and re-established political dialogue. An EU–PA foreign ministers troika meeting took place in September 2007. At a meeting in Ramallah in November 2007 the Commission and the PA decided to convene the Joint Committee in the first half of 2008 and to formally re-launch the implementation of the Action Plan.

These difficulties also overshadowed initiatives under the CFSP. The EU Police Mission in the occupied Palestinian Territory (EUPOL COPPS) re-engaged with the Palestinian civil police after June 2007, focusing its efforts on support to the modernization of the police in the West Bank (Gaza being beyond reach during this period). In October 2007, EUPOL COPPS convened the first joint seminar of Israeli and Palestinian police officers aiming at discussing accident prevention and building mutual confidence. Whereas this work is seen as a contribution to help the Palestinians meet their Roadmap obligations in the area of security, Israel started accrediting the mission only in December 2007. The EU Border Assistance Mission at Rafah on the border between Gaza and Egypt worked under significant constraints and has been on standby since the violent events in Gaza in June 2007.

Jordan's parliamentary elections in November 2007 were criticized for leading to an uneven allocation of seats in relation to population among electoral districts and for the absence of an independent electoral body and international electoral observers were not let in. Notwithstanding these political concerns, on 30 November the Council authorized the Commission to open negotiations with Jordan for establishing a Euro-Mediterranean Aviation Agreement.

North Africa

Energy and migration also formed the focus of sectoral co-operation with the North African ENP countries. At the 5th Euro-Mediterranean Ministerial Conference on Energy in December, ministers reaffirmed their commitment to enhancing reciprocal energy security, competitiveness and sustainability for the Euro-Mediterranean region and endorsed a 2008–13 Priority Action Plan for Euro-Mediterranean co-operation in the field of energy. In November, the first Euro-Mediterranean Ministerial Meeting on Migration was held under the Portuguese Presidency. In their declaration, ministers agreed to facilitate legal migration, to enhance the link between migration and development and to combat illegal migration.

Morocco, the frontrunner among the Mediterranean ENP countries, agreed on the implementation of five projects in the framework of the EU Twinning Programme. The selected projects focus on different sectors such as agriculture, consumer protection, or competition. In the September 2007 legislative elections, Morocco made progress on the transparency of the electoral process and on allowing political opponents access to media. Negotiations on a readmission agreement concerning irregular migrants went into their fifth year, as yet without results.

Co-operation with *Tunisia* focused again less on political and more on economic and technical issues, reflecting Tunisian priorities. Tunisia moved forward with its economic, social and regulatory reforms contributing to further economic growth and increasing economic exchange with the EU. On the other hand, the new ENP subcommittee on human rights and democracy, after several years of controversies over its working procedures, finally held its first session in autumn. Still, agreed commitments concerning freedom of association and expression and the modernization of the justice system were not implemented. Likewise, Tunisia so far resisted co-operation on irregular migration and readmission.

Egypt joined Morocco and Tunisia with the adoption of an ENP Action Plan in March 2007. Following the President's pledges of political reform in 2005, a package of amendments to the 1971 Constitution was adopted in April 2007 after a referendum. The constitutional amendments covered a wide range of issues including a call for a new election law regarding the eligibility of candidates of political parties and independent candidates to participate in elections. The government presented these amendments as paving the way for the promised ending of the state of emergency, which has been in place since 1981, before the end of the current legislative session in July 2008. Mid-term elections in June 2007 of Egypt's upper chamber of parliament were the first elections after the constitutional amendments entered into force. Alarmed by the low turnout and widespread allegations of irregularities, an EU Presidency statement called on Egypt to conduct an investigation, which has however not taken place. In the meantime, sectoral co-operation focused on energy matters with the preparation of a Memorandum of Understanding on energy, to be signed in 2008.

IV. European Economic Area and Switzerland

There were no major developments of note in the EU's relations with the European Economic Area (EEA) during 2007. The new energy dialogue launched in 2006 with *Norway* progressed with a focus on research and technological development, such as carbon capture and storage and relations with other energy producing countries. Closer co-operation was also sought in climate goals.

Relations with *Switzerland* were dominated by the discussions on certain company tax regimes in Swiss Cantons. The Commission argued that these schemes offering tax advantages to foreign companies established in Switzerland for profits generated in the EU were a form of state aid incompatible with the proper functioning of the 1972 Agreement between the EU and Switzerland. Swiss authorities maintained that the EU's intervention infringed the freedom of tax competition and the Swiss cantons' fiscal sovereignty. Together with the negotiations on the extension of freedom of movement for the new Member States Bulgaria and Romania, these talks reflected once more that such close forms of association blur the boundaries of membership.

Conclusions

EU relations with the (potential) candidate countries demonstrate growing problems for the effectiveness of accession conditionality. Above all the legacies of ethnic conflict (amplified by the close connection between EU accession criteria and issues of national identity), but also general transition and governance problems and a reduced credibility of the EU's threats and promises are responsible for these problems.

With regard to the ENP, in 2006 the main question was the relationship between its sectoral approach, providing new opportunities for the flexible horizontal integration of neighbouring countries, and its overarching foreign policy goals. In 2007 this discrepancy was carried further – yet accompanied by a series of high level initiatives to bolster the incentives the ENP has to offer in pursuing political change. Whereas the Commission and the EP as well as the German Presidency and the French government affirmed their willingness to pay greater tribute to the partner countries' interests, tedious bargaining on limited visa facilitations in exchange for readmission agreements and halting negotiations on trade in agricultural products are illustrative of the difficulties implied in reaching common foreign policy objectives in a multilevel and polycentric polity.

Further reading

Noutcheva (2007) and Pridham (2007) analyse the current problems of the EU's political conditionality in the candidate and potential candidate countries. Plümper and Schneider (2007) offer a rationalist explanation of EU enlargement based on the argument that losers among the Member States are compensated through the temporary discrimination of new Member States. Weber, Smith and Baun (2007) scrutinize the ENP from the point of view of its innovative potential as a form of regional governance and compile chapters on the various sectoral policies under the ENP.

References

Commission of the European Communities (2006) 'Communication: Strengthening the European Neighbourhood Policy'. COM(2006)726, 4 December.

Commission of the European Communities (2007a) 'Enlargement Strategy and Main Challenges, 2007–2008'. COM(2007)663, 6 November.

Commission of the European Communities (2007b) 'Instrument for Pre-Accession Assistance (IPA). Multi-Indicative Financial Framework for 2009–2001'. COM(2007)689, 6 November.

Commission of the European Communities (2007c) 'Communication: A Strong European Neighbourhood Policy'. COM(2007)774, 5 December.

Commission of the European Communities (2007d) 'European Neighbourhood and Partnership Instrument (ENPI) Funding 2007–2013'. Available at «http://ec.europa.eu/world/enp/pdf/country/0703_enpi_figures_en.pdf».

Council of the European Union (2007a) 'Strengthening the European Neighbourhood Policy'. Presidency Progress Report, 18/19 June.

Council of the European Union (2007b) 'Presidency Conclusions', Brussels European Council of 8/9.3.2007, Doc. 7224/1/07 of 2.5.2007.

European Parliament (2007) 'Report on Strengthening the European Neighbourhood Policy'. Rapporteurs: Charles Tannock, Raimon Obiols i Germ, A6-0414/2007.

Lavenex, S. and Schimmelfennig, F. (2007) 'Relations with the Wider Europe'. *JCMS*, Vol. 45, s1, pp. 143–62.

Noutcheva, G. (2007) 'Fake, Partial, and Imposed Compliance. The Limits of the EU's Normative Power in the Western Balkans'. *CEPS Working Document* 274, Brussels.

Plümper, T. and Schneider, C. (2007) 'Discriminatory European Membership and the Redistribution of Enlargement Gains'. *Journal of Conflict Resolution*, Vol. 51, pp. 568–87.

Pridham, G. (2007) 'Change and Continuity in the European Union's Political Conditionality'. *Democratization*, Vol. 14, pp. 446–71.

Weber, K., Smith, M.E. and Baun, M. (eds) (2007) *Governing Europe's Neighbourhood. Partners or Periphery?* (Manchester: Manchester University Press).

JCMS 2008 Volume 46 Annual Review pp. 165–182

Relations with the Rest of the World

DAVID ALLEN and MICHAEL SMITH
Loughborough University

Introduction

Last year we drew attention to the failure of the European Union (EU) to develop consistent and coherent strategies towards the wider world despite a great deal of external activity (Allen and Smith, 2007). We argued that this failure was partly explained by a weak institutional capacity. Thus it might be suggested[1] that agreement in 2007 on the details of the Lisbon Treaty represents a positive step towards dealing with this problem. The test of this institutional change will come in the years ahead, however, the need for, but continued lack of, more effective strategic thinking on the part of the EU is evident in almost all of the following developments.

I. General Themes

Foreign, Security and Defence Policy

The Lisbon Treaty that was finally agreed in October 2007 retains most of the proposed changes to the EU's external policy-making system that were originally contained in the Constitutional Treaty. Those states that had problems with the Constitutional Treaty can, however, argue that their sovereignty over foreign affairs is preserved. The proposed European Foreign Minister is renamed as the High Representative of the Union for Foreign Affairs and

---

[1] *European Voice*, 6–12 December 2007, p. 9.

Security Policy and two declarations (30 and 31) effectively state that nothing in the treaty affects the responsibilities of the Member States for the formulation and conduct of their own national foreign policies. As Whitman (2008), in an excellent analysis of the Lisbon Treaty points out, however, the Member States have reminded themselves that they are both obliged to seek a common approach to foreign and security matters and to consult one another on any national foreign policy stances or actions that might impact on collective EU policy.

The Lisbon Treaty, unlike the Constitutional Treaty, merely amends the previous EU Treaties, but a significant proportion of the amendments (25 out of 62) relate to the EU's 'external action', which is the new generic term for the totality of the EU's Common Foreign and Security Policy (CFSP), European Security and Defence Policy (ESDP) and external relations activities. Despite abolishing the pillar structure (see Dinan, this volume), the Lisbon Treaty retains the distinctive decision-making of external action, which means that there is still no role for the European Court of Justice (ECJ) and most decisions will continue to be made unanimously by all the Member States except where the treaty provides for either structured co-operation or, more interestingly, for actions by 'coalitions of the able and willing'.

The EU is now to have legal personality for the first time and it is to have an elected President of the European Council charged among other things with representing the EU in foreign and security matters at 'his or her level'. The elected President will however be joined in the European Council by the High Representative of the Union for Foreign Affairs and Security Policy (HR) whose powers are more clearly articulated than, and are not to be 'prejudiced' by, the president – a potentially interesting relationship that will be significantly influenced by the personality mix of the two incumbents. The HR was originally charged in 1999 with 'assisting the presidency' on CFSP matters, but under the Lisbon Treaty he or she will in effect replace the presidency on these matters by chairing the newly established Foreign Affairs Council, by appointing the chair of the Political and Security Committee, by representing the CFSP/ESDP to the European Parliament (EP) and by representing the EU with third parties and in international organizations. Furthermore the HR is also to become a Vice President of the Commission effectively taking on the former role of the Commissioner for External Relations (RELEX). The HR will be supported by the new European External Action Service (EEAS), which will be made up of officials drawn from the Commission, the Council Secretariat and the diplomatic services of the Member States. Although the Commission's external delegations are to be renamed as EU delegations and although they will effectively also serve the HR, they have not specifically been made a part of the EEAS. Thus the EEAS looks more like the basis of a foreign ministry, a 28th diplomatic service in the EU, than an extensive body charged with the staffing of EU external delegations – in other words more concerned with policy-making than policy implementation.

Along with the EEAS the HR will also become formally responsible for the appointment and management of the EU's Special and Personal Representatives. Finally, with regard to the CFSP, the Lisbon Treaty removes the Common Strategies that Javier Solana, EU High Representative for CFSP, has been so dismissive of and makes it probably easier for the HR to access the resources of the EU budget especially for ESDP operations.

The treaty contains a number of changes related to the ongoing evolution of ESDP with greater emphasis placed on the obligation of Member States to enhance their military capabilities – to be a member of a coalition of the willing, a Member State must not just demonstrate willingness but also relevant capability. Although the notion of collective defence remains firmly rooted in the North Atlantic Treaty Organization (NATO), the EU Member States agreed a mild version of the NATO/WEU (West European Union) Article V obligation to 'aid and assist' any one of their number who becomes the victim of armed aggression. More significantly the list of Petersberg tasks was expanded to include 'joint disarmament operations, humanitarian and rescue tasks, military advice and assistance tasks, conflict prevention and peace-keeping tasks, tasks of combat forces in crisis management including peace-making and post-conflict stabilization and the fight against terrorism including supporting third countries in their territories'. The European Defence Agency (which already exists with Alexander Weis replacing Nick Whitney as Director in 2007) is given a formal role in the treaty, charged amongst other things with trying to ensure that the EU gets a more effective military capability than at present from the total of €193 billion that the Member States spend annually on defence. Provision is made both for permanent structured co-operation (under extremely complex, possibly prohibitive arrangements) and for 'coalitions of the willing and able' (under much more permissive arrangements). The Treaty is expected to come into force by the start of 2009.

In 2007 the EU agreed on 80 CFSP joint actions and common positions (see Commission, 2008, pp. 198–205 for details). There were four new ESDP operations in Afghanistan, the Democratic Republic of the Congo, Kosovo (DRC), Chad and the Central African Republic. In Afghanistan[2] the EU Member States already contribute over 17,000 troops to the United Nations-mandated NATO force and will provide €600 million for reconstruction between 2007 and 2010. In addition, the EU established a police mission (EUPOL Afghanistan) although arguments continue as to whether it should

---

[2] *European Voice*, 1–7 March 2007, p. 13.

undertake work away from Kabul. In the DRC police and security missions (EUPOL RD Congo) were established. In Kosovo an EU planning team (EUPT Kosovo) was at work in anticipation of an EU police operation following the declaration of Kosovan independence. As well as sending 75 diplomats to Kosovo to establish the International Civilian Office, the EU police mission will involve over 100 police officers[3] (see Lavenex and Schimmelfennig, this volume). There was also a new military mission in Chad and the Central African Republic (EUFOR Tchad/RCA).

In addition, faced with Iran's continuing refusal to suspend uranium enrichment, the EU began towards the end of 2007 to consider strengthening its programme of sanctions. However, the majority of the Member States were reluctant to support French calls for further action without any progress in the UN Security Council, which appears unlikely to find support from Russia and China.

The Common Commercial Policy

As Alasdair Young (2007) has argued, the notion of 'European trade policy' needs now to be interpreted as multi-dimensional, encompassing elements of regulatory and social policy, and with the Common Commercial Policy – and thus the Directorate General (DG) Trade – sometimes only accounting for a relatively small part of what is going on. Yet even from a more restrictive version of commercial policy, there was plenty to observe during 2007. Alongside the global multilateral processes within the World Trade Organization (WTO), there was a strong upsurge of activity on inter-regional and 'plurilateral' trade negotiations, a series of trade disputes often with novel dimensions to them and a continuing review of the EU's 'trade defence' tools that reflected the Commission's attempts to respond to a changing global political economy. From a broader commercial policy perspective, there was plenty of evidence that the EU's regulatory 'model' could be deployed in an international context – with Charlie McCreevy, the Commissioner for the Internal Market and Services, adopting an increasingly active external role – and that purely commercial considerations were often accompanied by various aspects of human rights or by strong 'social' dynamics, for example, in policies on climate change. In November, the Commission (2007a; see also Howarth, this volume) adopted a Communication on 'A Single Market for 21st Century Europe' which brought a number of these issues together in the context of globalization. As evidence of the pervasive influence of globalization, the context in late 2007 was inexorably also shaped by the looming crisis

---

[3] *European Voice*, 6–12 December 2007, p. 13.

on global capital markets and the ways in which it might feed through into trade policy and trade disputes.

At the global multilateral level, the negotiations in the WTO's Doha Development Round remained dormant for much of the year, despite periodic attempts to revive them. At the beginning of the year, United States President George W. Bush and European Commission President José Manuel Barroso declared their common interest in re-invigorating the talks. New proposals emerged in February, with active support from the EU and Trade Commissioner Peter Mandelson, but it was clear that he was being closely watched to make sure that he did not become over-enthusiastic and offer additional concessions, especially on agriculture.[4] The EU was also active in pursuing negotiations through the newly-significant G-4 (the USA, the EU, Brazil and India), but hopes were progressively deflated during the summer and autumn. As the year went on, the pressures exerted by an increasingly protectionist Democratic Congress in the USA, by agricultural and other interests in the EU and by the approach of the US presidential election campaign made it increasingly difficult to maintain any momentum and the onset of the full US presidential campaign made it likely that little more would happen before the end of 2008.

The EU was much more active in pursuing inter-regional arrangements during the year – continuing a trend established in the wake of the unsuccessful WTO Ministerial meeting in Cancún in 2003. One dimension of this activity was constituted by renewed efforts to promote free trade agreements (FTAs) with a series of major emerging economies. In April, EU foreign ministers approved mandates for the opening of FTA negotiations with South Korea, India, the Association of Southeast Asian Nations (ASEAN), the Andean Community and the Central American countries. Significantly, these negotiations would focus on issues not covered by the WTO talks, including investment, intellectual property and the like; this could be interpreted as a renewed attempt to deal with the so-called 'Singapore Issues', which the EU had failed to advance in the WTO. Discussion of negotiations with specific partners or groups can be found below in the appropriate sections.

As noted above, during 2007 the Commission's DG for Trade reviewed the EU's 'trade defence' instruments, including anti-dumping. This review had been announced by Mandelson during 2006 and a Green Paper on the matter evoked a very strong response from both producer and consumer groups within the EU – so strong in fact that publication of the resulting report and proposals was deferred on several occasions. Whilst there had been a general decline in the use of anti-dumping and anti-subsidy measures – including their

---

[4] *European Voice*, 8–14 February 2007, p. 7.

use by the Commission – during 2006 and early 2007, there were signs of an upturn in their use as 2007 unfolded. When some advance details of possible proposals from the review surfaced at the end of the year, these included provision for exemptions for those EU manufacturers who had located production abroad. As might be expected, these exemptions led to an outcry from those producers who saw themselves as properly 'European'. By the end of the year no formal proposals had been made, but this was clearly an issue of considerable sensitivity.

Development Co-operation Policy and Humanitarian Aid

December 2007 was the deadline set by the Commission for the negotiation of (reciprocal) Economic Partnership Agreements (EPAs) to replace the EU's established system of unilateral preferential agreements (see Africa section below). In addition to complaints about its hasty implementation of the EPAs, the Commission was also criticized for its part in the likely failure of the international system to meet the UN's Millennium Goals for development.[5] In particular the EU will not meet its own target of allocating 20 per cent of all its development aid to education and health. Non-governmental organizations (NGOs) working in the development area have consistently criticized the Commission for its policy of giving large sums of its aid (over 30 per cent in the case of the European Development Fund, EDF) directly to governments as general budgetary support. This practice occurs particularly in Africa, whereas in Asia and Latin America aid is more specifically targeted. The suspicion is that the Commission is using this money to try to persuade governments to sign the EPAs.

In 2007 the ninth tranche of EDF money was due to expire and for the first time ever the Commission was able to report that it had committed all its available funds in advance of the start date (January 2008) of the next tranche. In 2007, €3.63 billion was made available under the EDF, although, as in previous years, there were arguments about the diversion of some funds from development aid to political and military assistance goals. Specifically the Commission was criticized for using EDF money (€45 million) to support the African Union force in Darfur, whose costs overran because of the delayed arrival of the promised UN force. This practice contradicted a 2006 agreement between the Commission and the EP not to divert development funding for political and security objectives. The Parliament also expressed concern early in 2007 that development funding destined for Asia and Latin America might be used to finance counter-terrorism in Indonesia, Malaysia, Pakistan, and Columbia.

[5] *European Voice*, 5–11 July 2007, p. 12.

The provisions for financing the CFSP in the Lisbon Treaty, mentioned above, seem designed to make access to the EU budget easier and thus reducing the scope for these financial conflicts in the future. Whilst the arrangements in the Lisbon Treaty could bring an end to these regular arguments about the legal basis for CFSP/ESDP-related expenditure, in the future the High Representative may well be able to exploit his dual role in the Commission and the Council to increase quite legally the budget for the CFSP at the expense of development projects.

In 2007 the EU distributed €768 million in humanitarian aid to 85 projects around the world, as well as €270 million in food aid that reached some 25 million recipients. Nevertheless, NGOs and the European Court of Auditors criticized the EU for a lack of consistency and transparency in its management of its €200 million-plus Refugee Fund. The Court of Auditors noted that the Commission's rules for spending this money were interpreted in very different ways by the Member States. The Commission for its part argued that this 'flexibility' was one of the Refugee Fund's strengths, given that the member states faced a wide range of differing problems with regard to refugees and asylum seekers.

II. Regional Themes

Russia

Relations between the EU and Russia worsened over the year as the Russian government became increasingly preoccupied with the internal politics associated with parliamentary elections in December 2007 and presidential elections in March 2008 (see also Light, this volume). Two EU–Russia summits were held: in Samara, Russia in May and in Mafra, Portugal in October, but increased tensions ensured that little progress was made either with the renewal of the Partnership and Co-operation Agreement or with giving substance to the concept of the four economic spaces. Signs of increasing tensions included Russia's hostility towards Estonia over the removal of a Soviet war memorial; its refusal to accept Polish meat products (and its implicit threat to extend this ban to all EU meat products); and its aggressive and restrictive approach towards the supply of oil to Lithuania and gas to Ukraine throughout the year soured the atmosphere. Divisions also surfaced within the EU, with some of the older Member States seemingly reluctant to demonstrate significant solidarity with those newer members (but also the UK which expelled four Russian diplomats following Russia's refusal to co-operate over the murder of Alexander Litvinenko in London) who were the target of Russian hostility (for details see Light, this volume).

The EU sought to contain these internal divisions[6] by adopting firmer and more united stands on a number of issues, including Russian membership of the WTO,[7] Russia's behaviour in Chechnya and Russian intransigence with regard to the activities of EU energy companies operating in Russia. The Russian government took exception to EU proposals that restrictions be placed on Russian ownership of EU-based energy production and logistic enterprises if the rights of EU firms operating in Russia were not respected and to date nothing has come of a Commission proposal for a telephone hot-line between Brussels and Moscow[8] to deal with any future energy crises between Russia and either the EU or, more likely, individual EU Member States.

Africa

The EU's strategic approach to Africa in 2007 was given an additional incentive by a growing awareness of the influence that China is beginning to exert on that continent.[9] The major event of the year was the second EU–Africa summit conference (the first met in Cairo in 2001), which was held in Lisbon in December (see Ferreira-Pereira, this volume). The summit agreed a programme of eight strategic partnerships, which make up a large part of the EU–Africa strategy that was the centrepiece of the summit conclusions. The eight partnerships cover: peace and security; democratic governance and human rights; trade and regional integration, including infra-structure; the millennium development goals; climate change; migration, mobility and employment; science, information society and space and, significantly given the Chinese and Indian interest, energy.[10]

The summit established the African Union as the EU's most significant institutional partner in Africa and this was underlined by the decision to appoint an EU envoy to Africa with a comprehensive brief to cover security, development and humanitarian aid. Despite British attempts to have Baroness Amos, a former Foreign Office Minister, appointed to this new post, Solana decided to give it to Koen Vervaeke, a member of his cabinet previously responsible for Africa. Vervaeke's post is a double-hatted one and he is both the EU special representative to Africa and the Head of the EU delegation to the African Union – jobs previously held by representatives of the Council and the Commission respectively. The British government did not send a minister to the EU–Africa summit because of the presence there of President

[6] *Financial Times*, 18 May 2007, p. 15.
[7] *European Voice*, 3–9 May 2007, p. 1.
[8] *European Voice*, 8–14 March 2007, p. 4.
[9] *European Voice*, 6–12 September 2007, p. 9, 29 November–5 December 2007, p. 20 and 6–12 December 2007, p. 17).
[10] *European Voice*, 21 November–9 December 2007, p. 21.

Robert Mugabe of Zimbabwe, who is generally prevented from travelling to EU states by EU sanctions against him and other senior Zimbabwean officials.[11]

Towards the end of 2007 the Commission was criticized by some Member States for its determination to persuade African countries to sign EPAs by 1 January 2008 to replace the ACP unilateral preferential schemes, which were deemed to be incompatible with WTO rules. The Dutch, German, Irish and Swedish governments have argued[12] that the African states are being forced to reciprocate the EU's own tariff cutting too quickly and in a way that will significantly disadvantage them. The French and Spanish governments have adopted a less generous approach and have sought to exploit transitional arrangements to protect their agricultural producers.

The EU's growing interest in political and military security issues in Africa, in addition to its heavy engagement with economic development issues, was reflected in its continuing involvement in the conflict in Darfur and in Somalia using resources drawn form the African Peace Facility. The EU's military mission to Chad is designed to complement UN–AU (AMIS 1 and 11) action in Darfur by providing security for the 200,000-plus refugees from Darfur who are sheltering in Chad. The police mission to the Democratic Republic of the Congo (EUPOL RD Congo) is designed to build on the groundwork laid down by the previous mission (EUPOL Kinshasa).

Asia

In the *General Report on the Activities of the European Union* for 2007 (Commission, 2008), Asia is dealt with under two headings: 'emerging countries' and 'regional approaches'. This sums up the tenor of relations with the continent during the year. On the one hand, major – if not obsessive – attention was devoted to China and India, whilst on the other hand there were key moves towards the revival or the initiation of inter-regional relationships. Both of these processes could be subsumed under the general heading of the 'search for partnership' in the EU's external relations. Although both processes undeniably have political and security overtones, the activities of 2007 were led by commercial interests and they encapsulated the kinds of multi-dimensional commercial realities noted earlier.

There is no doubt that China claimed the lion's share of attention from the EU during 2007. This is not surprising, given the ways in which China enters both into the specific commercial interests of the EU and also (and increasingly) into the broader management of the global political economy. During

[11] *European Voice*, 2–28 November 2007, p. 4.
[12] *Financial Times*, 23 November 2007, p. 8.

2007, the EU made consistent efforts to underpin its growing partnership with Beijing and to act on issues of specific significance. The partnership was buttressed by the results of the annual EU–China summit meeting at the end of November, which saw a movement towards what was described as a 'strategic economic dialogue'[13] focused on the management of trade deficits and the improvement of access for European investment in China itself. As in other areas of commercial policy, the regulatory framework formed a significant part of exchanges between Brussels and Beijing both at the summit and throughout the year. These exchanges extended to the management of currencies, with a visit by a financial 'troika' consisting of the European Central Bank president, the chair of the 'Eurogroup' and the commissioner for monetary affairs in November. The aim was to establish an ongoing dialogue about currencies and their management.

There was also a series of specific issues and disputes arising from China's super-competitive exporting prowess. One such issue concerned the continuation of the quotas on textile imports to the EU from China, imposed in 2005. These were due to expire at the end of 2007 and not surprisingly some EU producers wanted them to be extended. There was also a suspicion that these interests would wait until the Portuguese Presidency in the second half of the year to show their hand, since the Portuguese were assumed to be more sympathetic to textile producers' concerns than the Germans. Nonetheless, the quotas were not extended; instead, a system of close monitoring was established combined with improved communication between the Commission and Chinese producers. A second trade issue arose over the export of potentially dangerous toys from China. This issue was also picked up in the USA during the year, and was seized upon by Commission officials as a potential area of EU–US collaboration in relations with China. At the same time, a potential anti-dumping case concerning the export of energy-efficient light bulbs from China was temporarily averted by extending deadlines for a year. Typically of the 21st century, this dispute ranges EU firms producing in Europe (particularly Osram/Siemens) against those who actually produce in China (especially Philips), a situation that makes it hard for the Commission to find a comfortable solution. A more traditional concern was that with massively increased steel exports from China to the EU, which had doubled in 2007 compared with 2006[14] and led to threats of anti-dumping action. Trade Commissioner Peter Mandelson spent considerable time during the year warning the Chinese about a European backlash if such issues were not resolved.[15]

---

[13] *Financial Times*, 27 September 2007, p. 8.
[14] *Financial Times*, 28 September 2007, p. 10.
[15] *Financial Times*, 12 June 2007, p. 8.

India is at an earlier point on its 'partnership trajectory' than China. Whilst a proclaimed 'strategic partner' of the EU, it poses a number of problems for Brussels given its resistance to calls for market-opening (both bilaterally and within the WTO) and its reluctance to develop a political dialogue as opposed to commercial links.[16] Thus, when negotiations for an EU–India FTA and for a Partnership and Co-operation Agreement were opened in May 2007, they almost immediately encountered issues of market access and also of human rights. The EU includes human rights and 'good governance' clauses in its agreements as a matter of course, but the Indians were very reluctant to go along with this. So the main theme of the year was whether a FTA could actually be concluded, and if so whether there was any prospect at all of moving beyond a purely commercial arrangement into full 'partnership and co-operation'. During 2007, a lingering dispute over India's import duties on wines and spirits was resolved, with improved access for EU producers.

Alongside these two key bilateral partnerships, the EU was busy during 2007 in the cause of promoting group-to-group inter-regional relations. There were two key focuses to this. First, the EU, as already noted, moved to develop its relationship with ASEAN by initiating negotiations for a FTA. These proceeded during the second half of the year, but were troubled by ASEAN members' determination to have Burma (Myanmar) included. This condition was a particular problem in the autumn, when the Burmese dictatorship violently clamped down on dissidents, to international condemnation from the EU, amongst others. But in general, the commercial aspects of the FTA were elevated above those of the more general political situation.

A second area of inter-regional activity saw the EU further develop its approach to the countries of central Asia. On 27 March, the EU troika (Commission president, Council president, High Representative) met with the foreign ministers of Kazakhstan (the EU's favourite partner in the region), Kyrgyzstan, Tajikistan, Turkmenistan and Uzbekistan[17] (the EU's least favourite partner).[18] Unsurprisingly, issues of energy security and human rights featured large on the agenda, as well as EU commitments to double the levels of aid for the period 2007–13 (from €375 to €750 million). In June, the European Council adopted a new Central Asia strategy, which can be anticipated to lead to further actions in 2008. As a final contribution to inter-regional relations between the EU and Asia during 2007, the EU was granted

---

[16] *European Voice*, 3–9 May 2007, pp. 19–23; *Financial Times*, 5 March 2007, p. 9.
[17] *European Voice*, 2–29 August 2007, p. 147.
[18] *European Voice*, 16–23 May 2007, p. 9.

observer status in the South Asian Association for Regional Co-operation (SAARC), and attended its summit in New Delhi on 3–4 April.

Latin America

In keeping with themes exposed elsewhere in this article, EU activity towards and with Latin America followed two major strands during 2007: bilateral and inter-regional. The most significant development took place at the bilateral level, with the inauguration of a new EU policy towards Brazil. At the end of May, the Commission adopted a new Communication, 'Towards an EU–Brazil Strategic Partnership' (Commission, 2007b), which demonstrated clearly the intention to deal with Brazil on a basis similar to that adopted for China and India. The partnership was formally proclaimed at the first EU–Brazil summit on 4 July 2007 and enabled the Commission to claim that this completed the 'set' of strategic partnerships with the BRIC countries (Brazil, Russia, India, China) (see also Ferreira-Pereira, this volume). Also at the bilateral level, the EU continued its established links with Chile and Mexico, through meetings respectively of the EU–Chile Association Council and the EU–Mexico Joint Committee.

This growth of bilateralism, however, has to be seen alongside the continuing inter-regional engagements of the EU in Latin America. As noted earlier, FTA negotiations were initiated with the Andean Community and with Central American countries, whilst there were meetings with the Rio Group in Santo Domingo during April. The EU–Brazil strategic partnership itself included the aim of concluding association talks between the EU and Mercosur (the 'southern common market'). At the same time, preparations for a further EU–Latin America Summit took place. The reality of EU–Latin American relations is that of a multi-layered inter-regionalism bringing together bilateral, plurilateral and inter-continental relationships.

The United States, Japan and other Industrialized Countries

In a way, the United States is the EU's oldest, most comprehensive and most significant 'strategic partner' and the events of 2007 confirmed this assertion. The relationships between the EU and the US span the political, the economic and the security domains; often, these link together in a complex mesh of competition and convergence which makes it difficult to distinguish between what is 'European', what 'American' and what is concerned with the broader global arena (McGuire and Smith, 2008). Whilst in some ways 2007 might have appeared a relatively calm year in transatlantic relations, there was ample evidence of their continuing complexity and ambiguity. When Commission President Barroso and High Representative Solana visited

Washington in January 2007, they reflected on what they saw as a 'turning point' in transatlantic relations.[19] Equally, the incoming German Presidency placed transatlantic relations at the top of its list of priorities. As the year progressed, it was clear in all aspects of the relationship that the US mattered greatly to the EU, but there were suggestions in some American quarters that the EU might not matter quite so much to the US.[20] The suspicion that the EU might be taken just a little for granted could have grown. It was also clear by the end of 2007 that adverse developments in the US economy still had the potential to severely affect the EU as a whole, without Europeans being able to exert significant leverage on events. As a result, the priority given to EU–US relations did not guarantee an easy or stable ride.

This said, the initiatives produced and the energy injected by German Chancellor Angela Merkel and the German Presidency clearly had a significant payoff in the realm of 'transatlantic governance'. Merkel pushed for a new 'transatlantic economic partnership' that had its centre of gravity in regulatory co-operation – precisely one of the issues that contributes to the broadening scope of EU commercial policy as a whole.[21] As the regular EU–US summit approached in April, there was increasing attention paid to the content and mechanisms of such a renewed partnership, with Commissioner McCreevy playing an active role in promoting partnership in the regulation of financial services. The summit, held on 30 April in Washington, adopted a 'framework for advancing transatlantic economic integration between the USA and the EU' (TEC, 2007a). The framework identified a set of priority areas for collaboration – intellectual property, secure trade, financial market regulation, innovation and technology and investment – and the mechanism through which this was to be taken forward: the Transatlantic Economic Council (TEC).

Whilst the TEC could be seen as the logical successor to the Senior Level Group that had monitored progress on the New Transatlantic Agenda established in 1995, in fact it is designed to muster much more high-level political commitment and to focus on the delivery of results rather than on simply monitoring progress and the process. It is co-chaired by Günter Verheugen, a Commission Vice-President, and Allen Hubbard, Assistant to the President for Economic Policy and Director of the US National Economic Council and supported by an Advisory Group representing three key sets of stakeholders: the Transatlantic Business Dialogue, the Transatlantic Consumer Dialogue and the Transatlantic Legislative Dialogue.[22] The first meeting of the TEC

---

[19] *European Voice*, 21 December 2006–10 January 2007, p. 4.
[20] *European Voice*, 4–11 April 2007, p. 16.
[21] *European Voice*, 11–17 January 2007, p. 14.
[22] *Financial Times*, 22 June 2007, p. 6.

took place on 9 November 2007, and reported progress not only on defining its agenda but also on implementing measures in the priority areas (TEC, 2007b, 2007c). On the face of it, this progress represents a further enhancement of 'transatlantic governance,' and a recognition by both the US and the EU that they have strongly convergent interests in key areas of regulatory policy, as well as on central issues of broader commercial policy. It is likely to face some severe tests in 2008 and beyond in the context of global financial uncertainty.

Inevitably, alongside this upsurge in co-operation at the broad commercial and regulatory level, a number of important disputes and negotiations continued between the EU and the US. One of the most significant was the so-called 'open skies' negotiations, which led to a first-stage agreement in March. This agreement, to be implemented from 30 March 2008, opens up US and EU airports to new carriers, and is designed to lead on to further agreements after 2010 on such issues as the ownership of airlines (a special problem for the US, where national security and other considerations come into play). The agreement can best be described as partial and preliminary, but it is likely to lead to further consolidation in the EU airline market for those carriers involved in the transatlantic trade and to open up significant new routes between the transatlantic partners.

The partial success of 'open skies' went alongside continuing tensions over the 'Airbus dispute' in which the US accuses European governments of unfairly subsidizing the manufacture of Airbus aircraft. Washington had complained to the WTO – and the EU had counter-complained – about this in 2006, and proceedings started in 2007 with the gathering of information. This led to mutual accusations of unfair play involving very large amounts of claimed subsidy, with Boeing claiming a cumulative total of €200 billion given to Airbus particularly in the form of launch-aid, and Airbus responding via the Commission that Boeing also received subsidies from the US. By the end of the year, curious things were happening: as the US dollar declined, Airbus (whose products are sold in dollars) looked increasingly seriously at the possibility of moving significant production to the US, whilst some of its products – notably the A320 model – were scheduled for production in China and elsewhere. In such a context, arriving at a definitive judgement on who was subsidizing whom and for whose benefit became a very complex matter.

Other EU–US disputes during the year included one very old one – the banana dispute which was resurrected in the middle of the year – a very new one, about biodiesel exports and their tariff treatment and a continuing confrontation about the legality of online gambling, in which the US was accused of discriminating against EU-based operators. Finally, there was a confrontation embodying many of the aspects of a globalizing world, in which the US claimed that under the Information Technology Agreement reached in the WTO during the late 1990s there should be tariff-free entry into the EU for such items as flat-screen televisions, digital cameras and computer games (these being based on what in the 1990s appeared to be very high technology). This confrontation remained unsolved at the end of 2007.

The EU and the US have been embroiled in disputes over the ways to manage climate change since the late 1990s, and in 2007, this mutual entanglement came to a fresh head with the approach of the Bali conference at which a successor to the Kyoto Protocol was to be set in motion. During the year, the Commission and the German Presidency in particular tried to persuade the US to relent on its opposition to the setting of targets for emissions, using the Germans' chairing of the G8 summit at Heiligendamm in June to exert additional pressure. Meanwhile, President Bush set out to arrange a 'spoiler' meeting in Washington during September, which made no progress but did deflect attention from the broader efforts. At one point during the year, it was also reported that the Commission had held informal talks with California with a view to joint efforts on emissions trading.[23] Whatever the significance of such novel channels, by the time the Bali conference met in December the stage was set for confrontation. This duly occurred until, at the last moment, the US delegation caved in and appeared to sign up to a negotiation for a Kyoto successor. Much remained to be clarified about the real meaning of this change, but it seemed to herald at least some possibility of progress along the EU's preferred lines.

One feature of the climate change discussions during 2007 was the way in which as time went by they became infused with a linked debate about energy security. Indeed, it seemed to be a US tactic to link the two areas and to use the security argument to offset the environmental case. Whether or not this would succeed, it did demonstrate the ways in which security matters for the EU have become inexorably linked to many of its more traditional concerns. So the EU has become much more of a security organization because the nature of security has shifted. In terms of relations with the US, the energy security issue is only one example of the ways in which US policies have created new linkages and pressures.

More familiar, perhaps is the 'war on terror' and the ways in which this has created new challenges for the EU. During 2007, the Europeans found themselves engaged in continuing frictions with Washington over the use of 'extraordinary rendition' when dealing with terror suspects – an issue in which the EP has an abiding interest – and over the use of 'passenger name records' (PNR) to gather information on air travellers. The latter issue, and an

---

[23] *European Voice*, 2–29 August 2007, p. 12.

earlier agreement between the Commission and Washington to release data on Europeans heading for the US, had been the subject of legal challenge, and as a result, a new agreement was concluded during the summer of 2007.[24] Significantly, this agreement was arrived at through use of 'pillar three' mechanisms, which gave it a different and less challengeable legal base from the previous agreement. Nonetheless, it aroused similar suspicions about the uses to which the data transferred to the US might be put and about the length of time (up to 15 years) for which it would be held. Alongside this set of tensions, similar issues arose about the transfer of banking records to the US by the SWIFT interbank clearing organization – again, only partly resolved by an agreement during the year. And finally, there continued to be frictions about the US 'visa waiver' system, which does not extend to all new Member States of the EU. Proposals passed by Congress for further restrictions, including online 'pre-registration' for those wishing to visit the US, added to the feeling that some Europeans were being discriminated against, but the US continued to insist on its tests for admission to the waiver scheme, including (for example) the rate of visa refusals for those wishing to become part of it (see also Monar, this volume).

Finally, what of 'traditional' diplomacy and security policies in this picture of complexity and linkages? Some of the relevant issues are dealt with elsewhere (for example, the activities of the EU in the Middle East), but it is important to note the extent to which the EU was able to keep step with the US on some key outstanding issues. First, the problem of Iran's nuclear weapons potential, which had created tensions for several years, saw relatively little open confrontation between the EU and the US during 2007. Part of the reason for this was that by the end of 2006, the EU had swung at least partly behind the US's call for stiffer sanctions and these had been ratified by the UN. Another reason was that during 2007, the Iranian government, and particularly President Ahmadinejad, became increasing provocative in their claims to be on the verge of significant breakthroughs in the search for nuclear weapons capacity; as a result, there was a move to impose even stiffer sanctions than those already in place. There were still EU–US tensions, especially over a US threat to punish business people dealing with Iran and EU governments providing export credits to Tehran, but this threat did not lead to open confrontation.

Alongside the EU–US relationship, the rest of the 'industrial world' received fairly short shrift in 2007. Relations with Japan remained constructive and it is to be noted how far Japan has receded from the consciousness of EU policy-makers (compared with China in particular). As noted earlier, FTA negotiations were opened with South Korea and dialogues were maintained

---

[24] *European Voice*, 20–26 September 2007, p. 18.

with Australia and New Zealand. Canada made efforts to move towards the same kind of relationship with the EU as that encompassed by the new 'transatlantic economic partnership'. But it is fair to say that in 2007, the EU–US relationship dominated and that there is every sign that it will continue to do so.

Conclusions

At the beginning of this chapter, we noted that activity on the part of the EU in its relations with the rest of the world does not necessarily add up to a strategy. Significantly, as can be seen from the chapter itself, even the promulgation of formal strategies can be subject to this criticism – new 'strategic partners' or umbrella strategies towards key regions fall foul of the complexities, linkages and politicization processes we have observed throughout our review. By the end of 2007, there were a number of important elements contributing further to this problem: the increasing preoccupation of the USA with presidential elections, the consequent inattention to processes such as the Doha Development Round and the financial turbulence created by the sub-prime mortgage crisis and its ramifications (see Johnson and Verdun, both this volume). Meanwhile, the impact of a new regime in Russia and of political changes in other regions from the Balkans through southwest Asia to Latin America remained to be seen. In many ways, this exemplifies a key issue surrounding the EU's external policies in the 2000s: the ways in which an essentially deliberative process of institution-building and consolidation within the Union can be effectively related to a turbulent if not chaotic world.

Key Readings

Commission (2008) provides a good review of the external activities of the EU (pp. 158–94) along with footnoted links to all the relevant EU documentation. The *European Voice* (2007) provides a useful summary of recent ESDP developments. Whitman (2008) provides an excellent analysis of the external relations reforms proposed in the Lisbon Treaty. *CFSP Forum* is published bi-monthly by FORNET («http://www.fornet.info») and contains numerous articles on current CFSP and ESDP activities.

References

Allen, D. and Smith, M. (2007) 'Relations with the Rest of the World'. *JCMS*, Vol. 45, s1, pp. 163–81.

Commission of the European Communities (2007a) 'A Single Market for 21st Century Europe'. COM(2007)24, 20 November.

Commission of the European Communities (2007b) 'Towards an EU–Brazil Strategic Partnership'. COM(2007)281, 30 May.

Commission of the European Communities (2008) *General Report on the Activities of the European Union, 2007*. SEC (2007) 1000 final, 25 January.

European Voice (2007) 'Security and Defence: Special Report', 7–13 June 2007, pp. 25–31.

McGuire, S. and Smith, M. (2008) *The European Union and the United States: Competition and Convergence in the Global Arena* (Basingstoke: Palgrave Macmillan).

TEC (2007a) 'Framework for Advancing Transatlantic Economic Integration Between the European Union and the United States of America'. Adopted at the EU–US Summit, Washington DC (Transatlantic Economic Council), 30 April. Available at «http://ec.europa.eu/trade/issues/bilateral/countries/usa/index_en.htm».

TEC (2007b) 'Joint Statement of the Transatlantic Council, November 9, 2007'. Available at «http://ec.europa.eu/trade/issues/bilateral/countries/usa/index_en.htm».

TEC (2007c) 'Review of Progress Under the Framework for Advancing Transatlantic Economic Integration Between the United States of America and the European Union'. Available at «http://ec.europa.eu/trade/issues/bilateral/countries/usa/index_en.htm».

Whitman, R. (2008) 'Foreign, Security and Defence Policy and the Lisbon Treaty: Significant or Cosmetic reforms?' Global Europe Papers 2008/1, University of Bath.

Young, A.R. (2007) 'Trade Politics Ain't What it Used to Be'. *JCMS*, Vol. 45, No. 4, pp. 789–811.

JCMS 2008 Volume 46 Annual Review pp. 183–213

Political Developments in the EU Member States

KAREN HENDERSON
University of Leicester

NICK SITTER
The Norwegian School of Management BI

Introduction

Domestic politics are becoming increasingly important in a 27 Member State strong European Union (EU) where at least half a dozen national parliamentary elections take place each year. Whereas the work of a 12- or 15-state EU was interrupted by the occasional election, or even change of prime minister or governing coalition, hardly a month now goes by without a national election, a cabinet crisis or change of government in one of the Member States. In this respect 2007 was an average year: national elections were held in eight states, and brought about substantial government change in six of these and another five states saw a partial change of government. In short, as shown in Table 1, 14 Member States saw elections, changes in the governing coalition, a new prime minister, or a government's temporary resignation. In addition, two presidents were directly elected. Some of the changes – including the fall of the politically awkward government in Poland and the election of President Nicolas Sarkozy in France – are inevitably more important to the EU than others (see Dinan, this volume).

EU politics have long been a two-level game, in which domestic political developments shape policy-making at the EU level and vice versa. Enlargement has affected the process in both directions, but not in the way that had generally been feared. A recent extensive investigation of the EU's institutional practices since 2004 (Wallace, 2007) found that the increased number of Member States has not led to gridlock or more blocking minorities in the

Table 1: Elections and Government Change in the EU Member States in 2007

	No or minor government/coalition changes		New prime minister	Changed coalition	Entirely new coalition
No parliamentary elections	Germany Luxembourg Cyprus Malta Italy[a] Spain Portugal	Lithuania Slovenia Hungary Slovakia Bulgaria Romania Sweden	UK Latvia[a]	Netherlands Austria Czech Rep.	
Parliamentary elections	Greece	Denmark	France	Estonia Ireland Finland	Belgium[b] Poland

Source: Author's own data.

Notes: [a] The Italian and Latvian governments collapsed in 2007, but the same coalition returned to office; [b] The June 2007 election left Belgium without an effective government at the end of the year; a temporary three-month caretaker coalition was agreed in December.

Council of Ministers. However, even if the commeasurably larger number of elections and changes of government since enlargement has not affected EU-level decision making detrimentally, the sheer number and frequency of national domestic political events have raised the profile of such events in Brussels.

At the same time European integration has become politically more contested in the Member States over the last decade and populist domestic opposition is often coupled with euroscepticism (Taggart and Szczerbiak, 2008). In 2007, European questions played a role in the Polish and French elections, and Dutch, Swedish and British parties were divided over how to proceed with ratification of the Lisbon Treaty. In many of the new Member States the governments' need to manage relations with its EU partners and the EU institutions at times seems to take precedence over domestic political management and communication. In Britain and Italy, the reverse is sometimes the case: the effect of domestic political games on Brussels is not always taken into account. Thus this is a two-way relationship: the EU provides a second arena for domestic political competition and EU politics shapes domestic political developments. Recent changes in this two-way, two-level game are a central theme in this article.

2007 was a comparatively quiet year in terms of the political contestation of European integration in the Member States after the political turbulence that followed in the wake of French and Dutch voters' rejection of the EU

Table 2: Share of Respondents (%) who Describe EU Membership as a 'Good Thing'

| | 2007 | | 2006 | | 2005 | |
	Autumn	Spring	Autumn	Spring	Autumn	Spring
Luxembourg	82	74	74	72	82	80
Netherlands	79	77	72	74	70	77
Belgium	74	70	69	65	59	67
Ireland	74	76	78	77	73	75
Poland	*71*	*67*	*62*	*56*	*54*	*53*
Romania	*71*	*67*				
Denmark	69	66	61	65	56	59
Spain	68	73	62	72	66	66
Germany	67	65	58	57	53	58
Lithuania	*65*	*63*	*62*	*59*	*57*	*59*
Greece	62	55	57	53	54	56
Estonia	*61*	*66*	*56*	*51*	*41*	*48*
France	60	52	50	49	46	51
EU-27 (25 until 2007)	**58**	**57**	**53**	**55**	**50**	**54**
Portugal	58	55	50	47	54	61
Slovakia	*58*	*64*	*61*	*55*	*50*	*54*
Slovenia	*56*	*58*	*57*	*54*	*43*	*49*
Sweden	55	50	49	49	39	44
Malta	*54*	*51*	*45*	*44*	*43*	*40*
Bulgaria	*52*	*55*				
Italy	50	51	52	56	50	56
Finland	45	42	39	39	38	45
Czech Republic	*45*	*46*	*51*	*52*	*44*	*49*
Cyprus	*40*	*44*	*47*	*49*	*41*	*43*
Hungary	*40*	*37*	*39*	*49*	*39*	*42*
Austria	38	36	36	34	32	37
Latvia	*37*	*37*	*43*	*37*	*36*	*42*
UK	34	39	34	42	34	36

Sources: Standard Eurobarometer, nos. 63–8, available at «http://ec.europa.eu/public_opinion».
Note: 2004 and 2007 accession states in italics.

Constitutional Treaty in referendums in 2005. By the end of the year only Ireland (which is constitutionally obliged to do so) was set to hold a referendum on the new Lisbon Treaty, although the question was subject to considerable political debate in the UK, as well as in Denmark, France, the Netherlands and Sweden. As for public opinion, the two 2007 *Eurobarometer* surveys showed a general improvement in attitudes towards the EU across the board (see Table 2). The share of respondents expressing approval for the EU increased in the EU-27 as a whole in 2007 compared to the EU-25 in 2006 and in 16 individual Member States.

I. Central Western Europe – Power Sharing and Public Policy Reform?

2007 saw a return to normal politics in central western Europe after a period of considerable political uncertainty. The 'no' votes in the French and Dutch referendums on the Constitutional Treaty in the summer of 2005 were part of a broader pattern of instability and a backlash against the mainstream centre-right and -left political parties. In 2002 the success of the far-right List Pim Fortuyn in the Netherlands' parliamentary elections and of Jean-Marie Le Pen in the first round of the French presidential elections had raised questions about the future impact of the far right, particularly in the light of the participation of the Austrian Freedom Party in that country's governing coalition and the Flemish far right's campaign for secession from Belgium. Even the German mainstream parties were being challenged from the flanks, by the greens and the socialist left. Only Luxembourg seemed an island of political stability. Jean-Claude Juncker completed his 12th year as Prime Minister in 2007.

Come 2007, the political stability of the early 1990s seemed to be returning. The challenges from the left and right flanks may not have diminished, but the mainstream centre-right and -left parties looked more confident addressing these challenges. A grand coalition between Social Democrats and Christian Democrats had been established in Germany in 2006, and by early 2007 similar coalitions were in place in the Netherlands and Austria. In the latter two cases the grand coalitions partly reflected a return to the consociational democracy (or power-sharing) that had given rise to right-wing populist protest in the first place; a sign that the mainstream parties were once again dominating the political stage. In Belgium the lack of a functioning government in the second half of 2007 was dealt with relatively calmly, and a caretaker government was eventually put in place.

The most dramatic development in central western Europe in 2007 was Nicolas Sarkozy's victory in the French presidential election. The centre right's subsequent triumph in the parliamentary elections signalled the beginning of a period of radical reform, which had not fizzled out by the year's end. With the main contenders in the presidential election taking different stances on how to handle the new EU treaty then under negotiation, the European question was defused once the presidential election was complete and the political turbulence brought about by the 2005 referendum came to an end (see also Dinan in this issue).

The French Presidential and Parliamentary Elections

The central themes in the presidential and parliamentary elections in France were political stability and policy change. After the shock of National Front candidate Le Pen making it to the second round in the 2002 presidential elections, the 2007 election was very much a contest between the mainstream parties. The main centre-right and -left candidates worked hard to unite their camps and to prevent serious challenges from their respective flanks. In this, they were successful. At the same time, however, all three leading candidates for the presidency promised a renewal for French politics – a *rupture* with the 12 years of Jacques Chirac's presidency. The past two years' anti-government protests and the president's poor poll ratings had contributed to a sense of crisis on the centre right. Therefore, although Nicolas Sarkozy represented the incumbent Union for a Popular Movement (UMP), he resigned from the government and ran a campaign that promised renewal and radical reform. On the centre-left the Socialists' Ségolène Royal, who hoped to become France's first female president, had won the party's primary election on a modernizing platform. In the centre, François Bayrou of the Union for French Democracy (UDF) offered a strong third alternative to the two main parties and promised a bipartisan government.

The main surprise in the 2007 electoral campaign was Bayrou's strong showing in successive opinion polls, which at times indicated that he would be likely to win the second round if he made it to the run-off. During the six weeks before the first round Bayrou gained considerable ground, particularly as Ségolène Royal's campaign suffered from internal divisions and defections. In contrast, the Sarkozy campaign was better run, and it presented a more coherent programme that focused on economic liberalization and being tough on law and order. In the end however, on 22 April, the two main candidates carried the day (see Table 3), helped by a high turnout and tactical voting among right- and left-wing voters for Sarkozy and Royal respectively. The fear of seeing their side fail to make it to the second round, as in 2002, prompted left-wing voters to rally behind Royal. As Deloy (2007) observed, 'the political arena is bipolar again'. Apart from the three front-runners only one other candidate polled more than 5 per cent: the National Front's Le Pen. Sarkozy took a greater share of the first round vote than any other candidate since 1974.

With the centrist Bayrou out of the race, but refusing to endorse either of his erstwhile rivals, the campaign for the second round became a contest between clearly defined centre-left and centre-right alternatives. Although both candidates argued that the country faced a crisis and emphasized the need for change, they did so from distinct platforms. The central theme in Sarkozy's campaign was economic liberalization, with a focus on the need for

Table 3: French Presidential Elections, May/June 2007

	1st round 2007, 22 April (%)	*2nd round 2007,* 6 May (%)
Nicolas Sarkozy (UMP)	31.2	53.1
Ségolène Royal (PS)	25.9	46.9
François Bayrou (UDF)	18.6	
Jean-Marie Le Pen (FN)	10.4	
Oliver Besancenot (LCR)	4.1	
Philippe de Villiers (MPF)	2.2	
Others	7.6	

Source: Deloy (2007); Marthaler (2007a).
Notes: LCR: Communist Revolutionary League; MPF: the conservative Movement for France.

more radical reforms and flexible labour markets. Opinion polls, however, showed that it was on law and order and immigration that he enjoyed the biggest lead over Royal (Marthaler, 2007a). Royal's less coherent campaign, lesser political experience and weaker performance in debates combined to yield a decisive victory for Sarkozy and a strong mandate for radical reform. The centre right carried this momentum into the campaign for the parliamentary elections, whereas questions about the future leadership of the Socialist party were raised immediately after Royal's defeat. In the centre Bayrou lost no time in organizing a centrist alternative for the parliamentary elections: on 10 May the new Democratic Movement (UDF-MD) split from the increasingly pro-Sarkozy UDF, which contested the parliamentary elections as the New Centre (UDF-NC).

The parliamentary elections of 10 and 17 June were fought in the shadow of the presidential election, which meant that the result was a question of how strong the UMP's victory would be. The UMP campaign was led by Sarkozy's newly appointed Prime Minister, François Fillon, a moderate with a reformist reputation. It focused on providing the newly elected president with a working majority in parliament. On the left, Socialist party leader François Hollande was in charge of the campaign, but his party fared poorly in the opinion polls and the campaign was largely a matter of damage limitation (Marthaler, 2007b). The first round of the parliamentary elections reflected this (see Table 4): an exceptionally high number of UMP candidates (109) won a seat outright in the first round. The second round, however, held some surprises. France's electoral system allows candidates with more than 12.5 per cent of the votes to progress to the second round and therefore rewards parties that agree pacts in which rival parties from the same side of the political spectrum withdraw candidates to avoid three-way races.

Table 4: French Parliamentary Elections, June 2007 (Votes in first round, seats after the second round)

	Votes (%) 2007	Seats 2007	Votes (%) 2002	Seats 2002
UMP	39.6	313	33.3	350
PS	24.7	186	24.1	138
UDF-NC	2.4	22	4.9[a]	29[a]
UDF-MD	7.6	3		
PCF	4.3	15	4.6	21
FN	4.3	0	11.3	0
Greens	3.3	4	4.5	3
Others	13.8	2	17.3	19
others left		22		8
others right		10		9

Sources: French Ministry of Interior, available at «http://www.interieur.gouv.fr/sections/a_votre_service/elections/resultats»; the National Assembly, available at «http://www.assembleenationale.fr/elections/»; Marthaler (2007b).
Note: [a] UDF in 2002.

Deprived of allies for the second round, Bayrou's Democratic Movement won only three representatives, whereas the New Centre won 22 seats despite wining far fewer votes in the first round. Meanwhile the Socialists' focus on economic and social issues paid off and they were able to use a controversy about possible increases in value-added tax to pay for tax cuts to mobilize its supporters for the second round. Although the election provided an absolute majority of seats for the UMP, it won fewer seats than in 2002 whereas the Socialist increased their representation substantially.

The presidential and parliamentary elections in France thus provided the centre-right with a clear mandate for reform and the parliamentary majority required to carry it forward. Yet Sarkozy signalled early that his approach would be consensual: his cabinet was relatively broad-based, including the appointment of Bernard Kouchner (a Socialist, although the party said he was no longer a member) as foreign minister. The reform process began with consultations on institutional reform and consensus building for economic reform. Although labour market flexibility was on the top of Sarkozy's agenda, he also signalled his commitment to France's traditional industrial policy and protection of national champions. As 2007 came to a close, the main challenge for the president and government appeared to be how to avoid the kind of mass demonstrations that have prevented French governments over the past two decades from pushing through radical reforms. The Socialist Party, by contrast, was in disarray. The couple that had led the party, Hollande and Royal, split after the parliamentary election, and Royal announced that she would challenge Hollande for the leadership of the party in 2008. By the end of the year, Hollande had decided not to seek another term as party leader.

The presidential election also settled one important European question: Sarkozy's victory allowed French politicians to put the 2005 referendum on the EU Constitutional Treaty behind them. During the electoral campaign Sarkozy had advocated a lightly revised treaty, to be ratified in parliament, while Royal had argued for a more substantial revision of the treaty and ratification by referendum. The election result could therefore be seen as providing a mandate on this question, and in October the Socialists agreed to support the new Reform Treaty when a parliamentary vote of ratification is held (although the party was far from united on this matter).

Power-Sharing and Grand Coalitions: Germany, Austria and the Netherlands

By the end of February 2007, Germany, Austria and the Netherlands were all led by coalition governments that spanned the left–right divide. The Social Democrat (SPD)-Christian Democrat (CDU/CSU) government in Germany is only the second grand coalition since 1966–69. Grand coalitions have been more common in Austria and the Netherlands, but in both cases the return to such coalitions after a period of centre-right rule proved somewhat contentious.

Although Angela Merkel's coalition government in Germany ended the year intact, and looked set to survive until the 2009 elections, tension between the two coalition parties grew stronger during the second half of 2007 as the two government parties sought to mark the distance between them with a view to the regional elections in 2008 and the national elections of 2009. 2007 proved a more difficult year for the SPD than the CDU. Both parties performed poorly in the Bremen elections, the only state election held in 2007, but Chancellor Merkel managed to remain above the internal divisions in the CDU and her personal popularity helped the party remain relatively strong in opinion polls throughout the year. In contrast the SPD suffered poorer opinion polls, both because of its more severe internal disputes and because the new Left Party got nearly 10 per cent in opinion polls. The SPD thus saw the kind of challenge from the left with which Scandinavian Social Democratic parties have long been familiar.

Both Austria and the Netherlands had held elections in the autumn of 2006 and both saw coalitions of Social Democrats and Christian Democrats take office in early 2007. In both cases this meant a return to centrist governments after a spell of somewhat unstable centre-right coalitions and brought seemingly robust coalitions into office. Whereas this was accompanied by a degree of party stability in Austria, it brought more turbulence in the Netherlands. In Austria, the Socialists (SPÖ) and Austrian People's Party (ÖVP) agreed a grand coalition led by the SPÖ under Alfred Gusenbauer, with a policy programme that promised considerable continuity from the outgoing ÖVP-led government. Although the ÖVP chose a new leader, Wilhelm Molterer, in April, and the two parties hardly hid their policy differences, their first year in office was characterized primarily by stability.

In contrast, the Netherlands saw changes both on the left and the right of the political spectrum. Peter Balkenende of the Christian Democrats (CDA) remained prime minister, but now leading a coalition with Labour (PvdA) and the small ChristenUnie. The PvdA suffered the most divisive debates on policy and leadership. Its party chairman and executive resigned in April and policy disputes continued to pit deputy prime minister (and finance minister) Wouter Bos against Jaques Tichelaar, the new parliamentary leader. The PvdA's decision in September to join its coalition partners in ruling out a referendum on the new EU treaty deepened this division as Tichelaar and several PvdA deputies (and three-quarters of the electorate) favoured a second referendum. Meanwhile, the Liberals (VVD), now out of office, expelled the outspokenly critical right-winger Rita Verdonk in September. However, polls indicated that if Verdonk established a new party on the populist right it could outperform the VVD, taking votes both from her old party and the far-right Freedom Party. By the end of the year this process was well under way: Verdonk had set up a new political organization temporarily named 'Proud of the Netherlands'. In short, although the 2006 election and the grand coalition seemingly closed the chapter in Dutch politics dominated by the Fortyun phenomenon, Verdonk's new party promised to keep the populist right alive and well in the country.

Belgium: Governing Without Government

By the end of 2007 Belgium had been without a government for 174 days. The elections on 10 June (see Table 5) did not so much produce an incon-clusive outcome as lead to political stalemate. As expected, Guy Verhofstadt's Liberal-Socialist government was defeated at the polls with the centre right performing well, and the parties on the far right seeing little change in their fortunes. Negotiating a new coalition, however, proved difficult. A Socialist-Christian Democrat coalition had been expected to take over, but on the left both the Francophone (PS) and Flemish (SPA + Sprint) parties were hit so hard that this was not an option. A three-way grand coalition of Liberal, Socialist and Christian Democratic parties (which governed the Flemish region) was also discussed, but the purpose of such a coalition would have

Table 5: Belgian Parliamentary Elections, June 2007

	Votes (%) 2007	Seats 2007	Votes (%) 2003	Seats 2003
CDV & NVA[a]	18.5	30	13.2 + 3.1	21 + 1
MR	12.5	23	11.4	24
Vlaams Belang	12.0	17	11.6	18
VLD	11.8	18	15.4	25
PS	10.9	20	13.0	25
SPA + Sprint	10.3	14	14.9	23
CDH	6.1	10	5.5	8
Ecolo (greens)	5.1	8	3.1	4
Groen (greens)	4.0	4	2.5	0
Dedecker list	4.0	5	–	–
National Front	2.0	1	2.0	1
Others	2.9	0		0

Source: Belgian Federal Public Services, available at «http://polling2007.belgium.be/en».
Notes: [a] On separate lists in 2003.

been to muster the two-thirds majority required to pass constitutional reform. The deep divisions between the Francophone and Flemish parties over constitutional reform and further devolution, however, made agreement all but impossible. Although only the extreme-right Vlaams Belang demanded full Flemish independence, all the Flemish parties advocated considerably more regional autonomy, particularly on issues related to social security and labour market flexibility. Because the Flemish parties seek decentralization of elements of tax policy, social security, health care and labour regulation, all of which include a considerable financial dimension, negotiations proved particularly problematic. This was exacerbated by the intractable question of the bilingual Brussels-Halle-Vilvoorde constituency, which the Flemish parties wanted to split along provincial lines. Both sides saw the BHV question as a major matter of principle.

Negotiations continued without much progress during the autumn. Yves Leterme, the leader of the Flemish Christian Democrats (CDV), which ran on a joint list with the more nationalist New Flemish Alliance (NVA), was named *formateur* twice, but failed to put together a viable coalition. Leterme's efforts centred on a Liberal–Christian Democrat coalition, to include his own party and Verhofstadt's Liberals and Democrats (VLD), as well as their Francophone counterparts, the Humanist Democratic Centre (CDH) and the Reform Movement (MR). Although this made agreement on the social and economic programme easier than in three-way negotiations, devolution and constitutional reform proved too divisive.

This stalemate, however, hardly spelled the end of the country, some press reports notwithstanding. Belgium survived its half-year without government remarkably well. Verhofstad remained prime minister in a caretaker capacity, continuing the outgoing government's programme and preparing to extend the 2007 budget into 2008 on a month-by-month basis. In December Verhofstad was appointed for a fixed-term three-month period. Only in April 2008, at the earliest, almost ten months after the election, would Belgium get its new government.

II. Southern (Mediterranean) Europe – Polarized Party Competition?

It is perhaps not common to present southern Europe as a paragon of political stability. Yet in 2007 this was very much the case, and 2007 was not an exceptional year. Apart from the continuing political drama that Italian party politics provides, the Mediterranean states saw few or no momentous party political developments. The Greek government won re-election with a reduced majority; the governments of Spain, Portugal, Malta and Cyprus saw out the year without much change; and even Italy started and ended the year with the same government. However, 2007 also saw political polarization in several of the states. All six feature remarkably stable two-bloc party competition. Although different issues divide the left- and right-wing blocs – devolution in Spain, the Berlusconi factor in Italy, the economy in Portugal and the government's public policy reforms in Greece – two-bloc contests between clearly defined government and opposition blocs have been the rule in the Mediter-ranean states for the past two decades. Moreover, European integration has been less contentious than in western and northern Europe and there has been relatively little far-right or socialist-left radical populism. To be sure, Italy's centre-right is largely made up of populist parties, the Portuguese centre-right signalled a more populist turn in 2007 and in Greece the far right saw some success in the September election. Yet this hardly compares with the radical right and left's fortunes elsewhere in Europe.

The Reorganization of the Italian Party System

The line-up of political parties in Italy looked very different in January and December 2007. Within the familiar lines of division, there was considerable organizational change as Italy's political parties prepared for the seemingly inevitable early elections (and the government did finally fall on 24 January 2008). By the end of 2007 the two largest parties in the governing centre-left *Unione* had merged to form the Democratic Party (PD) and the two main parties on the centre-right had announced their intention to merge into the

Popolo della Libertà (People of Freedom, PDL). One smaller party defected from each bloc and decided to run separately at the political centre: the Christian Democrat Udeur fell out with Silvio Berlusconi's centre-right bloc; and on the left opponents of the PD-merger left to form the new Democratic Left party (which joined the Greens and two communist parties in a new Rainbow Left coalition). Whereas some of the previous political reorganizations in Italy have been driven by changes in the electoral law, the organizational changes of 2007 reflected political divisions within the main political blocs.

2007 proved a year of trials for Romano Prodi's centre-left coalition and his government resigned briefly in February after losing a vote of confidence on foreign policy in the Senate. The *Unione's* main problems came from its own internal divisions: over foreign policy, fiscal policy, liberalization of service markets, pension reform and same-sex civil unions; and over the two main parties' decision to merge and form a new political party – the Democratic Party (PD). The centre-right response to the left's reorganization came in November, when Berlusconi announced his intention to turn the *Casa* into a fully-fledged political party. The new party's name was announced in December, as it became clear that the post-fascist National Alliance would join the new party: the *Popolo della Libertà*. The third *Casa* partner, the Northern League, soon followed suit. The line-up for the expected 2008 elections thus became clear.

Greece: Reform-Oriented New Democracy Re-elected, but High Protest Vote

Costas Karamanlis's New Democracy government won re-election on 16 September and secured a mandate for continuing its economic and constitutional reform (see Table 6). Both the main parties lost seats in the election, however, while the three parties on the left and right flanks more than doubled

Table 6: Greek Parliamentary Elections, September 2007

	Votes (%) 2007	Seats 2007	Votes (%) 2004	Seats 2004
New Democracy	41.8	152	45.4	165
Pasok	38.1	102	40.6	117
KKE	8.2	22	5.9	12
Syriza	5.0	14	3.3	6
Laos	3.8	10	2.2	0
Others	3.1	0	2.6	0

Source: Greek Ministry of Interior, available at «http://ekloges.ypes.gr».

their representation in parliament. The emergency services' weak perform-ance in response to the forest fires that devastated the country during the first week of the electoral campaign hurt both the main parties, with voters pun-ishing both the socialist Pasok (in office 1993–2004) and the governing New Democracy (in office since 2004) for the poor state of public services. Pasok recorded its worst result since 1977; New Democracy returned to its average from the 1990s, after its peak performance in 2004. The protest vote – for the Communists (KKE), the Coalition of the Radical Left (Syriza), and the right-wing Popular Orthodox Rally (Laos) – increased from 11.4 per cent to 17.0 per cent. Nevertheless, Karamanlis claimed a renewed mandate for the government's economic reform programme and committed the government to continued reform.

The election had been due by March 2008 in any case, but after a politi-cally turbulent spring and summer Karamanlis called a snap election arguing that the government needed a clear mandate for further economic and admin-istrative reform. Until early 2007 the government had sought broad consensus for gradual reform, but relations with Pasok broke down and the spring saw widespread protests against the government's higher education reforms. With 152 seats in the 300-seat parliament, New Democracy emerged from the election weakened numerically, but with a four-seat majority and facing a fragmented opposition. Moreover, Pasok's poor performance left the party divided over whether to continue George Papandreou's modernization drive. On 11 November Papandreou saw off a leadership challenge from Evangelos Venizelos from the party's traditionalist left-wing, thus signalling a degree of continuity in both the major parties. At the end of 2007 the Greek political scene thus looked set to continue along the reform path that both the major parties advocate, away from Greece's recent history of clientelist and polarized party politics.

Spain, Portugal, Cyprus and Malta: Stable Politics and Preparing for Forthcoming Elections

The other four Mediterranean EU Member States began and ended 2007 with the same governments and saw little party system change. In Spain and Malta the parties prepared for parliamentary elections due in the spring of 2008, which in both cases promised to be closely fought. Cypriot politics was dominated by the candidates' positioning for the 2008 presidential elec-tion; Portugal saw a classical mid-term political year; the opposition Social Democratic Party surprisingly chose a new, more populist, leader; and both the main parties quietly abandoned plans for a referendum on the new EU treaty.

The main political event in Cyprus and Malta was the decision, formally made in July, to introduce the euro on 1 January 2008. With elections due, both governments developed strategies for the transition to the new currency that were designed to prevent the kind of political backlash that took place in some of the old Member States. This included issuing currency converters and establishing rules, guidelines and control systems to ensure that shops did not use the changeover to increase prices.

Much of Spanish politics during 2007 was oriented toward the 2008 election. The main political development was the failure of the Basque peace process, which had more or less come to an end when ETA broke its cease-fire with the Madrid airport bombing in December 2006. ETA's formal ending of its cease-fire came in June and prompted Spain's socialist government to take a much harder stance against minority nationalism than it had done in the three years since the 2004 elections. The government's drive toward further devolution to Catalonia provoked hostility from both sides: from the Catalan nationalist parties that consider the new statute insufficient and from the centre-right Popular Party which had been critical of the government's devolution project. What already looked set to be a close electoral contest was made even more uncertain by the establishment of a new political party in September, when the Progressive and Democratic Union (UPD) was established by centre-left politicians critical of the government's soft stance against regional nationalists in Catalonia and the Basque country. A cabinet reshuffle in July was geared toward improving the government's profile in the run-up to the election. When the election date was announced in December the government and opposition ran neck and neck in the polls, which suggested that the small regionalist parties might come to hold a balance of power.

III. Eastern Central Europe – Dysfunctional Elites and Alienated Voters

With the accession of Bulgaria and Romania on 1 January 2007, the number of post-communist states in the EU increased to ten. According to Eurobarometer, support for the EU remained extremely mixed (see Table 2). In autumn 2007 it ranged from highs of 71 per cent in Poland and Romania (nearly approaching the levels of support in the traditionally europhile Benelux countries and Ireland) to lows of 40 per cent or less in Latvia and Hungary (similar to the eurosceptic United Kingdom and Austria, although it is notable that the number of citizens who actually believed membership a 'bad thing' was lower in the new Member States). Interestingly, this reproduced trends from the

Eurobarometers for east central Europe of the mid-1990s, when Poland and Romania – the states which had had the most negative experience of communist rule – had also been the most supportive of EU membership. Since Poland and Romania contain substantially more citizens than the other eight states together, any comparison of the percentage of citizens supportive of the EU in the new and the old Member States became meaningless: the former was so heavily influenced by positive Polish and Romanian views that the complex variations in opinion elsewhere were concealed. However, one could conclude that the new Member States are converging with the old insofar that they could not reasonably be viewed as a block.

Nevertheless, it is possible to trace some similarities in political developments in the post-communist Member States. The two new members reinforced the pattern of post-accession domestic turbulence, most particularly in Romania, where the animosity between Prime Minister and President reached such intensity that a move to impeach the president was put to a popular referendum in May. Political elites who had successfully coped with the complex legislative agenda necessary during negotiations to join the EU in many cases proved unable to master the more basic art of conducting domestic political competition with each other. The infighting between and sometimes also within parties, and the rampant incidence of corruption allegations against serving politicians, frequently left voters alienated from politics, and often still willing to try new party alternatives rather than accept the continuation in power of more experienced political groups.

Bulgaria and Romania: Shifting Party Allegiances

Whether Bulgaria and Romania would accede to the EU in 2007, or be made to wait until 2008, had not been decidedly definitely until the autumn of 2006. The positive decision on 2007 accession was accompanied by a 'Co-operation and Verification' mechanism to help 'remedy shortcomings' in the areas of judicial reform and the fight against corruption (and, in the Bulgarian case, organized crime). This provision meant that, just as in the pre-accession period, the European Commission regularly reported on the states' progress towards achieving 'benchmarks.' It was therefore manifest that both countries had effectively been allowed to become EU members before they were ready. Politically, the decision had been made that further progress in achieving the required standards would be better promoted by permitting accession than by delaying it. Reports by the Commission in June 2007 and February 2008 indicated that during 2007 both countries had 'continued to make efforts to remedy weaknesses that would otherwise prevent an effective application of EU laws, policies and programmes', but that 'in key areas such as the fight

Table 7: Bulgarian European Parliament Election, May 2007

	Votes (%)	Seats	Votes (%) 2005
Citizens for the European Development of Bulgaria (GERB)	21.7	5	–
Platform of European Socialists (PES)	21.4	5	34.2
Movement for Rights and Freedoms (DPS)	20.3	4	14.2
Ataka	14.2	3	8.8
National Movement Simeon II (NDSV)	6.3	1	22.1
United Democratic Forces (SDS)	4.7	0	8.3

Source: Bulgarian Central Electoral Commission, available at «http://www.izbori2007.org/results/».

against high-level corruption', convincing results had not yet been demonstrated (Commission, 2008a, p. 9; 2008b, p. 7).

In both countries, 'high-level corruption' remained a major concern of citizens. EU accession gave voters the chance to express their opinion on political parties since they were required to vote for their members of the European Parliament (EP) in May 2007, which were in both states 'midterm elections' approximately half-way through the four-year parliamentary period.

In the case of Bulgaria, the EP election took place on 20 May. Following the June 2005 elections, the government had been led by Sergei Stanishev of the Bulgarian Socialist Party (BSP), which had won over a third of the votes and parliamentary deputies. One of its coalition partners was the National Movement Simeon II, led by the Bulgarian king-in-exile Simeon Sakskoburggotski, who had been Prime Minister from 2001 to 2005. The other was the Movement for Rights and Freedoms, which represented the country's Turkish minority. Since the opposition centre right had led the government from 1997 to 2001 (the period when EU accession negotiations began), all the major political forces in Bulgaria had at some point been involved in ensuring the country's road back to Europe.

The EP election in Bulgaria was in many ways fairly ordinary: the turnout was low (less than 29 per cent, but higher than most post-communist states had managed in 2004) and the campaign focused on domestic politics. What was most interesting were major shifts in the support for individual parties (see Table 7).

The ruling BSP, standing in the election as the Platform of European Socialists, was narrowly pushed into second place by the newly-formed Citizens for the European Development of Bulgaria (GERB), which had only been registered in December 2006. The BSP had suffered from both disappointment on economic issues during the run-up to, and early months of,

EU accession, and a major corruption scandal, although the Prime Minister succeeded in defusing the latter problem sufficiently to retain most of the party's support (Savkova, 2007). The GERB played both a right-wing nationalist and a left-wing anti-corruption card, and eventually joined the European People's Party in the EP, thereby taking over the centre-right space vacated by the United Democratic Forces which had led the government from 1997 to 2001, but failed to enter the EP. A further casualty of the GERB's election success was the National Movement Simeon II, which returned only one MEP, continuing its gradual decline since its spectacular election success as a new party in 2001. The EP elections were, by contrast, fairly successful for two further parties. The Turkish minority Movement for Rights and Freedoms was the only governing party that did not suffer in the elections. It benefited from the generally low turnout because it had a firm ethnically-based core electorate that was easier to mobilize, which compensated for the fact that Bulgarian citizens resident in Turkey were not permitted to vote in these elections. Finally, the right-wing Ataka party, which had first entered parliament in 2005 as a nationalist party and which campaigned as the major eurosceptic force in 2007, also increased its vote.

Romanian party politics was more spectacularly unstable. While Bulgaria demonstrated the volatility of the party systems in accession states, Romania illustrated the inability of inexperienced political elites to conduct party political competition within the institutional channels normal for established democracies. The EP elections had to be delayed until late November 2007 to make way for a 19 May referendum on the impeachment of President Traian Băsescu. The overwhelming 74.5 per cent majority in favour of the president demonstrated just how far out of line with public opinion the country's legislators had been when they impeached him. As so often in eastern central Europe, issues of corruption and trust emerged prominently in Romania's dispute between president and prime minister.

The roots of the 2007 debacle lay in the surprise result of the November/December 2004 elections. While the parliamentary election appeared to have been very narrowly won by the Social Democrats, the simultaneous presidential election of the joint candidate of the National Liberal Party and the Democratic Party – mayor of Bucharest Traian Băsescu of the Democratic Party – led to the new president initiating the formation of a coalition government under the premiership of National Liberal Party leader Călin Popescu-Tăriceanu. The relationship between President and Prime Minister, however, broke down completely during the next two years amid allegations of corruption and arguments over 'lustration' – investigating politicians' communist pasts. When, in January 2007, the Social Democrats initiated impeachment proceedings against the president (on somewhat flimsy

Table 8: Romanian European Parliament Election, November 2007

	Votes (%)	Seats	Votes (%) 2004[a]
Democratic Party (PD)	28.8	13	31.5 (with PNL)
Social Democratic Party (PSD)	23.1	10	36.8 (as National Union)
National Liberal Party (PNL)	13.4	6	31.5 (with PD)
Liberal Democratic Party (PLD)	7.8	3	–
Hungarian Democratic Union of Romania (UDMR)	5.5	2	6.2
László Tökés (Independent)	3.4	1	–
Greater Romania Party (PRM)	4.2	0	13.0

Notes: [a] Results for the Chamber of Deputies.
Source: Adapted from Maxfield (2007b).

grounds), they were joined by the nationalist Greater Romania Party, which was also in opposition, and also the ruling National Liberals.

The voters, however, placed their trust in the politics of personality and backed the president. Opinion polling showed that while Democratic Party voters were overwhelmingly in favour of the president and Social Democratic voters against, the president also enjoyed the trust of a majority of voters from other parties that had campaigned in favour of his impeachment (Maxfield, 2007a).

Against this background, the EP election was eventually held on 25 November. The failed referendum increased the popularity of the president's Democratic Party, which won nearly 29 per cent of the EP vote, almost as much as it had obtained standing together with the National Liberals in the 2004 parliamentary elections (see Table 8). Both the Prime Minister's National Liberal Party (which had split, and lost some of its support to the breakaway Liberal Democrats who were closer to the Democratic Party) and the opposition Social Democrats lost substantially. It was noticeable, however, that despite worries in Romania that its citizens were regarded as 'second class' in the EU, the nationalist vote declined and the Greater Romania Party failed to return any MEPs.

It is obviously unwise to read too much about Romanian domestic politics into the EP election result as the turnout was just under 25 per cent. Some sense of the political alienation felt by Romanian voters was, however, given by a referendum held simultaneously. Over 83 per cent of voters opted for an electoral reform proposal that would have introduced single-member constituencies and thus substantially weakened the power that political parties enjoyed under proportional representation. The proposal had been introduced by President Băsescu in retaliation against the attempted impeachment. While the referendum result was not binding because of low turnout, it nonetheless gave an indication of the low regard in which the population held political parties.

Poland's Critical Election

Polish political developments attracted far more attention than those in the two most recent accession states. This was not merely because it was the largest new Member State, but also because it continued to project itself within the EU as the new 'awkward partner'. This image had been formed in the run-up to accession under the previous Social Democrat-led government, and continued during negotiations on the Lisbon Treaty. Furthermore, the politics of the rather maverick nationalist right government (which was made even more curious by the presence of the Law and Justice party's Kaczyński twins as prime minister and president) led to considerable concern about the direction the country was following.

Domestic politics also continued to be marked by considerable instability, and it was no great surprise when Law and Justice took the country to new elections in October 2007, two years before they were due. Its government coalition with two eurosceptic right parties, Self-Defence and the League of Polish Families, had temporarily broken down the year before, and survived largely because the two junior partners were aware that their very low opinion poll ratings would most likely lead to their elimination from parliament when the next elections took place.

Domestic disputes took place on several different levels. The public and opposition parties criticized the government's policies, particularly its confrontational foreign policy. Disputes with Russia over the latter's ban on Polish meat exports were augmented by the intention of Poland (along with the Czech Republic) to permit the stationing of the US missile defence system on its territory. Ongoing hostility towards Germany also culminated in Prime Minister Jarosław Kaczyński arguing, during the June European Council meeting chaired by Germany, that Poland's voting weight should reflect the millions of Poles killed in the Second World War. Many Polish citizens also had a more general feeling that Poland was making itself look ridiculous, with plans by the education minister (from the League of Polish Families) to add the works of nationalist and Catholic authors to the school syllabus being just one of many domestic disputes. Law and Justice also had a number of intra-party disputes as well, losing its defence minister and interior minister in February and the speaker of the lower chamber (*Sejm*) in April.

It was, however, a renewed dispute with Andrzej Lepper, leader of Self-Defence, who was dismissed from the government for a second time in July, that finally led the Prime Minister to announce in August that there would be

Table 9: Polish Parliamentary Election (Sejm), October 2007

	Votes (%)	Seats	Votes (%) 2005
Civic Platform (OP)	41.5	209	24.1
Law and Justice (PiS)	32.1	166	27.0
Left and Democrats (LiD)	13.2	4	17.7[a]
Polish Peasant Party (PSL)	8.9	53	7.0
Self-Defence	1.5	0	11.4
League of Polish Families (LPR)	1.3	0	8.0

Notes: [a] Combined vote of constituent parties in 2005.
Source: Polish State Electoral Commission, available at «http://www.pkw.gov.pl».

early elections. Since the dispute with Lepper related to corruption allegations, this enabled Law and Justice to enter the election campaign still promoting itself as opponents of corruption and hoping to gain re-election on the
grounds of the country's good economic results. For much of the campaign,
there were opinion poll indications that it could indeed succeed, and the party
in fact increased both its share of the vote and seats in the *Sejm*.

As shown in Table 9, however, the election result brought victory to Civic
Platform, led by Donald Tusk, who had been Lech Kaczyński's main presidential rival in 2005. Although centre-right and economically liberal, he soon
formed a majority government with the Polish Peasants' Party of former
Prime Minister Waldemar Pawlak, which had previously been a coalition
partner of the Social Democrats.

There were a number of reasons for the election result. In the campaign,
Tusk outperformed Kaczyński in a key television debate. An attempt to
exploit a corruption scandal involving a Civic Platform deputy backfired
on Law and Justice because of the obvious way it was staged politically
(Szczerbiak, 2007). More crucially, however, Polish politics had been polarized by the controversial nature of the Kaczyńskis' rule. The seemingly
unimpressive turnout of 53.9 per cent was the highest ever in a post-
communist Polish parliamentary election, and the higher participation by
younger and urban voters assisted Civic Platform. In addition, the Left and
Democrats, a reformed grouping of centre-left parties, did less well than it
might have expected. Some leftist voters are likely to have switched their vote
to Civic Platform as the surest way of ousting Law and Justice. Finally, the
almost total collapse of Self-Defence and the League of Polish Families left
Law and Justice isolated.

The outcome of the election was greeted enthusiastically within the rest of
the EU, as new Prime Minister Tusk immediately set about repairing relations
and the apparent demise of the two eurosceptic government partners removed

Poland from the equation of post-accession nationalist resurgence in eastern central Europe. However, Polish assertion of national interests within the EU did not begin nor is it likely to end with the Law and Justice-led government. The major difference will be in negotiating style. Domestically Polish politics will remain conflictual since the new government faces both a very hostile opposition, and a presidency, dominated by the Kaczyńskis.

Polarized Party Systems in the Czech Republic, Hungary, Slovakia and Slovenia

The other four central eastern European states did not experience major political events such as elections, but all showed signs of highly conflictual and dysfunctional relationships between government and opposition.

In two cases – Slovakia and Slovenia – governments had to moderate their behaviour to cope with specific EU-related challenges apart from ensuring entry to the Schengen zone, which all the 2004 accession states except Cyprus achieved in December 2007. In Slovakia's case, left-wing Prime Minister Robert Fico, who had come to power in July 2006, had realized within days of his election that he was bound politically by public and elite expectations that he should achieve the previous government's goal of joining the euro area at the beginning of 2009. This commitment circumscribed his scope to make major changes in economic policy and throughout 2007 he did little to reverse the previous rightist government's radical reforms, even retaining Slovakia's renowned 19 per cent flat tax.

Fico remained plagued by the Party of European Socialists' decision not to readmit his Direction-Social Democracy (*Smer-SD*), which it had suspended from the PES in 2006 for entering a coalition government with the Slovak National Party. Fico was hence denied the special access to other socialist Prime Ministers that PES membership would have permitted, and he tended to compensate by developing particularly warm relations with states such as Cuba, Libya and Russia.

Domestic political competition in Slovakia was highly conflictual. While Fico never went as far as his coalition partner Vladimír Mečiar had when prime minister in the mid-1990s in excluding the opposition from parliamentary committees, his government's total refusal to accept any opposition input into legislation took lack of government-opposition co-operation to a particularly high level. His opinion poll ratings were high and rising, however, despite all three government parties being subject to major corruption allegations.

In 2007 Slovenia became the first post-communist state to join the euro-zone, and prepared for becoming the first 2004 accession state to take over the

EU presidency, at the beginning of 2008. The presidency was a particular challenge for a small state of only two million and problems were exacerbated by the traditionally rather consensual Slovene political scene having been altered when Janez Janša's Slovene Democratic Party came to power in a four-party centre-right coalition in late 2004. By 2007 the government's unpopularity was on the increase. Opponents objected to issues such as a perceived restriction of press freedom and rising inflation, and supporters were disappointed at the lack of major economic reform. In a bitter political environment, government and opposition parties eventually negotiated an 'agreement of co-operation' whereby they would prevent campaigning for the 2008 elections from interfering with the EU presidency.

The presidential election due in October and November 2007, however, did nothing to reduce political tensions. President Janez Drnovšek, previously the long-serving prime minister, declined to stand for a second time (he died within two months of leaving office), and the major contest was between three nominally independent candidates with party backing. In a second-round run-off, Danilo Türk, a former United Nations diplomat supported by the centre-left opposition parties, won an impressive 68 per cent of the vote against the candidate of the centre-right government parties, former prime minister and foreign minister Lojze Peterle. This result was a surprise given that in the first round Peterle had led Türk by 28.7 per cent to 24.5 per cent and was evidence of a strong anti-government mood amongst all but its supporters.

The Czech Republic and Hungary were also marked by very sharp conflicts between government and opposition. In the Czech Republic tensions were evident in that it took more than six months to form a new government after the June 2006 elections. The coalition government of Mirek Topolánek, the leader of the rightist Civic Democratic Party, finally received a parliamentary vote of confidence only in January 2007. By the end of the year, however, the country was heading for yet another display of political confrontation as parties selected their candidates for the February 2008 presidential elections.

Political conflict in Hungary did not reach the levels of the demonstrations against Socialist Prime Minister Ferenc Gyurcsány in October 2006, but the commemoration of the 1956 revolution was again marked by major demonstrations led by the opposition Fidesz party of Viktor Orbán, which had never entirely come to terms with losing power in 2002. Problems with the Hungarian economy contributed both to increasing public dissatisfaction with the government and to the conspicuous ambivalence towards EU membership demonstrated in Eurobarometer polls. Ironically, it was precisely on an EU issue that Hungarian political elites managed to demonstrate a notable consensus: in

December 2007, the Hungarian parliament became the first Member State to ratify the Lisbon Treaty with an overwhelming vote in favour.

The Baltic States: Stabilization within Fragmented Party Systems

The three Baltic states had long had fairly volatile party systems; it was unknown for a government coalition or Prime Minister to survive an entire parliamentary term. Accordingly, in 2007 only Lithuania did not see a change in Prime Minister.

Estonia faced parliamentary elections on 4 March (see Table 10), which were hailed as the first national election anywhere in the world to use internet voting. The development may have raised the turnout slightly, as it increased by about 3 per cent, although only 5.4 per cent of voters used this method (OSCE, 2007). The result was also a first for Estonia, as Andrus Ansip of the Estonian Reform Party became the first incumbent Prime Minister to be returned to power. His new government, however, differed notably from his previous one, with the Estonian Social Democratic Party and the Union of Pro Patria and Res Republica, rather than the Centre party and the People's Union, as coalition partners. The recently formed Green Party initially joined negotiations but then withdrew.

As in 2003, the ethnic Russian vote was split and no party representing the Russian minority entered parliament. This failure to mobilize was perhaps rather surprising as the elections coincided with the controversy surrounding the removal of the 'bronze horseman'. This was a statue that depicted a Second World War Soviet soldier as a liberator, though the Russians were perceived by Estonians as occupiers. In May, the statue was moved from the centre of Tallinn to a more discrete park location, sparking riots by ethnic Russians, in which one person died, and leading to tense relations with Russia (see Light, this volume).

Table 10: Estonian Parliamentary Election, March 2007

	Votes (%)	Seats	Votes (%) 2003
Estonian Reform Party (ER)	27.8	31	17.7
Estonian Centre Party (EK)	26.1	29	25.4
Union of Pro Patria and Res Publica (IRPL)	17.9	19	31.9[a]
Estonian Social Democratic Party (ESDP)	10.6	10	7.0[b]
Estonian Green Party (EER)	7.1	6	–
Estonian People's Union (ERL)	7.1	6	13.0

Notes: [a] Combined vote of constituent parties in 2003. [b] Standing as the Moderates.
Source: Estonian National Electoral Committee, available at «http://www.vvk.ee».

In Latvia the parliament elected a new president in May to succeed Vaira Vīke Freiberga, who had been in office for eight years. The new president, Valdis Zatlers, was supported by the four parties of the government coalition and defeated an opposition candidate supported by both the (ethnically Latvian) New Era party and the two parties representing the Russian minority in parliament. The position of Prime Minister Aigars Kalvītis, however, became increasingly insecure as the year progressed. Controversy over attempts to increase the prime minister's national security role was followed by an attempt by the prime minister to remove the director of the anti-corruption bureau in the autumn. This intervention provoked the largest anti-government demonstration since the fall of communism, and although Kalvītis survived a no-confidence vote, after a number of ministerial resignations, he announced in November that the government would resign in December. Kalvītis was replaced as prime minister by Interior Minister Ivars Godmanis of Latvian Way, who had previously been Prime Minister in 1990–93, but the parties comprising the government remained the same.

IV. Northern Europe – Centripetal Party Competition

The five northern European Member States have, in important respects, become more similar over the past two decades, although this has little or nothing to do with EU membership. Whereas even in the 1980s it made sense to speak of the Scandinavian states as consensus democracies and Britain and Ireland in terms of adversarial politics, the 1990s and 2000s have changed both groups. In Ireland party coalitions have been more flexible in the past two decades than in earlier times, and in the UK and Scandinavia the Social Democrats' modernization has brought the centre-left closer to the centre-right, so that these states all feature considerable cross-bloc consensus on important public policy questions. Consequently, the Irish, Finnish and Danish elections were closely fought, but none led to major policy change.

The UK: Gordon Brown Succeeds Tony Blair;
Devolution in Northern Ireland

The only change of Prime Minister in a northern European Member State was also the most expected. On 27 June Gordon Brown succeeded Tony Blair as Prime Minister of the UK. Although the change initially led to a boost for Labour in the opinion polls, by the end of the year the Conservatives were ahead in the polls and seemed a more credible political alternative than at any point since the 1997 election.

When Gordon Brown took over the Labour leadership unopposed he signalled broad policy continuity with the past ten years, but also a change in leadership style. The cabinet saw few surprising changes, but inevitably a number of close Brown associates were promoted. The change clearly improved the government's poll ratings, as did its handling of terrorist attacks on London and Glasgow. Yet this set the scene for the main political event of the autumn; the government-fuelled speculation that Brown would call an early election and his subsequent climb-down after the Conservatives' successful party conference. The main European question, the challenge of ratifying the Lisbon Treaty in parliament, was left to 2008. Whether a drawn-out ratification debate would damage the government or the Conservatives more remained open.

In Northern Ireland five years of direct rule from Westminster ended on 8 May when a power-sharing government led by the old arch-enemies, the Democratic Unionist Party (DUP) and Sinn Fein, took office. The DUP's Ian Paisley became first minister and Sinn Fein's Martin McGuinness deputy first minister. Both parties had done well in the March elections to the Northern Ireland Assembly (the DUP took 36 of the Assembly's 108 seats, and Sinn Fein became the second largest party with 28 seats), and agreed to share power shortly after the election. The government was still in office by the end of the year, although DUP defectors had established a new anti-agreement party and the agreement to devolve police and justice powers proved contentious. By the end of the year Ireland's Fianna Fail party announced its intention to organize in Northern Ireland and eventually field candidates in future Assembly elections.

Ireland: Bertie Ahern Re-elected for a Third Term

Even though very little changed from the 2002 election, the Irish election of 24 May was a major triumph for the ruling Fianna Fail and prime minister Bertie Ahern (see Table 11). The main uncertainty had been whether the closely fought election would lead to a change of government – Labour and Fine Gael formed a pre-election 'the Alliance of Change' in order to achieve this – or whether Ahern would return for a third term. In the end Fianna Fail performed better than the pre-election polls had predicted, and despite the poor performance of the junior coalition party, the Progressive Democrats (PD), the coalition was able to retain power by inviting the Greens to enter government for the first time. A strong economy contributed to Fianna Fail's solid performance, and the party's track record of working with a range of the smaller parties over the past two decades opened the way for widening the coalition. The Green Party's softening of its eurosceptic stance and its change

Table 11: Irish Parliamentary Elections, May 2007

	Votes (%) 2007	Seats 2007	Votes (%) 2002	Seats 2002
Fianna Fail	41.6	77	41.5	81
Fine Gael	27.3	51	22.5	31
Labour	10.1	20	10.7	20
Greens	4.7	6	3.9	6
Sinn Fein	6.9	4	6.5	5
PD	2.7	2	3.9	8
Others	6.9	5	11.0	14

Source: Gallagher and Marsh (2007).

in party leadership facilitated the coalition; Trevor Sergeant, who had ruled out participating in a coalition government, was replaced by John Gormley (Holmes 2007). By the end of the year the three-party coalition had survived a few minor mishaps and poorer opinion polls, and Ahern survived an opposition motion of no confidence that followed his appearance before a judicial corruption investigation.

The election confirmed the central, if not dominant, position of Fianna Fail in the Irish party system, both in terms of votes and coalition games. Gallagher and Marsh (2007) suggest that the de-alignment of the Irish electorate over the past decade or two has not had the detrimental effect on the three largest parties that might have been expected. Fianna Fail has maintained its leading position and attracted a high number of floating voters. Moreover, as Fianna Fail has now governed with the Greens as well as PD and Labour, it has a broad set of options for coalitions. Although both the main opposition parties performed well in the election, Labour's co-operation with Fine Gael failed to secure a change of government. It subsequently chose a new leader (Eamon Gilmore) and announced that it would fight the next election on its own. The Irish party system thus looked more stable at the end of 2007 than might have been expected in the run-up to the election.

The Nordic Member States: Two Elections and a Small Crisis

Two of the three Nordic Member States held elections in 2007: Finland on 18 March, as part of its regular electoral cycle, and Denmark, when Prime Minister Anders Fogh Rasmussen called an early election on 13 November. By April 2007 all three countries were governed by the centre right, and in Denmark the minority government was dependent on support from the radical right. In Sweden the centre-right four-party coalition that won office in 2006 struggled through its first full year in office. The coalition of the conservative Moderates, the Swedish People's Party, the Centre Party and the Christian

Table 12: Finnish Parliamentary Elections, March 2007

	Votes (%) 2007	Seats 2007	Votes (%) 2003	Seats 2003
KESK	23.1	51	24.7	55
KOK	22.3	50	18.6	40
SDP	21.4	45	24.5	53
Left Alliance	8.8	17	9.9	19
Greens	8.5	15	8.0	14
Chr. Democrats	4.9	7	5.3	7
Swedish PP	4.6	9	4.6	8
True Finns	4.1	5	1.6	3
Others	2.3	1[a]	2.8	1[a]

Notes: [a] Includes the single representative from the Åland Islands (who sat with the Swedish People's Party group in both legislatures).
Source: Statistics Finland, available at «http://www.stat.fi».

Democrats continued to suffer from its political inexperience, having taken office after 12 years of Social Democrat government, and Prime Minister Fredrik Reinfeld suffered criticism for poor party management. By the end of 2007 it had lost five ministers or junior ministers (under-secretaries) since the September 2006 election, all but one linked to political scandals. On the other side of the political spectrum the opposition Social Democrats chose their new leader after the 2006 election defeat. Mona Sahlin, who hails from the right wing of the party, but has a moderate track record, became the party's first female leader.

The main surprise in Finland's parliamentary elections was that they led to a broad four-party coalition including the Greens, rather than a three-party coalition of the Centre Party (KESK), the Conservatives (KOK) and the Swedish People's Party (Table 12). Although the previous KESK–Social Democrat (SDP)–Swedish People's Party government had presided over a period of reasonable economic growth, only KESK and the Swedish party managed to sustain their shares of the vote. With the electoral campaign centred on improving public services, a goal on which all parties agreed, the KESK and the SDP's different fortunes came down in large part to the two party leaders: Prime Minister Matti Vanhanen's popularity translated into a strong performance for the KESK and a mandate to continue governing with a new coalition (Raunio, 2007). KOK and the Greens were the two main winners of the election and both were invited into the new coalition, with the Greens promising not to leave the coalition over the question of nuclear power, as they had done in 2002. Although KESK and KOK held a majority of seats together, and the coalition had the Swedish groups' ten seats, Vanhanen cited the need for smooth government as the basis for his decision to

Table 13: Danish Parliamentary Elections, November 2007

	Votes (%) 2007	Seats 2007	Votes (%) 2005	Seats 2005
Liberals	26.2	46	29.0	52
Social Democrats	25.5	45	25.8	47
Danish PP	13.9	25	13.3	24
Socialist PP	13.0	23	6.0	11
Conservatives	10.4	18	10.3	18
Radical Liberals	5.1	9	9.2	17
New Alliance	2.8	5	–	–
Unity List	2.2	4	3.4	6
Others	0.9	4[a]	3.0	4[a]

Notes: [a] Includes two representatives from Greenland and two from the Faroe Islands.
Source: Danish Ministry of Interior, available at «http://www.valgresultat.dk».

invite the centre-left Greens to join the coalition. He thus maintained Finland's tradition of over-sized coalitions that cross the left–right divide (Raunio, 2007), and left a fragmented opposition. Although the far-right (and eurosceptic) True Finns increased their vote by half, they remained thoroughly marginalized from Finnish party politics.

As in the Irish and Finnish elections, the main surprise in the Danish election was that it did not feature more political change (see Table 13). The creation of a new political party, the New Alliance, designed to wean the centre-right minority government off its reliance on the far-right Danish People's Party (DPP), turned out to have remarkably little effect on Danish party politics. The party had been established in May 2007 by three politicians from the Radical Liberals (RV) and the Conservatives, and positioned on the left flank of the Conservative–Liberal (Venstre) government. This new competitor prompted the Radical Liberals, and even the Social Democrats and Socialist People's Party, to adopt a more flexible stance on possible future coalitions and play down their opposition to the government's tough immigration policy (Christensen, 2007).

After six months of speculation, Prime Minister Fogh Rasmussen of the Liberals called an early election for November, justified with the need to provide a solid political basis for public sector reform. Yet by the end of the year his government found itself on ever shakier ground, and on the brink of collapse. If the New Alliance was counted as part of the parliamentary basis for the minority Liberal–Conservative government, the government was left with almost exactly the same support as before the election. Taking into account the tension between the new party and the DPP, the government was left in a far more precarious state. Counting the one representative from the Faroe Island who joined the Liberal group in parliament, the coalition had a majority of one (including the DPP, but not the New Alliance). It was propelled toward a crisis when one deputy left the Conservative group in December, but recovered in early 2008 by securing support from the New Alliance.

Come the end of 2007, Danish party politics was, if anything, less stable than it had been at the beginning of the year. Yet its European policy remained on track, and geared toward cross-party consensus. On 4 December the Ministry of Justice advised the government that there was no need to put the Lisbon Treaty to a referendum; and most parties were prepared to accept parliamentary ratification. Shortly after the election, Fogh Rasmussen had announced his government's intentions to call a referendum on scrapping Denmark's four opt-outs relating to the Maastricht treaty (the common currency, defence, citizenship, and supranational decision-making on justice), and by the end of 2007 the government was seeking to build a broad political consensus behind its European policy, attempting even to reach agreement with the eurosceptic Socialist People's Party (but not the DPP or the left-wing Unity List).

Conclusion

Political developments in the EU Member States continued to defy regional patterns in 2007. Although there are some common themes in each of the four groupings of Member States presented above, they are defined by geography rather than common dynamics of party politics or political stability. To be sure, there are some common themes such as the Nordic Member States' similar party systems or the tendency for voters in post-communist states not to re-elect their governments. Both the predictable sources of government change (regular elections) and its unpredictable sources (early elections, coalitions that break up, corruption scandals) vary as much within as between the four groups. For example, polarization between government and opposition characterizes Hungarian, but also Italian politics. Coalition negotiations were drawn-out in the Czech Republic, but lasted even longer in Belgium. Developments in 2007 thus confirm the patterns that emerged in 2005 and 2006; the role of domestic politics in the EU may have changed because there is a larger number of elections and governments crises in any given year, but there is little to indicate that enlargement to post-communist states has changed the nature or dynamics of domestic politics in the EU. Moreover, after the turbulence of 2005, with one or two significant exceptions, the political parties in both the old and new Member States proved surprisingly successful in 2007 in their attempt to minimize the effect of domestic politics on European integration by building broad domestic consensus on the handling of the Lisbon Treaty.

Key readings

Taggart and Szczerbiak (2008) give background on domestic political reactions to EU-related issues in the Member States, while Wallace (2007) looks at adaptation at the EU level. For citizens' views of the EU, a wide range of public opinion surveys are available at «http://ec.europa.eu/public_opinion/index_en.htm». For recent elections in most European states, see reports provided by the Sussex European Institute «http://www.sussex.ac.uk/sei» and the OSCE «http://www.osce.org/odihr-elections».

References

Christensen, J. (2007) 'Danish Election Summary'. PSA Scandinavian Group. Available at «http://www.psa.ac.uk/spgrp/Scandinavia/Previous.htm».

Commission of the European Communities (2008a) 'Interim Report from the Commission to the European Parliament and the Council on Progress in Bulgaria under the Co-operation and Verification Mechanism'. COM(2008)63, 4 February.

Commission of the European Communities (2008b) 'Interim Report from the Commission to the European Parliament and the Council on Progress in Romania under the Co-operation and Verification Mechanism'. COM(2008)62, 4 February.

Deloy, C. (2007) 'France: Presidential Elections'. European Elections Monitor, Fondation Robert Schuman. Available at «http://www.robert-schuman.org».

Gallagher, M. and Marsh, M. (eds) (2007) *How Ireland Voted: The Full Story of Ireland's General Election* (London: Palgrave).

Holmes, M. (2007) 'Europe and the General Election in the Republic of Ireland, May 24 2007'. EPERN Election Briefing No. 35, Brighton: Sussex European Institute. Available at «http://www.sussex.ac.uk/sei/».

Marthaler, S. (2007a) 'The French Presidential Election of 22 April and 6 May 2007'. EPERN Election Briefing No. 33, Brighton: Sussex European Institute. Available at «http://www.sussex.ac.uk/sei/».

Marthaler, S. (2007b) 'The French Legislative Elections of 10 and 17 June 2007'. EPERN Election Briefing No. 34, Brighton: Sussex European Institute. Available at «http://www.sussex.ac.uk/sei/».

Maxfield, E. (2007a) 'Europe and Romania's Presidential Impeachment Referendum, May 2007'. EPERN Referendum Briefing No. 15, Brighton: Sussex European Institute. Available at «http://www.sussex.ac.uk/sei/».

Maxfield, E. (2007b) 'The European Parliament Elections in Romania November 24th 2007'. EPERN European Parliament Election Briefing No. 24, Brighton: Sussex European Institute. Available at «http://www.sussex.ac.uk/sei/».

OSCE (2007) 'Republic of Estonia: Parliamentary Elections 4 March 2007: ESCE/ODIHR Election Assessment Mission Report', Warsaw 28 June. Available at «http://www.osce.org/documents/odihr/2007/07/25385_en.pdf».

Raunio, T. (2007) 'Europe and the Finnish Parliamentary Elections of March 2007'. EPERN Election Briefing No. 32, Brighton, Sussex European Institute. Available at «http://www.sussex.ac.uk/sei/».

Savkova, L. (2007) 'The European Parliament Elections in Bulgaria May 20th 2007'. EPERN European Parliament Election Briefing No. 23, Brighton, Sussex European Institute. Available at «http://www.sussex.ac.uk/sei/».

Szczerbiak, S. (2007) 'Europe and the October 2007 Polish Parliamentary Election'. EPERN Election Briefing No. 37, Brighton, Sussex European Institute. Available at «http://www.sussex.ac.uk/sei/».

Taggart, P. and Szczerbiak, A. (eds) (2008) *Opposing Europe? The Comparative Party Politics of Euroscepticism, vols 1 and 2* (Oxford: Oxford University Press).

Wallace, H. (2007) *Adapting to Enlargement of the European Union: Institutional Practice since May 2004* (Brussels: Trans European Policy Studies Association). Available at «http://www.tepsa.be/».

JCMS 2008 Volume 46 Annual Review pp. 215–231

Economic Developments in the Euro Area

AMY VERDUN
University of Victoria

Introduction

Turmoil and turbulence characterized economic developments in the euro area in 2007. A financial crisis struck the European markets in August 2007 and the European Central Bank (ECB) felt compelled to take swift action. The economy during the remainder of 2007 continued to be frail as the financial market crisis unfolded and as multiple shocks hit the markets throughout the autumn. These developments came against the backdrop of the so-called sub-prime mortgage crisis in the United States (US). In the euro area, economic growth continued, but nervousness about the strong euro, the financial crisis and a possible US recession influenced governments and the ECB.

In the Member States of the euro area, the economic growth of 2006 continued for the most part into 2007 as the world economy continued to expand strongly. The overall growth rate for the world as a whole was projected to be about 5.2 per cent for 2007 and 4.8 per cent for 2008 (IMF, 2007b, p. 5). Growth in the first half of 2007 was strong (globally above 5 per cent) but eased slightly in the second half.

The euro area witnessed its second expansion with Slovenia joining on 1 January 2007 as its 13th member. In the euro area as a whole, economic growth over the year 2007 stood at 2.6 per cent, whereas the European Commission spring forecast revised the forecast for growth downwards to end up at 1.7 per cent in 2008 and 1.5 per cent in 2009 (Commission, 2008a).

Strong growth and a sharp increase in energy and food prices meant that there remained a concern about rising inflation rates.

The real crisis came following the turmoil in financial markets when it became apparent that liquidity was drying up in the euro money market. On 9 August 2007 the ECB responded to the lack of liquidity by injecting €95 billion ($131 billion) into the economy – the biggest ever loan and much more than the US Federal Reserve had done in the same period (twice lending $12 billion).

In currency markets the real effective exchange rate of the euro strengthened further whilst the US dollar continued to weaken. Whereas the euro had been worth $1.29 on 11 January, by the end of November 2007 it was at a high of $1.49.

This article looks at the economic developments in the euro area by highlighting a few core characteristics of the euro area as a whole and those of its largest five economies (Germany, France, Italy, Spain and the Netherlands). Section I provides some key economic performance indicators such as economic growth, employment, inflation, and public finances. Sections II and III briefly discuss respectively ECB decisions in 2007 and the external dimension of the euro. Section IV looks at the five selected countries. Section V offers a reflection on the developments with Economic and Monetary Union (EMU) over the reviewed time period. The final section closes with a brief summary and outlook for 2008.

I. Economic Developments in the Euro Area –
Main Economic Indicators

Economic Growth

In April 2007, the International Monetary Fund (IMF) reported that the average rate of economic growth for advanced economies in the year 2006 was projected to be 2.6 per cent, which is down a little from 2.8 per cent the year before (IMF, 2008, 2007b, p. 8). 2007, however, showed a break in the trend. Unlike in previous years, the performances of euro area countries did not lag behind those of the advanced economies; the euro area performed on a par with other advanced economies for the first time in years (see Table 1). The recovery in the euro area in 2007 was strong, with output growth surpassing the US and Japan (see Table 1). However, as was the case in previous years, the EU as a whole performed better than the euro area, largely due to the catch up of central and eastern European countries that joined the EU in 2004 and 2007.

The euro area economies that performed well in 2007 included Austria, Finland, Germany, Greece, Ireland, Luxembourg, Slovenia and Spain

Table 1: World Economic Outlook Update Projections (Annual % Change Unless Otherwise Stated)

	2005	2006	Estimated 2007	Projected 2008	Difference from October 2007 projections 2007	2008
World output	4.4	5	4.9	4.1	0.2	−0.3
Advanced economies of which	2.5	3	2.6	1.8	0.1	−0.4
United States	3.1	2.9	2.2	1.5	0.3	−0.4
Euro area (15)	1.5	2.8	2.6	1.6	0.1	−0.5
Japan	1.9	2.4	1.9	1.5	−0.1	−0.2
Other advanced economies	3.2	3.7	3.8	2.8	0.1	−0.2
Emerging market and developing economies	7	7.7	7.8	6.9	0.2	−0.2
Africa	5.9	5.8	6	7	–	−0.2
Central and eastern Europe	5.6	6.4	5.5	4.6	−0.3	−0.6
Commonwealth of Independent States	6.6	8.1	8.2	7	0.5	–
Developing Asia of which	9	9.6	9.6	8.6	–	−0.1
China	10.4	11.1	11.4	10	−0.1	–
Middle East	5.6	5.8	6	5.9	0.1	−0.1
Western Hemisphere	4.6	5.4	5.4	4.3	0.5	–

Note: Real effective exchange rates are assumed to remain constant (4 December 2007–2 January 2008). *Source*: IMF (2008).

(Commission, 2007). Others are still performing poorly, such as France, Italy and Portugal (see Table 2). In 2007 it was no longer as clear-cut that the old Member States that are not part of the euro area did better than the average of the euro area countries. This result was mainly due to the fact that growth in Denmark lagged behind (Sweden and UK are still performing at the same level of growth as for instance Germany).

Employment

The employment situation in the euro area improved sharply in 2007 thereby breaking the trend of the very small gradual improvement seen over the previous three years. From 2003 to 2005 the euro area average unemployment hovered around 8.7 per cent dropping to 8.3 per cent in 2006. The finalized statistics for 2007 are expected to show unemployment in the euro area at 7.3 per cent, the lowest level in 26 years (Trichet, 2007; ECB, 2008, p. 19). The forecasted figures for 2007 suggest that the euro area's employment perform-ance is at 7.1 per cent – closely trailing the performance of other EU countries

Table 2: GDP per capita (% Change on Preceding Year, 1992–2009)

	2003	2004	2005	2006	2007	2008
Belgium	0.6	2.5	1.1	2.1	2.5	1.9
Germany	−0.3	1.1	0.8	3.0	2.6	2.2
Ireland	2.6	2.5	3.6	3.1	2.9	2.3
Greece	4.7	4.2	3.2	4.0	3.8	3.4
Spain	1.4	1.6	1.9	2.3	2.4	1.6
France	0.4	1.8	1.1	1.4	1.3	1.5
Italy	−0.7	0.2	−0.6	1.4	1.5	1.2
Cyprus	0.1	1.8	1.4	2.1	1.9	2.0
Luxembourg	0.9	3.4	3.4	4.4	4.2	3.8
Malta	−0.9	−0.6	2.5	2.6	2.6	2.3
Netherlands	−0.1	1.9	1.3	2.9	2.6	2.5
Austria	0.8	1.6	1.3	2.7	2.8	2.3
Portugal	−1.4	0.9	0.0	0.9	1.4	1.6
Slovenia	2.7	4.4	4.0	5.3	5.5	4.2
Finland	1.5	3.4	2.6	4.6	3.9	3.1
Euro area	1.5	1.4	0.9	2.2	2.2	1.9
Bulgaria	5.6	7.2	6.8	6.6	6.8	6.5
Czech Rep	3.6	4.4	6.1	6.0	5.6	4.7
Denmark	0.1	1.9	2.8	3.2	1.7	0.9
Estonia	7.7	8.3	10.8	11.4	8.0	6.5
Latvia	7.8	9.3	11.2	12.5	11.0	7.7
Lithuania	10.8	7.9	8.6	8.3	9.0	7.6
Hungary	4.5	5.0	4.3	4.0	2.3	2.8
Poland	4.0	5.4	3.7	6.2	6.5	5.7
Romania	5.5	8.8	4.4	7.8	6.3	6.3
Slovakia	4.1	5.4	5.9	8.2	8.6	6.9
Sweden	1.3	3.7	2.5	3.6	2.6	2.3
United Kingdom	2.4	2.8	1.2	2.3	2.6	1.8
EU-27	0.9	2.0	1.3	2.6	2.6	2.2
USA	1.5	2.7	2.1	1.9	1.1	0.8
Japan	1.2	2.7	1.9	2.3	2.0	2.0

Source: Commission (2007), Table 4, p. 144.

over the past four years. The statistical improvement was caused by an increase in employment (the labour force is growing) as much as a decrease in unemployment caused by the improvement in the cycle, which has benefited all types of employees (ECB, 2008, pp. 68–9). The Member State with the lowest unemployment in 2007 was the Netherlands; Austria, Ireland, and Luxembourg also had relatively low unemployment rates (see Table 3). Despite rapid growth, unemployment in Germany was still rather high, but falling. Belgium, France, Greece, and Portugal had similar levels of unemployment to Germany. The Member States outside the euro area have

Table 3: Percentage of the Civilian Labour Force Unemployed in the EU-15, 2003–08

	2003	2004	2005	2006	2007	2008 projected
Belgium	8.2	8.4	8.2	8.2	7.5	7.2
Germany	9.3	9.7	10.7	9.8	8.1	7.7
Ireland	4.7	4.5	4.3	4.4	4.5	5.3
Greece	9.7	10.5	9.8	8.9	8.4	7.9
Spain	11.1	10.6	9.2	8.5	8.1	8.5
France	9.5	9.6	9.7	9.5	8.6	8.2
Italy	8.4	8.0	7.7	6.8	5.9	5.7
Luxembourg	3.7	5.1	4.5	4.7	4.7	4.5
Netherlands	3.7	4.6	4.7	3.9	3.1	2.7
Austria	4.3	4.8	5.2	4.7	4.3	4.2
Portugal	6.3	6.7	7.6	7.7	8.0	8.0
Slovenia	6.7	6.3	6.5	6.0	4.9	4.7
Finland	9.0	8.8	8.4	7.7	6.7	6.4
Euro area	8.7	8.9	8.9	8.3	7.3	7.1
Denmark	5.4	5.5	4.8	3.9.	3.0	2.7
Sweden	5.6	6.3	7.4	7.1	6.1	5.8
UK	4.9	4.7	4.8	5.3	5.3	5.4
EU-27	9.0	9.1	8.9	8.2	7.1	6.8

Source: Commission (2007), p. 155, Table 28.

markedly lower levels of unemployment than either the euro area average or the EU average (see Johnson, this volume).

Inflation

Overall the inflation rate in the euro area has stayed more or less the same over the past four years (see Table 4). The performances of individual countries, however, continue to diverge a little. The average inflation rate of the euro area countries in 2007 was 2.1 per cent with a maximum of 3.8 per cent for the newcomer Slovenia and a minimum of 1.6 per cent for Finland and the Netherlands.

If we compare the inflation performance of the euro area countries with those in the rest of the EU we find quite wide divergence between the euro area Member States and the three old Member States outside on the one hand, and the new Member States on the other, although the average inflation rate for the EU-27 was still close to that of the euro area.

Public Finances

In 2007, public finances in the euro area stabilized. It was the first year that no euro area Member State was in excess of the 3.0 per cent budgetary deficit

Table 4: Harmonized Consumer Price Index (Annual % Change)

	2001	2002	2003	2004	2005	2006	2007
Belgium	2.4	1.6	1.5	1.9	2.5	2.3	1.8
Bulgaria	7.4	5.8	2.3	6.1	6.0	7.4	7.6
Czech Republic	4.5	1.4	−0.1	2.6	1.6	2.1	3.0
Denmark	2.3	2.4	2.0	0.9	1.7	1.9	1.7
Germany	1.9	1.4	1.0	1.8	1.9	1.8	2.3
Estonia	5.6	3.6	1.4	3.0	4.1	4.4	6.7
Ireland	4.0	4.7	4.0	2.3	2.2	2.7	2.9
Greece	3.7	3.9	3.4	3.0	3.5	3.3	3.0
Spain	2.8	3.6	3.1	3.1	3.4	3.6	2.8
France	1.8	1.9	2.2	2.3	1.9	1.9	1.6
Italy	2.3	2.6	2.8	2.3	2.2	2.2	2.0
Cyprus	2.0	2.8	4.0	1.9	2.0	2.2	2.2
Latvia	2.5	2.0	2.9	6.2	6.9	6.6	10.1
Lithuania	1.6	0.3	−1.1	1.2	2.7	3.8	5.8
Luxembourg	2.4	2.1	2.5	3.2	3.8	3.0	2.7
Hungary	9.1	5.2	4.7	6.8	3.5	4.0	7.9
Malta	2.5	2.6	1.9	2.7	2.5	2.6	0.7
Netherlands	5.1	3.9	2.2	1.4	1.5	1.7	1.6
Austria	2.3	1.7	1.3	2.0	2.1	1.7	2.2
Poland	5.3	1.9	0.7	3.6	2.2	1.3	2.6
Portugal	4.4	3.7	3.3	2.5	2.1	3.0	2.4
Romania	34.5	22.5	15.3	11.9	9.1	6.6	4.9
Slovenia	8.6	7.5	5.7	3.7	2.5	2.5	3.8
Slovakia	7.2	3.5	8.4	7.5	2.8	4.3	1.9
Finland	2.7	2.0	1.3	0.1	0.8	1.3	1.6
Sweden	2.7	1.9	2.3	1.0	0.8	1.5	1.7
United Kingdom	1.2	1.3	1.4	1.3	2.1	2.3	2.3
Euro Area-15	2.4	2.3	2.1	2.1	2.2	2.2	2.1
EU-27	3.2	2.5	2.1	2.3	2.3	2.3	2.4
Euro Area-12	2.4	2.3	2.1	2.1	2.2	2.2	2.1
EU-25	2.5	2.1	1.9	2.1	2.2	2.2	2.3
EU-15	2.2	2.1	2.0	2.0	2.1	2.2	2.2

Source: Commission (2008b).

ceiling laid down in the Treaty on European Union and further clarified by the Stability and Growth Pact (SGP), which was reformed in 2005 (see Heipertz and Verdun, 2006; Verdun, 2007; and see Table 5). The only country at the 3 per cent threshold in 2007 was Portugal. Italy had corrected its excessive deficit of 2006 in 2007, which had been partly due to anomalies causing a somewhat inflated deficit in 2006 (see Verdun, 2007). Otherwise the improvements in public finances can be traced to higher tax revenues, so whether

Table 5: Net Lending (+) or Net Borrowing (−) General Government as a Share of GDP in EU-15, 2003–08

	2003	2004	2005	2006	2007 projected	2008 projected
Belgium	0.0	0.0	−2.3	0.4	−0.3	−0.4
Germany	−4.0	−3.8	−3.4	−1.6	0.1	−0.1
Greece	−5.6	−7.3	−5.1	−2.5	−2.9	−1.8
Ireland	0.4	1.3	1.2	2.9	0.9	−0.2
Spain	−0.2	−0.3	1.0	1.8	1.8	1.2
France	−4.1	−3.6	−2.9	−2.5	−2.6	−2.6
Italy	−3.5	−3.5	−4.2	−4.4	−2.3	−2.3
Luxembourg	0.5	−1.2	−0.1	−0.7	1.2	1.0
Netherlands	−3.1	−1.7	−0.3	0.6	−0.4	0.5
Austria	−1.6	−1.2	−1.6	−1.4	−0.8	−0.7
Portugal	−2.9	−3.4	−6.1	−3.9	−3.0	−2.6
Finland	2.5	2.3	2.7	3.8	4.6	4.2
Euro area	−3.1	−2.8	−2.5	−1.5	−0.8	−0.9
Denmark	−0.1	1.9	4.6	4.6	4.0	3.0
Sweden	−0.9	0.8	2.4	2.5	3.0	2.8
UK	−3.3	−3.4	−3.3	−2.7	−2.8	−3.0
EU-27	−3.1	−2.8	−2.4	−1.6	−1.1	−1.2

Source: Commission (2007), p. 160, Table 37.

there may be problems with meeting the stipulations of the SGP will remain to be seen in future years once there is an economic downturn.

II. Policies of the European Central Bank

The Governing Council of the ECB sets the key interest rates for the euro area. Since its creation, the ECB has taken the euro area as a whole as its reference point, weighting the Member States' economies proportionally to their size. Although Slovenia's addition is thus only a minor change in the size of the euro area economy, the governor of the Slovenian central bank has nevertheless the same vote as the governor of any other national central bank (for a general discussion of ECB policy see Verdun, 2006).

The crisis that hit financial markets in August posed a serious challenge to the ECB. During the first half of 2007 the ECB raised interest rates twice, each time by 25 basis points (to 2.75 on 8 March 2007 and to 3.00 on 6 June 2007 (see ECB, 2008, p. 96), following on from a remarkable five increases in 2006 (see Verdun, 2007). These increases were responses to the concern that inflation was rising as the economy picked up steam. What was striking was that there have been no changes in interest rates in the autumn of 2007 in response to the credit crunch that originated in the sub-prime mortgage crisis.

The ECB has held the line on interest rates because it is seeking to balance the risk of inflation and the negative effects of the credit crunch and the risk of a major downturn in the US slowing down the global economy (Trichet and Papademos, 2007).

As in the past, the ECB has not been responsive to outside pressures. In these circumstances, however, keeping the interest rates unchanged during the autumn of 2007 (whilst the Federal Reserve was responding quickly) did not mean it was unresponsive to the situation in the markets. It is likely that the ECB would have raised interest rates if there had not been a financial crisis, as the average inflation was above the 2 per cent target (it was approaching 3 per cent in December 2007). But because the ECB needed to balance both the consequences of the financial market turmoil and the information about the rate of inflation it left interest rates unchanged (Trichet and Papademos, 2007).

III. External Dimension of the Euro

The euro gained considerably in value against most other major currencies during 2007. As in 2006, there was little criticism of the euro being overvalued, concern instead focused on the decline of the US dollar. In the early months of 2007 the euro appreciated further, following the trend set in 2006. The appreciation was briefly interrupted between May and mid-August, only to continue appreciating in the second part of 2007. At the end of the year in nominal effective terms, the euro was worth 6.3 per cent more than it had been at the beginning of the year and 8.2 per cent more than the average of 2006 (ECB, 2008, p. 78). Against the dollar the euro appreciated almost 12 per cent, whereas against the pound sterling it appreciated 9.3 per cent and against the Japanese yen about 5 per cent. The real effective exchange rate (based on cost and price measures) also increased. The euro was up 5.5 per cent compared to a year earlier.

IV. Developments in Selected Member States of the Euro Area

Since the EMU is an asymmetrical economic and monetary union (Verdun, 1996), with a strong central authority responsible for monetary policy and fiscal policy decentralized in the hands of national governments, its success depends more than most monetary unions on the economic performance of its constitutive states. Some of the criticism of the euro area has been that its economic growth, particularly that of the largest countries (Germany, France and Italy), has lagged behind that of other EU Member States and other advanced economies. The performance of the larger Member States is important as the ECB sets monetary policy based on a weighted average of the economies of the euro area. This section therefore discusses some economic developments in the largest five Member States of the euro area and assesses the differences in their performances on a number of characteristics, such as economic growth, investment and consumption, employment, public finances and inflation, and considers the forecasts for 2008.

Germany

Economic growth in Germany in 2007 was finally solid, continuing on from 2006 and likely to continue into 2008 (Commission, 2007, p. 70). Growth in 2006 was 2.9 per cent; 2.5 per cent in 2007; and is forecast to be 2.1 per cent for 2008 (Commission, 2008a, p. 70). Economic growth was boosted at the end of 2006 due to private consumption and housing investment (anticipating an increase in value added tax (VAT) from 16 to 19 per cent on 1 January 2007) and consequently slowed down a little in the early months of 2007. Exports, though still strong, contracted a little. Some of the reduced export growth in the later part of 2007 was due to the financial turbulence in the second half of the year.

Private consumption was stronger in 2007 and is expected to stay strong, at least for a while, as will household savings (Commission, 2007, p. 70). Corporate and government investment was also up and contributed significantly to growth. At the same time, the stronger euro puts pressure on the export sector, which has performed comparatively well during the past few years, as Germany managed to keep wages and prices under control. Regardless of these challenges, the German economy is unlikely to see a fall in housing prices, for instance. Inflation is somewhat on the rise with a number of factors contributing to price increases: the higher rate of VAT, increases in food and energy prices, and pressures from the need to renegotiate a number of collective wage agreements after 2007. Employment was up in Germany in 2007 in terms both of number of people employed and number of hours worked.

Public finances in Germany were very healthy in 2007 for the first time in several years. The government budget is projected to be in balance for the first time since 2000 (Commission, 2007, p. 71). The spring 2007 forecast envisaged a deficit of 0.6 per cent of gross domestic product (GDP), but government efforts to increase revenue and control expenditure improved the situation. The government had more revenue available this year, compared to last year, as a result of the higher VAT rate and due to an increase in revenues from direct taxes.

Though inflation in Germany over the past few years has been lower than in other euro area countries, in 2007 it was similar to the euro area average and in the EU-27 (German inflation stood at 2.3 per cent in 2007 compared to 2.1 per cent in the euro area and 2.4 per cent in the EU-27 in the same year). Although Germany's large economy has the greatest impact on ECB policies, euro area interest rates do not normally exactly reflect economic conditions in Germany. Contrary to the recent past, in 2007, ECB monetary policy was appropriate for Germany insofar as inflation rates in that country were concerned. Inflation was higher than in previous years mostly due to the VAT increase. However, even though there is uncertainty about the increase in food and energy prices, German inflation is expected to decline below the euro area average for 2008, which most likely has Germany returning to a situation of earlier years whereby ECB monetary policy would be a little too tight given the inflation rate in this country.

The economic forecast for Germany in 2008 is favourable. The government budget is projected to be in surplus (Commission, 2007, p. 73) According to the Commission's annual forecast, unemployment is projected to come down to 7.7 per cent in 2008 and 7.6 per cent in 2009 (down from 9.8 per cent in 2006 and 8.1 per cent in 2007).

France

Economic developments in Germany and France differed profoundly in 2007. France witnessed a disappointing performance with subdued economic growth, which is expected to stay below the euro area average in both 2008 and 2009. Measured as annual percentage of change at previous year prices, 2006 saw 2.0 per cent growth, whereas 2007 was projected to see growth in this country at 1.7 per cent and growth forecast to be at 2.0 per cent in 2008 (Commission, 2008, p. 84). This stagnation, particularly in the second quarter, was attributed to an unexpected slowing of business investment (Commission, 2008, p. 82), due to uncertainty about where the new government would take the country and to the crisis in the financial markets. As in 2006, strong domestic demand, facilitated by an increase in purchasing power, was an important driver of economic growth in France. Consequently, imports are likely to grow faster than exports.

The employment situation in France showed improvement in 2007. In 2006, job creation was about 0.7 per cent, whereas the projected increase in jobs in 2007 was 1.0 per cent. Similarly, whereas the rate of unemployment was 9.5 per cent in 2006, the forecast for 2007 is 8.6 per cent, with further reductions expected in the years to come (Commission, 2007, p. 84). Nevertheless, the unemployment rate in France is still high compared to other EU Member States. Thus, wage moderation is expected to continue.

Public finances in France improved further in 2007. The budget deficit fell to 2.6 per cent of GDP in 2007 and is projected to stay there in 2008 (see Table 5). Most of the reduction in the budget deficit was due to stronger economic growth, which contributed to improved revenues and reduced expenditures. The increase in revenue was largely due to taxes on corporations in a year in which VAT revenue fell a little behind and income tax revenue was a little lower because rates had been lowered by the government in the 2007 finance law. Further changes in taxation law (draft finance laws for the state and social security) may change the revenue – such as the abolition of the tax on inheritance, income tax credit for mortgage interests, a tax shield or *bouclier fiscal* (a ceiling of 50 per cent on the maximum amount of tax paid on income) and tax rebates on overtime – all of which will reduce the revenue basis for the government in the years to come (Commission, 2007, p. 83). The public debt to GDP ratio has been at 64 per cent in 2006 and 2007 and is forecast to stay stable at that rate in 2008 and 2009. France's budget deficit has stabilized below the SGP's 3 per cent threshold. It was 2.5 per cent in 2007 and is forecast to be 2.6 per cent in 2008 and 2.4 per cent in 2009.

Inflation in France has been steady and marginally lower than elsewhere in the euro area. Inflation in 2006 was at 1.9 and in 2007 projected to end up at 1.5 per cent, and is expected to pick up slightly to 1.7 per cent in 2008 (Commission, 2007, p. 84). Because inflation in France is relatively close to that of the euro area as a whole, the ECB's interest rate policy is not inappropriate for France insofar as inflation is concerned.

The economic forecast for France for 2008 is not as favourable as it was last year. Growth is expected to remain slightly subdued. Nevertheless, just like last year, it is expected that in the years 2008 and 2009 it will be better largely because of strong domestic demand (Commission, 2007, p. 82). Household disposable income should increase as a result of government tax deductions on mortgage loan interest mentioned above and other tax changes laid out in the law on work employment and purchasing power.

Italy

Economic growth in Italy in 2007 was weak compared to that in other Member States of the euro area. Real economic growth was close to zero in 2005 (0.1 per cent) and positive (1.9 per cent in both 2006 and 2007) which in both years is below the euro area average. Growth is forecast to drop to 1.4 per cent and 1.9 per cent respectively in 2008 and 2009 (Commission, 2007, p. 87). The main drivers behind the growth in 2007 were the improvements in employment and domestic demand. The performance of Italian exports remained a concern. Although Italy has seen an increase in the value of its exports, it has been losing market share in terms of volume, which has been offset by rising prices of exported goods. Thus, as in 2006 (Verdun, 2007), Italy was not able to maintain competitiveness.

After a spectacular employment growth of 1.6 per cent in 2006, 2007 did not see growth of the same magnitude, although the employment grew by 0.8 per cent (Commission, 2007, p. 86). The forecast (Commission, 2007, p. 87) is that unemployment will drop further from 6.8 per cent in 2006 to 5.9 and 5.7 per cent in 2008 and 2009 respectively, but this is mainly due to the stalling of the growth in the labour force.

The most notable change was in Italy's budget deficit. Whereas Italy ran a deficit of 4.4 per cent of GDP in 2006, well in excess of the SGP ceiling, the forecast for 2007 was 2.3 per cent of GDP. As mentioned in last year's report (Verdun, 2007), there were some important, one-off reasons for the disappointing budgetary situation in 2006, but it is nevertheless remarkable that Italy got out of the excessive deficit situation so quickly. The improvement was the result of greater than expected revenues as well as some one-off measures. The public debt to GDP ratio is still above 100 per cent, but is gradually dropping from its high of 106 in 2005 to 103 in 2007 and is projected to come down slowly in subsequent years (Commission, 2007, p. 87).

Inflation in Italy over the past few years has been around 2.3 per cent and is now expected to sit at or just below 2.0 per cent in 2007, 2008 and 2009. Italy, like France, has an inflation rate that is close to that of the euro area as a whole. As a consequence, the ECB's interest rate policy is appropriate for Italy as far as price stability is concerned. The economic forecast for Italy for 2008 suggests that growth will be a little weak, but the expectation for 2009 is rosier.

Spain

Growth in Spain had been faster than in most Member States of the euro area for a number of years, including in 2007, but the prospects for the future are not as rosy. Measured as annual percentage of change at previous year prices, 2005 saw 3.6 per cent growth, 2006 had 3.9 per cent growth, 2007 was forecast to have 3.8 per cent, but growth in 2008 is projected to drop to 3.0 per cent (Commission, 2007, p. 81), which is still well above the euro area and EU averages (see Table 2). Again, increased domestic demand was an important driver, but this factor is likely to lose force in 2008 as the credit crunch impacts on consumers. In Spain net exports are contributing negatively to growth, but less so than in 2005 and in 2006 (Commission, 2007, p. 79).

As was the case in 2006, the employment situation in Spain is still looking very good. Employment increased again in Spain in 2007 by 3.0 per cent (slightly down from 3.2 per cent in both 2005 and 2006). Similarly, whereas the rate of unemployment had been 10.6 in 2004, 9.2 per cent in 2005, and 8.5 in 2006, the forecast for 2007 was 8.1 per cent. The forecast for subsequent years, however, suggests that unemployment will rise again (contrary to what had been expected last year).

Public finance in Spain is and has been recently in line with the EMU requirements on deficits and public debt. The Spanish government will have a surplus in 2007 and a debt level below the reference value.

Over the past few years, inflation in Spain has tended to be relatively high, between 3.1 and 3.6 per cent in the period 2004–06. In 2007 inflation came down, and was projected to be 2.6 per cent. Even in 2008 inflation is due to stay below 3.0 per cent. The main reason for the higher inflation in earlier years was the strong economic growth in the country. The downward trend is a result of the cooling down of the economy and related factors. For example, an adjustment in the housing sector is contributing to the reduction in prices, as is the decline in the growth of private consumption and the reduction in the speed and quantity of jobs created.

So even though the economic forecast for Spain for 2008 is once again favourable, growth in 2008 and 2009 is expected to be somewhat lower than in recent years (Commission, 2007, p. 81). Inflation will gradually come down to about 2.7 per cent in 2008. With Spain's economic performance coming more closely in line with the euro area as a whole, ECB monetary policy is becoming more suitable for Spain.

The Netherlands

After strong economic growth in 2006 the Dutch economy continued to experience economic good times in 2007. Measured as an annual percentage change at the previous year's prices, 2006 featured 3.0 per cent growth, whereas growth in 2007 was projected to end up at 2.6 per cent and the forecasts for 2008 and 2009 show a similar level of growth (2.6 and 2.5 respectively) (Commission, 2007, p. 102). In the Netherlands there are multiple drivers of the growth, including consumer demand and exports (Commission, 2007, p. 100).

The employment situation in the Netherlands has improved with the economic recovery. The Netherlands is a little different in that the average number of hours worked per person is relatively low – at just below 1,400 hours per person per year it has the lowest rate of all OECD countries (compared to an average of 1,625 hours per person in the EU-15 or the OECD country average of 1,775; OECD, 2008, p. 153). Most of the variance between the Netherlands and other EU and OECD countries is, however, attributable to the large number of part-time workers. Corrected to full-time equivalents the unemployment rate in 2007 was about 1.8 per cent (similar to that in 2006). At the same time there was an increase in demand for labour. The regular rate of unemployment (persons) was 3.9 per cent in 2006 and 2.5 per cent for 2007 (Commission, 2007, p. 101). Given that the labour force has not been growing, the increased demand for labour means that the people already active in the labour market will need to work more hours – something the government is aware of and seeking to provide incentives for. The number of self-employed people is also rising quickly.

The Netherlands has performed admirably lately with regard to the SGP's budget deficit criterion. In 2006 the budget was in surplus (0.6 per cent of GDP), while in 2007 it was in deficit, but only slightly so (0.4 per cent of GDP) (see Table 5).

Inflation in the Netherlands has been dropping since the early 2000s, after a slight increase in 2006 to 1.7 per cent it was forecast to fall to 1.6 per cent for 2007, before increasing to 2.3 per cent in 2008. Thus, in 2007, as in the years before, inflation in the Netherlands has been low. With the forecast increase, however, one could conclude that the ECB's relatively tight interest rate policy is fine for the Netherlands.

The 2008 economic forecast for the Netherlands is positive. Since economic recovery took hold in 2005, productivity growth appears strong as well (Commission, 2007, p. 102). Overall, the Netherlands is doing very well indeed.

V. An Assessment of Economic and Monetary Union in 2007

After a number of years of speculation about whether EMU was good for the participating states, criticisms of EMU have been much less frequent in recent years, including in 2007. The more positive assessment of EMU can be traced back to the improvement of the economic performance of the larger economies of the euro area (particularly Germany's). Furthermore, in 2007, the euro area countries performed as well as most advanced economies in terms of growth and better than a few important partners (such as Japan and the US). Also the economic performances of the countries in the euro area started to compare favourably to those Member States that stayed out; except for unemployment the 'ins' and 'outs' were doing equally well.

The reality is that EMU through ensuring low inflation and low interest rates has enabled the euro area countries, on average, to borrow money more cheaply than prior to 1999. The ECB's decision to respond quickly and forcefully to the credit crunch crisis of August 2007, that is to provide €95 billion in loans to banks at a policy rate of 4.00 per cent at overnight maturity, revealed another advantage of having the ECB manage the euro area (ECB, 2008). Another benefit of EMU is the ease in comparing prices between countries, which promotes trade and foreign direct investment in the euro area.[1] Finally, the dynamic effects of EMU are such that other imperfections of market integration, such as the shortcomings in the integration of financial services, are now coming to the surface and are being discussed (see Howarth, this volume).

As in 2006 overall acceptance of EMU meant that there was no serious discussion of reform of EMU's institutional design. The only major institutional change was the accession of Slovenia. Part of the discussion in 2007 was the decision to have Cyprus and Malta join the euro area as of 1 January 2008 even though the decision was by no means controversial.

Conclusion

Despite financial turmoil in the summer and autumn, the economic developments in the euro area countries during 2007 were positive. The concerns about the lack of economic growth in the euro area that still dominated 2005 have withered away and the new concern is how long the euro area economies will be able to weather the storm in the financial market. The differences between the 'ins' and the 'outs' (as far as the old Member States are concerned) diminished, and Germany, a leading economy, continued to make clear improvements. Although not all large Member States are performing at the solid 2.5 per cent level of growth, all are making efforts to be ready for either a downturn (keeping deficits under control) and are looking for ways to increase growth (such as the French tax relief).

EMU seems to be gaining acceptance among the EU's citizens. 2007 saw no major discussion of the institutional structure, and criticism of the Stability and Growth Pact was all but absent, most likely because no countries were running against the budgetary deficit ceiling. A clear assessment of the euro area countries' commitment to EMU and the SGP, however, can be made only after their economies have been tested by a recession.

---

[1] Baldwin (2005) has calculated that trade has increased by between 5 and 10 per cent due to the introduction of the euro. Petroulas (2007) estimates that the introduction of the euro raised inward Foreign Direct Investment (FDI) flows by approximately 16 per cent within the euro area, by 11 per cent to non-members and by 8 per cent from non-member countries into the euro area. The European Commission and the European Central Bank have also stressed the connection between the introduction of the euro and increased trade (ECB, 2008; Commission, 2008c).

The ECB was very active in 2007 in addressing the challenges that emerged out of the credit crunch in August 2007, and it has not responded to threats of inflation in the autumn because it balanced stability in financial markets (access to credit) with increasing inflationary pressures.

The outlook for the euro area economy in 2008 is good, but not as good as for 2007, and may well be optimistic depending on the impact of the credit crisis. Although growth is likely to slow, the prospect is that the euro area economies will still experience strong economic growth, job creation and reduced unemployment. The countries in the euro area may look ahead to another good year.

Key Readings

Grauwe (2007) is a further updated version of his classic textbook on EMU that covers everything from a critique of the optimum currency area literature, to the costs and benefits of a single currency to the relationship between monetary and political union. Dyson (2007) assesses the first decade of the euro area from the perspective of the extent to which, and ways in which, the creation of the euro has affected EU Member States, 'insiders' and 'outsiders' alike. Jones *et al.* (2007) examine various legitimacy and efficiency issues of EMU, reflecting on the eight years since the start of its stage three and looking ahead to its future expansion. Hansen and King (2007) argue that the distribution of seigniorage from issuing euro notes to national central banks will initially benefit the new EU members from central and eastern Europe a lot, but large unintended redistribution through seigniorage cannot be expected in the future. Segers and van Esch (2007) discuss the Stability and Growth Pact from a political point of view and argue that the Franco–German leadership alliance, rather than the German financial elite, was crucial for the SGP.

References

Baldwin, R.E. (2005) 'The Euro's Trade Effects'. Available at «http://hei.unige.ch/~baldwin/RoseEffect/Euros_Trade_Effect_Baldwin_31May05.pdf».
Commission of the European Communities (2007) 'Economic Forecast'. *European Economy*, No. 7.
Commission of the European Communities (2008a) 'Economic Forecasts'. *European Economy*, No. 3, Spring.
Commission of the European Communities (2008b) 'Harmonized Index of Consumer Prices'. DG Ecfin Services, March 2008.

Commission of the European Communities (2008c) 'EMU@10: Successes and Challenges after 10 years of Economic and Monetary Union'. Available at «http:// ec.europa.eu/economy_finance/emu10/expert_en.htm».

de Grauwe, P. (2007) *Economics of Monetary Union* (Oxford: Oxford University Press).

Dyson, K. (ed.) (2007) *The Euro at Ten* (Oxford: Oxford University Press).

European Central Bank (2008) *Annual Report 2007* (Frankfurt: ECB).

Hansen, J.D. and King, R.M. (2007) 'How to Cut the Seignorage Cake into Fair Shares in an Enlarged EMU'. *JCMS*, Vol. 45, No. 5, pp. 999–1010.

Heipertz, M. and Verdun, A. (2006) 'The Dog That Would Bark But Never Bite? Origins, Crisis and Reform of Europe's Stability and Growth'. In Torres, F., Verdun, A. and Zimmermann, H. (eds) *EMU Rules: The Political and Economic Consequences of European Monetary Integration* (Baden-Baden: Nomos).

IMF (2007b) 'World Economic Outlook. Globalization and Inequality'. (Washington DC: International Monetary Fund), October.

IMF (2008) 'World Economic Outlook Update. An Update of the Key WEO Projections'. (Washington DC: International Monetary Fund), January.

Jones, E., Sadeh, T. and Verdun, A. (eds) (2007) *Review of International Political Economy*, Vol. 14, No. 5 (Special Issue), pp. 739–894.

OECD (2008) *OECD Factbook 2008: Economic, Environmental and Social Statistics*. (Paris: Organization for Economic Co-operation and Development).

Petroulas, P. (2007) 'The Effect of the Euro on Foreign Direct Investment'. *European Economic Review*, Vol. 51, No. 6, pp. 1468–91.

Segers, M. and van Esch, F. (2007) 'Behind the Veil of Budgetary Discipline: The Political Logic of the Budgetary Rules in EMU and the SGP'. *JCMS*, Vol. 45, No. 5, pp. 1089–109.

Trichet, J.-C. (2007) Transcript of the Press Briefing Following the Meeting of the Governing Council on 2 August 2007. Available at «http://www.ecb.int/press/pressconf/2007/html/is070802.en.html».

Trichet, J.-C. and Papademos, L. (2007) Introductory Statement with Q&A. Frankfurt am Main, 6 December. Available at «http://www.ecb.int/press/pressconf/2007/html/is071206.en.html».

Verdun, A. (1996) 'An "Asymmetrical" Economic and Monetary Union in the EU: Perceptions of Monetary Authorities and Social Partners'. *Journal of European Integration*, Vol. 20, No. 1, pp. 59–81.

Verdun, A. (2006) 'Economic Developments in the Euro Area'. *JCMS*, Vol. 44, s1, pp. 199–212.

Verdun, A. (2007) 'Economic Developments in the Euro Area'. *JCMS*, Vol. 45, s1, pp. 213–30.

JCMS 2008 Volume 46 Annual Review pp. 233–252

Developments in the Economies of Member States Outside the Euro Area

DEBRA JOHNSON
Hull University

Context

The strong global economic growth of 2006 carried over into 2007. The European Commission has estimated world growth of 5.1 per cent for 2007. This represents moderate slowdown and reflects strong momentum in emerging economies and sound economic fundamentals. By late 2007, however, disruptions in financial markets had increased downside risks to the world economy. The major problem was the turmoil in the United States (US) sub-prime mortgage market which left many financial institutions, including western European banks, exposed. As a result, credit conditions tightened not only in the US but also in Europe and elsewhere. The final impact will depend on how quickly market liquidity returns to normal and on the extent of retrenchment in individual credit markets. Countries of central and eastern Europe and the Commonwealth of Independent States (CIS) with large current account deficits dependent upon external financial inflows are also vulnerable to the knock-on effects of the US crisis.

The sub-prime and subsequent housing crises have slowed economic growth in the US. The impact on the world economy, however, may be less pronounced than previously because of strong expansion elsewhere. China, India and Russia alone accounted for half of world economic growth in 2007. China benefited from strong exports and investment to register real gross domestic product (GDP) growth of over 11 per cent in 2007 and is only marginally affected by US economic developments. India's growth eased slightly, but was still a healthy 7.6 per cent. Elsewhere in Asia, Japanese growth was moderate but the economies of South East Asia grew robustly.

In the rest of the world, the CIS, helped by rapidly growing domestic demand and higher oil prices, was the second fastest growing region behind developing Asia. The Middle East and North Africa performed well, as did sub-Saharan Africa, which grew by almost 7 per cent as a result of accelerating domestic demand. Latin America also managed to grow by 5 per cent.

Other factors that increase the risk of a downturn of the world economy include higher oil prices, which are here to stay, and hikes in world food prices, which are due to drought, the loss of agricultural land to bio-fuel production and enhanced demand for some food products from newly prosperous emerging markets.

I. Overall Economic Performance of the EU Member States Outside the Euro Area

The overall impact of global economic developments for the European Union (EU) is greater uncertainty. The recent strength of the European economy, both inside and outside the euro area, however, has led the Commission to reduce its forecast for the region only marginally. It warns, however, of a potentially serious downside risk.

In 2007, real EU GDP growth declined moderately both inside and outside the euro area; notable exceptions were the United Kingdom (UK), Lithuania, Poland, Slovakia and Bulgaria, which performed better (see Table 1). In most cases, growth remained strong early in 2007, but slowed towards the end of the year. It was largely domestic demand that provided the main growth impetus and led to a decreasing contribution of net exports to growth as imports increased to satisfy this demand.

Despite its continuing strong performance, the UK remains highly vulnerable to the US-induced uncertainty because of the importance of the financial sector to its economy. Other economies at risk are those with widening current account deficits, such as Bulgaria and Romania, and those with high levels of foreign currency debt, such as Latvia and Hungary. On the whole, however, banks in the post-2004 accession states were not involved in the US sub-prime market and their economies are more directly integrated with the EU than the US.

Notable changes outside the euro area in 2007 include slower growth in Estonia and Latvia. Their growth, along with that of Lithuania, remains extremely robust and the slowing of their growth represents a move to a more sustainable long term growth path. Poland and Slovakia have also performed

Table 1: Real GDP Growth (% Annual Change) – Non-Euro Area

	1997–2001	2002	2003	2004	2005	2006	2007[a]	2008[b]
Bulgaria	2.0	n/a	5.0	6.6	6.2	6.1	6.3	6.0
Czech Republic	1.2	1.9	3.6	4.5	6.4	6.4	5.8	5.0
Denmark	2.4	0.5	0.4	2.1	3.1	3.5	1.9	1.3
Estonia	6.2	8.0	7.2	8.3	10.2	11.2	7.8	6.4
Cyprus	4.2	2.1	1.8	4.2	3.9	3.8	3.8	3.9
Latvia	6.2	6.5	7.2	8.7	10.6	11.9	10.5	7.2
Lithuania	5.0	6.9	10.3	7.3	7.9	7.7	8.5	7.5
Hungary	4.6	4.3	4.2	4.8	4.1	3.9	2.0	2.6
Malta	3.4	2.2	−0.3	0.1	3.1	3.2	3.1	2.8
Poland	4.4	1.4	3.9	5.3	3.6	6.1	6.5	5.6
Romania	−0.9	n/a	5.2	8.5	4.1	7.7	6.0	5.9
Slovakia	2.7	4.1	4.2	5.4	6.0	8.3	8.7	7.0
Sweden	3.2	2.0	1.7	4.1	2.9	4.2	3.4	3.1
UK	3.1	2.1	2.8	3.3	1.8	2.8	3.1	2.2
Euro area	2.8	0.9	0.8	2.0	1.5	2.8	2.6	2.2

Notes: [a] Estimate; [b] forecast.
Source: Commission (2007).

well. Poland grew at its fastest rate for a decade, leading to an improvement in public finances, which seemed improbable only a few years ago. Slovakia has become a major success story as the large inflows of foreign direct investment (FDI) have started to bear fruit in terms of exports. Hungary, on the other hand, has lost its position as the star performer of central and eastern Europe, largely as a result of its public finances: measures to correct the spiralling deficit were introduced in 2006 and took their toll on growth in 2007.

Labour markets continued to tighten in almost all the non-euro area Member States in 2007. This tightening took the form of lower unemployment and higher levels of employment (see Table 2). In Denmark, labour markets have become so tight that capacity constraints are holding back growth. Apart from Hungary, unemployment rates in the post-2004 accession states are at their lowest this decade. Poland and Slovakia have experienced particularly sizeable falls in unemployment. In Poland, for example, unemployment in 2007 was less than half the level of five years previously and is no longer the highest in the EU.

Labour market improvements have occurred as a result of sustained economic growth and net outward migration. It has taken time for labour markets to respond fully to the recent healthy growth in central and eastern Europe. In part, this is because the economic restructuring in these states initially resulted in the shedding of large quantities of labour. This increased

Table 2: Unemployment (% of the Civilian Labour Force) – Non-Euro Area

	1997–2001	2002	2003	2004	2005	2006	2007[a]	2008[b]
Bulgaria	16.4	n/a	13.7	12.0	10.1	9.0	7.5	6.8
Czech Republic	7.7	7.3	7.8	8.3	7.9	7.1	5.9	5.4
Denmark	4.8	4.6	5.4	5.5	4.8	3.9	3.0	2.7
Estonia	11.1	10.3	10.0	9.7	7.9	5.9	4.9	4.8
Cyprus	3.9	3.6	4.1	4.6	5.2	4.6	4.3	4.1
Latvia	14.0	12.2	10.5	10.4	8.9	6.8	5.8	5.5
Lithuania	13.3	13.5	12.4	11.4	8.3	5.6	4.2	4.2
Hungary	7.3	5.8	5.9	6.1	7.2	7.5	7.3	7.0
Malta	6.8	7.5	7.6	7.4	7.3	7.3	6.8	6.6
Poland	13.8	19.9	19.6	19.0	17.7	13.8	9.4	7.3
Romania	6.2	n/a	7.0	6.1	7.2	7.3	7.1	7.0
Slovakia	15.8	18.7	17.6	18.2	16.3	13.4	11.2	9.7
Sweden	7.1	4.9	5.6	6.3	7.4	7.1	6.1	5.8
UK	5.8	5.1	4.9	4.7	4.7	5.3	5.3	5.4
Euro area	9.2	8.3	8.7	8.9	8.9	8.3	7.3	7.1

Notes: [a] Estimate; [b] forecast.
Source: Commission (2007).

productivity rather than employment and absorbed increasing labour demand. This phase has ended and a more direct relationship between growth and labour markets has emerged.

Despite these improvements, however, labour markets in the new Member States have their problems. Even in countries where unemployment is high, there are reports of labour shortages and labour market inflexibility which could discourage further foreign investment and inhibit growth. The participation rate in most central and eastern European countries is also low compared to most other EU regions. Higher participation rates would increase the labour force but would also require a significant investment in training to update skills. In some cases, labour force shortages are being addressed by importing cheaper labour from further east. Moreover, as the central and eastern European economies continue to move closer to western European levels, the attraction of emigration will decrease and many migrants will return home.

The 2007 annual inflation figures for the non-euro area do not tell the whole story. Prices increased more quickly at the end of the year than at the beginning, for a mixture of domestic and external reasons. For example, domestic droughts pushed up food prices in Bulgaria and Romania. Romania also experienced currency depreciation. Towards the end of 2007, all countries had to absorb the impact of higher global food and energy prices. The

Table 3: Inflation – Non-Euro Area

	1997–2001	2002	2003	2004	2005	2006	2007[a]	2008[b]
Bulgaria	n/a	n/a	2.3	6.1	6.0	7.4	7.1	7.3
Czech Republic	5.6	1.4	−0.1	2.6	1.6	2.1	3.0	3.8
Denmark	2.1	2.4	2.0	0.9	1.7	1.9	1.7	2.4
Estonia	6.1	3.6	1.4	3.0	4.1	4.4	6.3	7.3
Cyprus	2.3	2.8	4.0	1.9	2.0	2.2	2.0	2.3
Latvia	3.9	2.0	2.9	6.2	6.9	6.6	9.6	9.8
Lithuania	3.9	0.3	−1.1	1.2	2.7	3.8	5.6	6.5
Hungary	12.3	5.2	4.7	6.8	3.5	4.0	7.7	4.9
Malta	3.1	2.6	1.9	2.7	2.5	2.6	0.8	2.5
Poland	9.8	1.9	0.7	3.6	2.2	1.3	2.5	2.8
Romania	63.2	n/a	15.3	11.9	9.1	6.6	4.7	5.6
Slovakia	8.5	3.5	8.4	7.5	2.8	4.3	1.7	2.5
Sweden	1.5	1.9	2.3	1.0	0.8	1.5	1.6	2.0
UK	1.3	1.3	1.4	1.3	2.1	2.3	2.4	2.2
Euro area	1.7	2.3	2.1	2.1	2.1	2.2	1.0	2.0

Notes: Figures are for the harmonized index of consumer prices; [a] estimate; [b] forecast.
Source: Commission (2007).

ability of non-euro countries to absorb these and other price shocks varies. The Baltic states and Hungary have particular inflationary problems whereas, so far, Cyprus, Malta, Slovakia, Denmark and the UK, among others, have not encountered acceleration in overall prices (see Table 3).

A combination of inflationary and public finance concerns has delayed the plans of several post-2004 accession states to adopt the euro. While Slovenia acceded to the euro area in January 2007 and Malta and Cyprus received the go-ahead to join from January 2008, the others, apart from Slovakia which is actively seeking to adopt the euro in January 2009, have abandoned official target dates and now refer only to earliest possible entry dates, usually in several years time.

II. Economic Developments in the Old Euro-Outsiders

The United Kingdom

Despite real GDP growth accelerating from 2.8 per cent in 2006 to 3.1 per cent in 2007 and continuing expansion of the economy for 60 successive quarters (the longest expansion since quarterly national accounts were first compiled in the 1950s) (UK Treasury, 2007), global financial volatility and the resulting credit crunch have placed a question mark over the outlook for the UK.

For the first three quarters of 2007, UK economic activity remained strong but slowed somewhat in the final quarter. The main growth driver was continuing vigorous private consumption growth, bolstered by the wealth effects of rising house prices and easy credit availability. Investment was growing steadily; inflation was close to target and unemployment had been falling steadily for 11 consecutive months (UK Treasury, 2007). Net exports were marginally negative but slower consumption growth will reduce import growth and, although the US slowdown does not help UK exports, the European market remains strong and the emerging markets of India and China continue to provide trade opportunities. In short, there was much to be positive about. In January, May and July, for example, interest rates were increased by 0.25 per cent in an attempt to restrain potential overheating. It was only in December that interest rates were reduced by 0.25 per cent.

By the end of 2007, the uncertainty created by disruption in global financial markets and the collapse of the sub-prime market in the US promoted a distinct change in consumer sentiment. The run on the Northern Rock bank in September reinforced this change and demonstrated the exposure of the UK financial sector to external financial developments. As a result, consumer and business confidence was dented; consumption weakened and precautionary savings became a bigger priority for households, a factor further depressing consumption. Moreover, as the exposure of UK banks to the US sub-prime market became apparent, the credit environment became more restrictive for mortgages, for general consumption and for business. The knock-on effects of this were slower house price rises, which turned into house price falls in early 2008.

After many years of confident growth, this new uncertainty has led to a lack of consensus about UK prospects; forecasts range from a gentle slowdown to a full scale recession. Indeed, the Treasury in its Pre-Budget Report got it about right when it reported, 'disruption in financial markets has meant economic prospects have become more uncertain and events need to unfold further before the impact on the economy can be rigorously quantified' (UK Treasury, 2007, p. 21). In other words, it is too early to say what impact the credit crunch will have on the UK: persistent disruption, especially if more financial institutions are destabilized, would seriously undermine the economy. However, the much vaunted flexibility of the UK economy could facilitate rapid absorption of these financial shocks and the European Commission's forecast of the moderation of growth to 2.2 per cent in 2008 may not be far off the mark.

Speculation about falling house prices and the increase in food and energy prices towards the end of 2007 present the possibility of a period of slow growth and rising inflation. Although there are inflationary pressures from global factors and a pound that has depreciated against the euro, falling house prices and containment of wages could help the UK avoid a surge in inflation and give the Bank of England scope to reduce interest rates and boost the economy. Even if interest rates fall, however, the amount of credit and the conditions under which it is made available will be much tighter than in the past. This will reduce the contribution of consumption to growth and slow investment activity.

Denmark

Denmark's real GDP growth rate decelerated to 1.9 per cent in 2007 from 3.5 per cent in 2006. Domestic demand, notably private consumption, had been the main engine of growth, but rising interest rates and a faltering housing market underpinned the slowdown. Investment growth rates also slowed. The economy is forecast to continue to grow moderately with domestic demand, although slowing, remaining the main driver.

Labour markets are imposing capacity constraints on key aspects of the economy; in 2007, unemployment fell to 3 per cent and employment rose by 2 per cent. Labour shortages are occurring in many sectors, particularly in construction, industry and the public sector. These shortages are constraining economic activity, especially in the export sector, and encourage high import growth to satisfy domestic demand. So far, Denmark has utilized foreign labour to ease pressures from tighter labour markets (National Bank of Denmark, 2008). Other possible solutions include investment to increase productive capacity or to substitute capital for labour. There may also be some respite if private consumption eases as forecast, but this effect will be limited as consumer and business confidence indicators remain relatively buoyant.

Another consequence of a tight labour market was a series of relatively generous private sector wage settlements. Higher wage increases than those in competitor countries, especially when combined with an appreciating currency, threaten Denmark's long-term competitiveness. These cost pressures have placed upward pressure on prices, also subject to global energy and food price increases. Given the low starting point of Danish inflation, however, the inflationary outlook remains relatively positive.

Sweden

Following 4.2 per cent growth in 2006, real GDP growth moderated in 2007. According to the latest official Swedish estimates that growth was 2.6 per cent in 2007 (Statistics Sweden, 2008), below European Commission forecasts and previous forecasts by the Swedish authorities. This still healthy growth helped maintain strong public finances and was underpinned by private consumption, which benefited from increases in disposable income arising from lower taxes, higher wages and employment increases. Growing uncertainty, however, meant that rising disposable incomes resulted in a higher savings ratio rather than an increase in domestic demand; such caution may spill-over into 2008. Investment also flourished in 2007, benefiting from high capacity utilization, buoyant corporate profitability and an expansion of residential construction.

The external sector did not fare so well and for the first time since 1998, the contribution of net exports to growth was negative. Strong consumer demand and investment resulted in imports growing more rapidly than exports. The growth in exports suffered from an appreciating currency, export capacity problems and a moderation of the prospects in the main markets for Swedish goods.

In 2007, labour markets strengthened significantly with employment growth of 2 per cent and unemployment falling from 7.1 per cent in 2006 to 6.1 per cent. An ongoing high demand for labour and an increasing number of firms reporting labour shortages have combined to push up real wages, a trend that could undermine competitiveness if joined with weaker productivity growth.

2007 also saw a gradual pick-up in the rate of inflation, albeit from a low base. Domestic cost pressures and, towards the end of the year, rising food and energy prices were all contributory factors. So far, the rate of price increase has been moderate and has presented no real cause for concern.

III. Economic Developments in the New Euro-Outsiders

Poland

In 2007, Poland's real GDP growth was 6.5 per cent, the highest for a decade and a continuation of the robust growth that began towards the end of 2005. Domestic demand – both in terms of consumption and investment – remains the key factor behind growth.

Private consumption has been strong as a result of higher employment and lower unemployment; accelerating real wage growth and credit expansion. Tax changes scheduled for 2008 and 2009 will also boost disposable income and thus maintain strong consumption growth. Public spending, however, has fallen significantly as the government has spent less on social transfers given falling employment and public finance reform. Investment growth of over 21 per cent in 2007 was driven by buoyant corporate profits and increasing construction activity. Public sector investment, on the other hand, decelerated in line with the reform of public finance. Investment is forecast to grow strongly as a result of continuing support by foreign investors and an increasing inflow of EU funds.

Strong domestic demand has undermined the contribution of the external sector to growth. Higher investment levels and strong consumption have encouraged a surge in imports whereas 2007 export growth was significantly down on 2006 because of lower import demand from the EU. The upshot was a deterioration in Poland's trade and current account deficits. This trend of thriving domestic demand and a negative contribution from the external sector is forecast to continue into 2008 and 2009.

Buoyant domestic demand has also contributed to significant improvements in labour markets. In 2007, employment grew by 4.4 per cent and unemployment fell from 13.8 per cent in 2006 to 9.4 per cent in 2007, representing a remarkable turnaround from almost 20 per cent unemployment five years earlier. In addition to higher economic activity, early retirements, more students and migration also contributed to labour market improvements. As labour markets begin to tighten, a growing number of employers report recruitment difficulties, both of skilled and unskilled workers. Some respite may come from the return of migrant Poles, attracted by the improved economic conditions in Poland.

As in many other European countries, inflation accelerated in Poland in 2007, particularly towards the end of the year when global factors pushed up food and energy prices. Strong domestic demand and tighter labour markets also increased inflationary pressure. There is some concern that average wages have started to increase faster than productivity, which could have a detrimental effect on competitiveness. Poland's inflationary problems, however, are not as severe as in some new Member States as they are, to an extent, kept in check by a nominal appreciation of the exchange rate and lower import prices from low-cost countries.

Accelerating GDP growth and labour market improvements have led to a much better situation than forecast in public finances, with the budget deficit falling below 3 per cent of GDP in 2007. Revenue exceeded expectations because of growth, whereas spending was below forecasts because of lower social transfers; lower growth of debt leading to lower interest expenditure; and reduced public investment.

Hungary

During the first decade of transition, Hungary's economy was the star of central and eastern Europe, but in recent years public finances have been a major drag on the economy. In 2006, the budget deficit reached almost 10 per cent of GDP and government debt increased in parallel. Accordingly, the government introduced measures designed to consolidate public finance and bring down the deficit and public debt.

The most immediate impact of this policy was a fall in domestic demand, resulting in a halving of real GDP growth in 2007 from 3.9 per cent to 2 per cent according to European Commission estimates and an end to labour market improvements (Commission, 2007). Subsequent data from Hungarian authorities suggest that growth fell even further in 2007 to between 1.5 and 1.7 per cent (Hungarian Ministry of Finance, 2008). By the end of 2007, a serious downturn in agriculture also contributed to lower growth.

Both private and public consumption were restrained by the new policy in 2007. Private consumption was also adversely affected by increasing inflation and falling employment. Although private sector wages rose by a nominal 10 per cent in 2007, their impact on demand was counterbalanced by a 4 per cent fall in public sector employment and a decrease in public consumption of nearly 5 per cent. Households increased their indebtedness and drew on their savings in partial compensation for falling real incomes.

Investment growth of 3.3 per cent occurred in 2007. Private sector investment was strong in the export-oriented manufacturing sector but was partially offset by a 9 per cent fall in construction and housing investments (Hungarian Ministry of Finance, 2008). Public sector investment experienced retrenchment as a result of the fiscal consolidation. In the immediate future, however, both private and public investment may benefit from increasing EU structural funds.

Most of the growth in 2007 was due to the strong performance of the external sector. Hungary's main trading partners, and thus its exports, continued to perform well, while the downturn in domestic demand reduced imports. Exports are expected to continue to grow, although there are considerable downside risks given the uncertainty surrounding the global economy. The gradual recovery forecast for domestic demand will give it a bigger role as a growth driver and boost imports.

The impact of the 2006 fiscal adjustment measures on public finances has so far exceeded expectations. According to figures from the Hungarian Ministry of Finance (2008), the 2007 budget deficit was 5.7 per cent of GDP, about four percentage points below the 2006 figure, and 1.1 percentage points below the target in the December 2006 convergence programme. Improvements in public finances have occurred as a result of better than expected revenues, lower debt service and reduced expenditure, including unpopular cuts in welfare expenditure. Further deficit reductions are anticipated for 2008.

Reform of public finance is essential if Hungary is to meet the criteria for euro area membership. Setting a target date for entry has been abandoned some time ago. 2014 is now most commonly suggested as the earliest possible date for euro adoption.

Inflation has also become a major cause for concern during 2007. Prices peaked in March. Their rate of growth decelerated until September when there were sudden increases in the price of energy and food imports. The result was an annual inflation rate for 2007 of 7.7 per cent. Although the forecasts are for inflation to be quickly brought under control, the events of 2007 demonstrate how fragile inflationary performance can be.

Czech Republic

In 2007 real GDP growth in the Czech Republic was slightly below 6 per cent, continuing the strong performance of the previous two years. Consumer demand (buoyed by higher real wages and increasing social transfers; rising employment and falling unemployment; cheaper credit and relatively restrained inflation) was the main driver behind growth. Manufacturing, especially sectors that have acted as magnets for FDI and dominate exports, such as transport equipment, automobiles and electronics, also made a significant contribution to growth. The external sector, although no longer the dominant force it was in 2005, continued to make a small but positive contribution to growth.

For most of 2007, despite global pressures, inflation was relatively contained. Towards the end of the year, a surge in key food prices, excise duty increases and strong consumer demand increased inflationary pressure. This pressure will continue into early 2008 as the result of further excise rises, new environmental taxes and an increase in the lower rate of value added tax from 5 per cent to 9 per cent. The continuing strength of the currency helps to offset these pressures by restraining import prices.

Initially, the Czech Republic had hoped to enter the euro area in 2009–10, a date that has long since been abandoned. The immediate stumbling block is the state of public finances but, according to the Czech Republic's updated euro accession strategy (Czech Government and Czech National Bank, 2007), it is public finances plus the limited flexibility of the economy that pose the greatest risk to successful euro area membership. In 2006, the government deficit fell below 3 per cent of GDP, but, despite the boost to revenue from stronger than forecast growth, it deteriorated again in 2007 to 3.5 per cent as the result of big increases in social expenditure. Early in 2008, Prime Minister Mirek Topolanek was reported to be against rushing into the euro area, stating that the Czech Republic needed to implement further reforms before adopting the euro.[1] These reforms include measures to improve the health of public finances and labour market flexibility and significant changes to the health care and pension systems.

[1] *International Herald Tribune*, 1 April 2008.

On the face of it, labour markets continue to improve. New jobs have been forthcoming from foreign-owned enterprises in particular and unemployment has fallen. Such factors, however, disguise potentially serious problems in labour markets. Low regional and professional mobility indicate limited labour flexibility, but so far, the potential constraint on growth has been counteracted by the relatively large number of foreign workers in the labour force. The government has also identified the lack of co-ordination between tax and benefit systems as removing the incentive for the long-term unemployed and low income families to seek work. Accordingly, the Czech Republic's stabilization package seeks to redress the balance by reducing personal and corporate income tax and lowering social benefits. Strict employment protection regulations, a rising minimum wage and high labour taxes are also seen as obstacles to greater labour market flexibility and will be targeted for reform.

Slovakia

Slovakia is one of the most dynamic of the 2004 accession states. Rapid productivity growth; a skilled and relatively cheap labour force and controlled inflation have created an attractive destination for FDI, especially in the automotive and electronics sectors. Nevertheless, Slovakia's long-term unemployment rate is the highest in the EU (OECD, 2007) as a consequence of difficulties in finding work for a large reservoir of unskilled workers and the big gap between the economically dynamic west of the country and the lagging east.

The European Commission's estimate for Slovakian real GDP growth in 2007 was 8.7 per cent compared to 8.3 per cent in 2006. According to more recently published figures from the Slovak Statistical Office (2008), growth in the final quarter of 2007 was 14.1 per cent. This acceleration is largely due to a one-off stockpiling of cigarettes prior to an increase in excise duty. Even after removing this effect from the figures, the build-up of production in new foreign-owned, export-oriented manufacturing capacity pushed growth to almost 10 per cent for 2007. This barnstorming end to the year contrasted sharply with other EU economies which tended to experience slower growth in the fourth quarter.

The major factor behind growth was domestic demand, especially investment and private consumption, but the contribution of the external sector picked up in 2007. Investment growth, buoyed by ongoing large corporate investment projects, was above 7 per cent with investment in machinery and equipment reaching over 10 per cent. A small decrease in investment is forecast for 2008 and 2009, but Slovakia remains attractive to foreign investors. Private consumption has benefited from real wage growth, a favourable credit situation, and falling unemployment and rising employment, but labour market improvements have a long way to go, as indicated above.

Slovakia, helped by the appreciation of its exchange rate, was able to withstand the inflationary pressures from higher energy and food prices better than most in 2007, although some acceleration of inflation is anticipated in 2008. Controlled inflation plus a budget deficit that fell below 3 per cent of GDP in 2007 and public debt that is roughly half the maximum of the Maastricht convergence criteria means that Slovakia has stuck to its long-held target of adopting the single currency on 1 January 2009 unlike other countries who have been forced to push their target dates back. This aspiration was confirmed by Slovak Prime Minister Robert Fico before the European Parliament in December 2007.

Estonia

Following two years of double-digit growth, Estonia's 2007 GDP growth rate was below 8 per cent and was 4.5 per cent in the final quarter, the lowest quarterly growth for eight years. Early in the year, private consumption and investment were the main drivers behind growth. By the second half of the year, however, domestic demand was clearly faltering; construction and the rental market slowed and the number of new housing loans fell.

The deterioration in the property markets hit household consumption and helped curb imports. Import and export growth rates both fell in 2007, but the fall was much steeper for imports, reducing the negative contribution of the external sector to growth. These trends are forecast to continue, resulting in a gradual improvement in the external sector. Exports should benefit from earlier investment growth, but may be restrained by the global developments and their impact on Estonia's export markets.

The external economic environment has taken its toll on inflation. Fuel and food price increases boosted inflation by almost two percentage points to 6.3 per cent for 2007 and by January 2008, prices were 11 per cent above January 2007 levels. The short-term inflationary position was exacerbated by the June 2007 decision to bring forward to 1 January 2008 all excise tax increases required by EU legislation, initially to be spread over 2008–10.

One effect of this inflationary surge will be further delays in Estonia's adoption of the euro. Estonia has no problems meeting the other convergence criteria, however. For example, it has the lowest level of public debt in the EU and runs a budget surplus. Estonia's official position has always been that it should enter the euro area as soon as possible and, at the time of accession to the EU, it was optimistic about euro area entry by 2007. At present, there is no official target date, although in March 2008, the Prime Minister said he was hopeful about 2011.

Inflation, along with skilled labour shortages, helped trigger real wage increases in 2007. In the final quarter of 2007, the gross average monthly wage was 20 per cent above the same period in 2006. Labour productivity growth still lags significantly behind real wage growth, although the latter has shown some signs of slowdown in early 2008. In the longer term, labour market inflexibilities in terms of skills and constraints on labour force increases could inhibit further increases in productive capacity.

Latvia

In the first three quarters of 2007, Latvia continued the double-digit growth of 2005 and 2006 with real GDP growth over 11 per cent, driven by private consumption and investment. In the final quarter of 2007, growth had fallen to around 9.5 per cent, bringing the overall growth rate for 2007 to 10.5 per cent. This slowdown has its roots in lower domestic consumption, a correction in the booming property market and slower growth in retail sales and new car registrations.

The Latvian economy faces two major downside risks – inflation and significant external deficits. The inflation rate accelerated throughout 2007 and by the end of the year prices were over 10 per cent higher than at the end of 2006. Domestic overheating, higher wages, global food and energy price increases and regulated price hikes created this situation.

The inflationary surge means Latvia's original plan to adopt the euro by 2008 has been superseded. Although no official target date has been set, Finance Minister Spurdzins and Prime Minister Kalvitis have stated that they do not expect Latvia to be ready for euro area membership until 2012 at the earliest.

The external downside risk comes from Latvia's widening trade balance. Although there was a strong increase in export values in 2007, the growth of imports was even faster and the foreign balance remains a major negative contributor to growth. At present the current account deficit is over 20 per cent of GDP. Thus far the deficit has been covered by FDI inflows and long term loans, but the country remains vulnerable to the current financial turmoil. Competitiveness and exports were also adversely affected by tight labour conditions, which raised wages and unit labour costs and started to impose capacity constraints on output.

In short, unless the external economic problems intensify greatly, Latvia appears to be set for a soft landing. Growth, albeit several percentage points below the double digit growth of 2005–07, is still forecast to settle at a more sustainable and healthy 6–7 per cent in the medium term.

Lithuania

Economic growth in Lithuania actually accelerated in 2007 to 8.5 per cent, up from 7.7 per cent in 2006. Domestic demand continued as the main driver. Investment growth of almost 20 per cent was particularly robust and benefited from strong construction and real estate sectors. Despite the anticipated slowdown in the housing markets resulting from tighter credit conditions and lower expectations, construction opportunities will continue to be available in infrastructure and non-residential business investment.

Consumption has also played its part in growth and is forecast to continue to do so. 2007 saw strong growth in credit and retail sales, in part because disposable income was boosted by income tax cuts in mid-2006 and further cuts were scheduled for January 2008. High real wage growth, rising employment and falling unemployment also stimulated private consumption. Some moderation of consumption is anticipated as a result of higher interest rates and tighter availability of credit. Overall, real GDP growth is forecast to weaken in 2008, but is expected to remain above 7 per cent.

The external situation deteriorated in 2007. A major factor was damage to Lithuania's trade balance caused by the disruption to production from a fire towards the end of 2006 at the Mazeikiu Nafta oil refinery and the ensuing closure and modernization. The refinery had returned to full capacity by the beginning of 2008: output of 10 million tonnes is expected in 2008 compared to less than 6 million tonnes in 2007, thereby boosting exports. Expatriate remittances, greater transfers from the EU and slower import growth as a result of consumption moderation should also help the external balance in 2008.

Lithuania has, like other Baltic states, been hit by accelerating inflation resulting from overheating, higher food and fuel costs and accession-related increases in excise duties. The inflationary outlook is not promising: electricity price hikes and further excise increases are in the pipeline, more food and fuel increases cannot be ruled out and the full impact of wage increases has yet to feed through.

Competitiveness is also under threat from tighter labour markets. Increasing participation rates boosted employment in 2007 and unemployment fell to just over 4 per cent, compared to double-digit unemployment only three years earlier. The result was growing labour shortages, accentuated by outward migration, vacancies at historically high levels and wage increases far above the growth in productivity. Supply-side constraints and deteriorating competitiveness therefore remain a real possibility.

Bulgaria

The Bulgarian economy has been sending out mixed signals. On the one hand, 2007 growth remained strong at 6.3 per cent, the fourth successive year of growth above 6 per cent, and investment, dominated by the inflow of foreign capital, grew by almost 30 per cent. On the other hand, inflation remained high and the trade and current deficits reached 24 per cent and 18 per cent of GDP respectively.

The main factor behind growth is strong domestic demand. Investment has been the main factor behind this but private consumption, which grew at 7.3 per cent during 2007, has also played its part. Public consumption growth, however, was moderate. In the second half of 2007, private consumption slowed slightly and the consumer confidence indicator, influenced by rising inflation, declined, overriding the positive impact on demand of improved labour markets (Bulgarian National Bank, 2007). Business confidence remains strong and underpins the robust growth forecasts for 2008–09. Growth has also allowed the government to maintain a budget surplus of around 3 per cent of GDP.

In 2007, real import growth was 12.6 per cent whereas real exports grew by 7.4 per cent. The outcome was a negative contribution to growth by net exports of 5.7 per cent. Import growth was buoyed by investment demand and by private consumption. Exports, however, were affected by ongoing economic restructuring and by lower energy exports following the partial closure at the end of 2006 of two reactors at Kozloduy nuclear power plant.

In 2007, employment rose and unemployment fell, resulting in increased reports of labour shortages, especially for skilled labour. This shortage has contributed to an accelerating growth in wages and has stimulated a real increase in unit labour costs, although they remain 70 per cent of 1998 levels (Bulgarian National Bank, 2007). The completion of so much new investment may inhibit falling productivity and competitiveness stemming from real wage growth in the short to medium term. In the longer term, labour supply problems may restrict economic growth and capacity utilization rates, but in the interim an increasing labour force participation rate – at 53.5 per cent still very low by European standards (Bulgarian National Bank) – is holding off these problems.

The outlook for Bulgaria is positive but is not without its downside risks. In the first half of 2007, inflation decelerated as the excise increases of early

2006 fell out of the index but price rises picked up again in the second half of 2007 as a result of domestic factors (drought-related increases in food prices and a hike in utility prices) and developments in global food and energy markets. Uncertainty about inflation, resulting from the world economy and the unclear international financial situation, creates some uncertainty about the short to medium outlook for Bulgaria's economy.

Romania

Following years as central and eastern Europe's most troubled economy, Romania averaged 6 per cent growth per year during 2001–06. Indeed, during its first full year of EU membership, Romania's economy was at risk of overheating; private consumption was strong, government spending and inflation were up and the current account deficit continued to grow.

Real GDP growth in 2007 fell from 7.7 per cent in 2006 to a still healthy 6 per cent. Domestic demand, which grew by 13.2 per cent in 2007, was the main driver behind growth, with both consumption and investment playing their part. Private consumption grew 11 per cent in 2007 as a result of nominal wage increases of 20 per cent plus, tighter labour markets and debt-fuelled spending as domestic credit growth averaged 55 per cent during 2005–07. Public consumption growth, albeit less strong than private consumption growth, was also significant. Investment growth was over 18 per cent in 2007, benefiting from continuing construction demand, FDI inflows and increasing EU funds.

Strong domestic demand accentuated the negative contribution of net exports to growth which was the equivalent of 7.3 per cent of GDP in 2007. Both strong domestic consumption and investment sucked in imports which grew over 22 per cent in 2007 whereas exports grew by only 8 per cent. Consequently, despite increases in inflows of EU funds and migrant remittances, the trade balance widened to 15.5 per cent of GDP and the current account balance to almost 14 per cent; and net borrowing continued to increase.

Inflation in 2007 averaged 4.7 per cent, continuing the downward trend of recent years. However, the rate of price increases reached 6.6 per cent by the end of the year. This acceleration occurred as a result of the currency depreciation that began during the summer; higher domestic food prices stemming from the severe drought; strong domestic demand and the impact of global food and energy price increases.

Labour markets continued to tighten in Romania. In 2007, employment grew by 1.2 per cent and unemployment fell slightly. Rapid growth and significant emigration have contributed to labour shortages in many sectors.

Indeed, since 1989, Romania has lost about 10 per cent of its population through migration, which could push wages upwards and introduce production constraints, thereby discouraging FDI. An option that companies are increasingly likely to choose is to import foreign workers, as in the case of a textile factory in Bacau that imported 670 Chinese workers in 2007.

Malta

In 2007, Malta continued its post-2004 recovery, experiencing real economic growth of 3.1 per cent. The main growth driver was domestic demand, particularly private consumption, which benefited from increases in disposable income from higher employment and earnings and lower income tax rates and inflation. Investment growth, on the other hand, turned negative in 2007: this, in part, reflected the completion of big infrastructure projects and private sector investments in pharmaceuticals, aviation, information and communication technology and financial sectors.

Despite a 1.4 per cent decrease in real exports in 2007, the proportionally greater fall in real imports meant that the external sector made a positive contribution to GDP for the second year in succession. The external balance led to some shrinkage of the current account deficit. The export slowdown was caused by a disappointing performance by the electronics sector which constitutes a major share of manufacturing output. The development of higher value-added manufacturing and services, notably electronics and, to a degree, pharmaceuticals, has been an important part of Malta's response to globalization. Imports have declined because of lower investment activity and reduced export-led import demand. Some export recovery is expected in 2008, namely from an expanded pharmaceutical industry and from the growth of service exports.

The official position has always been that the single currency was important for Malta because it offered the opportunity to replace the costs and vulnerability of managing a small national currency in a more and more competitive international environment with the greater security and credibility of an international currency (Central Bank of Malta, 2007). In May 2007, Malta attained its goal when it was given the go-ahead for entry into the euro area on 1 January 2008. Tight control of prices helped Malta's quest for euro adoption and has also kept wages down. Wage moderation, in turn, has facilitated the productivity growth from which Malta has benefited in recent years. In view of Malta's tightening labour markets and low participation rates, productivity growth represents the best prospect for continued growth.

Cyprus

Real GDP growth in Cyprus has hovered just below 4 per cent since 2005. Growth has been driven almost entirely by domestic demand, particularly private consumption, which has benefitted from low real interest rates and relatively easy credit conditions and ongoing employment and wage growth. Investment, especially construction, has also made a significant contribution to growth. These trends are expected to continue into 2008–09, although private consumption may moderate slightly as a result of rising interest rates and global credit tightening.

The anticipated slight decrease in domestic demand will constrain imports and perhaps transform the negative contribution made to GDP by the external sector in recent years into a positive or, at least, a neutral one. Export performance has been disappointing and the improved performance in 2007 was limited because of subdued re-exports. Re-exports are, however, expected to recover. Despite a marginal decline in the number of tourist arrivals throughout 2007, spending per tourist increased with positive effects on tourism revenues and on the external balance, which was also helped by good export performance of the financial services sector.

Employment continued to grow and unemployment to fall in 2007. Wages have increased sufficiently to stimulate economic activity but not enough to damage productivity. This has also helped Cyprus keep inflation down. Despite oil and commodity price increases, inflation, helped by the falling price of imported products, particularly motor vehicles (Central Bank of Cyprus, 2007), remained relatively low. Low inflation plus the steady reduction in the budget deficit and the impressive falls in public debt were significant factors in the European Commission's mid-2007 decision to admit Cyprus to the euro area on 1 January 2008.

References

Bulgarian National Bank (2007) *Economic Review*, 4/2007.
Central Bank of Cyprus (2007) *Monetary Policy Report*.
Central Bank of Malta (2007) *Malta's Economy on the Path to the Euro*.
Commission of the European Communities (2007) 'Economic Forecasts: Autumn 2007'. *European Economy*, No. 7.
Czech Government and the Czech National Bank (2007) *The Czech Republic's Updated Euro-Area Accession Strategy*.
Hungarian Ministry of Finance (2008) *Report on Economic and Financial Developments*. 17 January 2008.
National Bank of Denmark (2008) *Monetary Review 1st Quarter 2008*.

OECD (2007) *Economic Survey of Slovak Republic 2007*. Policy Brief (Paris: Organization for Economic Co-operation and Development).

Slovak Statistical Office (2008) 'Flash Estimates of Gross Domestic Product and Total Employment of Fourth Quarter 2007'. 14 February 2008. Available at «http://portal.statistics.sk/showdoc.do?docid=11185».

Statistics Sweden (2008) Press Release. Number 2008: 079.

UK Treasury (2007) *Pre-Budget Report and Comprehensive Spending Review*.

JCMS 2008 Volume 46 Annual Review pp. 253–259

Chronology: The European Union in 2007

ALTIN NAZ SUNAY
London School of Economics and Political Science

At a Glance

Presidencies of the EU Council: Germany (1 January–30 June) and Portugal (1 July–31 December).

January

1	Accession of Bulgaria and Romania to the EU.
1	Slovenia joined the euro area.
1	The new 'Northern Dimension Policy Framework Document' came into effect.
10	Ukraine ratified the 'Ukraine–EU Cooperation Agreement on Civil Global Navigation Satellite System'.
11	Alfred Gusenbauer became Chancellor at the head of an SPÖ–ÖVP grand coalition in Austria.
11	Oil dispute between Russia and Belarus is resolved, which had disrupted oil supplies to the Czech Republic, Germany, Hungary, Poland, Slovakia and Ukraine.
19	The Czech government received a parliamentary vote of confidence.
19	A new action plan was adopted with Lebanon.
26	'Friends of the Constitution' – the 18 countries that had already ratified the Constitutional Treaty, as well as Portugal and Ireland – met in Madrid.

February

14 The Commission published the communication 'The Internal Market for Goods: A Cornerstone of Europe's Competitiveness'.

22 A coalition government is formed in the Netherlands under Prime Minister Jan Peter Balkenende.

23 Lithuania threatened to block talks on a new EU–Russia agreement due to the problems experienced in a Russian pipeline managed by Transneft.

27 The Council adopted conclusions on 'the clearing and settlement of securities transactions'.

March

4 Parliamentary elections in Estonia; Andrus Ansip re-elected.

5 Negotiations of a 'New Enhanced Agreement' between the EU and Ukraine started.

6 A new Action plan was adopted with Egypt.

8 The European Central Bank raised interest rates to 2.75 per cent.

8–9 The European Council Spring summit. Energy action plan was adopted for the period 2007–09. The EU committed to reduce greenhouse gas emissions by 20 per cent and agreed to produce a fifth of its energy by renewable sources.

18 Finnish legislative elections; Matti Vanhanen re-elected.

25 Berlin Declaration ('Declaration on the Occasion of the 50th anniversary of the Signature of the Treaty of Rome').

27 The EU troika met with the foreign ministers of Kazakhstan, Kyrgyzstan, Tajikistan, Turkmenistan, Uzbekistan.

27 The Council agreed to a draft of the payment services directive that aimed to unify the EU's national payment regimes to eliminate the cost of cross-border transactions.

April

3–4 The EU attended the South Asian association for regional co-operation summit in New Delhi as an observer.

11 The Commission published the communication 'Black Sea synergy: a new regional co-operation initiative'.

12 The European Parliament's Industry Committee gave strong support to the introduction of tough limits on international mobile call fees.

22	First round of presidential elections in France.
25	The EU opened a 'Common Visa Application Centre' in Chisinau, Moldova.
26	A thematic group on 'Strategies, Forecasts and Scenarios' was set up within the framework of the Russian–EU Energy Dialogue.
26–7	Violent protests in Tallinn after the Estonian government's decision to relocate a bronze statue of a Soviet soldier.
30	EU–US summit held in Washington DC.

May

4	EU–ASEAN Free Trade Agreement negotiations started.
6	Nicolas Sarkozy won the second round of presidential elections in France.
8	A power sharing government took office in Northern Ireland.
8	Ecofin Council welcomed the Commission's white paper on enhancing the single market framework for investment funds.
16	Commission 'Proposal for a Directive Providing for Sanctions Against Employers of Illegally Staying Third-Country Nationals'.
16	Commission communication on 'Applying the Global Approach to Migration to the Eastern and South-Eastern Regions Neighbouring the European Union'.
16	Commission communication on 'Circular Migration and Mobility Partnerships between the European Union and Third Countries'.
17–18	EU–Russia summit in Samara.
19	Referendum in Romania to impeach the President Traian Băsescu failed.
20	European Parliament elections took place in Bulgaria.
24	Bertie Ahern won general elections in Ireland.
24	'European Patrol Network' became operational.
30	The Commission adopted a communication 'Towards an EU–Brazil Strategic Partnership'.
31	The Latvian parliament elected Valdis Zatlers as new president.

June

1	Two agreements between the EU and Russia on visa facilitation and re-admission of illegal immigrants entered into force.
6	Commission green paper on 'The Future Common European Asylum System'.
6	The European Central Bank raised interest rates to 3 per cent.
6	Commission report on 'The Evaluation of the Dublin System'.
6–8	G8 summit at Heiligendamm.
10	General elections in Belgium.
10	First round of French legislative elections.
12	Council decision on the establishment, operation and use of the second generation Schengen Information System (SIS II).
12	Council reached an agreement on 'The Visa Information System Regulation'.
13	Negotiations for a Stabilization and Association Agreements with Serbia resumed.
15	European Union Police Mission to Afghanistan launched.
17	Second round of French legislative elections; Nicolas Sarkozy's UMP retained its majority.
18	The EU–Ukraine Co-operation Council endorsed a new Justice and Home Affairs Plan, as well as signing a visa facilitation and readmission agreement.
18	The EU resumed normal relations with the Palestinian Authorities.
21–2	Brussels European Council.
27	Gordon Brown replaced Tony Blair as Prime Minister in the UK.
28	The EU–US Agreement on the processing and transfer of passenger name record (PNR) data by air carriers was concluded.

July

1	The European Security and Defence Policy police mission in Kinshasa, Democratic Republic of Congo was followed by EUPOL RD CONGO aimed at assisting authorities with police reform.
4	The EU–Brazil summit in Lisbon.

11	Council and Parliament adopted a regulation that establishes a mechanism for the creation of 'Rapid Border Intervention Teams'.
11	Rome II Regulation on the law on non-contractual obligations was adopted.
22	Tayyip Erdogan won the parliamentary elections in Turkey.
23	Start of the Intergovernmental Conference.

August

| 9 | The European Central Bank responded to the credit shortage by providing €95 billion to stimulate the economy. |
| 28 | Abdullah Gul was elected president of Turkey. |

September

4	The European Parliament adopts a resolution on the single market emphasizing the improvement of implementation and enforcement of existing rules.
11	Commission's third Annual Report on migration and integration.
11	European Court of Justice decision in *Hendrix*.
14	EU–Ukraine summit in Kiev.
16	Greek legislative elections; Costas Karamanlis re-elected.
17	Court of First Instance confirmed the Commission's March 2004 decision which found Microsoft guilty of abusing its quasi-monopoly position in the market.
18	EU signed visa facilitation and readmission agreements with Serbia, Bosnia-Herzegovina, Montenegro, and Former Yugoslav Republic of Macedonia.
19	Gilles de Kerchove appointed as EU Counterterrorism Co-ordinator.

October

1	EU transport ministers decided to open up postal services to full competition and end national monopolies on the delivery of lightweight letters and postcards in 2011.
10	EU–Moldova visa facilitation and readmission agreement signed.
12	The European Parliament adopted a report proposing a reallocation of seats between the Member States.

15	Montenegro and the EU signed Stabilization and Association Agreement.
18–19	European Council in Lisbon.
21	Donald Tusk's Civic Platform win the parliamentary elections in Poland.
21	Constitutional referendum on electoral reform took place in Turkey.
23	Commission 'Proposal for a Council directive on the conditions of entry and residence of third-country nationals for the purposes of highly qualified employment'.
23	European Court of Justice decision in *Morgan*.
26	EU–Russia summit in Mafra, Portugal.

November

1	The EU–Africa–Middle East Energy conference took place in Egypt.
6	Commission proposed a new counter-terrorism package.
7	The Stabilization and Association Agreement with Serbia was initialled.
9	The Justice and Home Affairs Council agreed on a general approach regarding the third pillar data protection directive.
9	The first meeting of the Transatlantic Economic Council took place.
13	Danish legislative elections; Anders Fogh Rasmussen re-elected.
13	The European Parliament and the Council adopted the final version of the payment services directive.
14	The European Parliament criticized the Russian NGO law in its 'resolution on the EU–Russia summit'.
16–17	The Russian–EU aviation summit was cancelled.
18–19	First Euro–Mediterranean Ministerial Meeting on migration was held in Portugal.
20	Commission adopted a communication on 'A Single Market for 21st Century Europe', and published a paper envisaging a 'new social vision' for the EU and a communication on services of general interest.
25	Elections to the European Parliament held in Romania.

26	Commission 'Report on the Application of Directive 2003/9/EC of 27 January 2003 Laying down Minimum Standards for the Reception of Asylum Seekers'.
27–9	The President of the Eurogroup, President of the European Central Bank and EU Commissioner for Economic and Monetary Affairs visited the People's Bank of China.
28	EU–China summit in Beijing.
30	EU–India summit in New Delhi.
30	The Council authorized the Commission to open negotiations with Jordan for a Euro–Mediterranean Aviation Agreement.

December

2	President Vladimir Putin's United Russia Party won the legislative elections in Russia.
3–14	United Nations Climate Change conference at Bali.
4	The Stabilization and Association Agreement with Bosnia-Herzegovina was initialled.
5	Interim progress report on 'The Global Approach to Migration'.
6	Council decision abolished the internal borders for all of the 2004 accession countries apart from Cyprus.
8–9	EU–Africa summit: agreement on a joint strategy and a series of action plans as part of the 'Africa–EU Strategic Partnership'.
11	European Court of Justice decision in *Viking Line*.
13	Lisbon Treaty (Reform Treaty) signed.
14	European Council adopted the 'EU Declaration on Globalization'.
17	Hungary ratified the Lisbon Treaty.
17	5th Euro–Mediterranean Ministerial conference on energy held in Cyprus.
18	European Court of Justice decision in *Laval un Partneri*.
18	The Commission published a White Paper on integration of EU mortgage credit markets.
19	Memorandum signed to lift the Russian ban on imported Polish meat.
21	The Czech Republic, Estonia, Hungary, Latvia, Lithuania, Malta, Poland, Slovakia and Slovenia joined the Schengen area.

Index

Note: Italicized page references indicate information contained in tables.